The Japanese Advantage?

The Japanese Advantage?

Competitive IT strategies past, present and future

Brian Hunt and David Targett

Butterworth-Heinemann Ltd
Linacre House, Jordan Hill, Oxford OX2 8DP

⋐ A member of the Reed Elsevier plc group

OXFORD   LONDON   BOSTON
MUNICH   NEW DELHI   SINGAPORE   SYDNEY
TOKYO   TORONTO   WELLINGTON

First published 1995

© Butterworth-Heinemann Ltd 1995

All rights reserved. No part of this publication
may be reproduced in any material form (including
photocopying or storing in any medium by electronic
means and whether or not transiently or incidentally
to some other use of this publication) without the
written permission of the copyright holder except
in accordance with the provisions of the Copyright,
Designs and Patents Act 1988 or under the terms of a
licence issued by the Copyright Licensing Agency Ltd,
90 Tottenham Court Road, London, England W1P 9HE.
Applications for the copyright holder's written permission
to reproduce any part of this publication should be addressed
to the publishers

British Library Cataloguing in Publication Data
Hunt, Brian
  Japanese Advantage?: Competitive IT
  Strategies Past, Present and Future
  I. Title II. Targett, David
  658.050952

ISBN 0 7506 1934 1

Printed in Great Britain by Clays, St Ives plc

Contents

Preface vii

Acknowledgements ix

Part One   Setting the Scene

 1 Competition between Japanese and Western organizations   3
 2 The strategic role of information technology   15
 3 Japanese culture and Japanese management   38

Part Two   Case Studies

 4 All Nippon Airways Ltd   57
 5 Daiwa Europe Ltd   70
 6 Hitachi Europe Ltd   78
 7 Japan Travel Bureau (Europe) Ltd   90
 8 JVC (UK) Ltd   101
 9 Kobe Steel Europe Ltd   110
10 Nissan Motor (GB) Ltd   117
11 Nissan Motor Manufacturing (UK) Ltd   135
12 Sony (UK) Ltd   146
13 Toshiba Information Systems (UK) Ltd   167

Part Three   Weighing the Evidence

14 Japanese management of IT   181
15 The business impact and strategic use of IT   199
16 Head office control   213
17 Eclipsing the sun?   233

Index   243

Preface

The embryo of this book was a modest research project at the School of Management, University of Bath. Originally, our focus was Japanese banks and financial services companies. The quantity and diversity of stimulating data encouraged us to extend our horizons. Consequently, we broadened our field of vision to encompass Japanese multinational companies in a variety of industries. Still, we would not claim that our choice of companies or industries is exhaustive. However, we believe that the companies described here are representative of the range of business activities undertaken by Japanese companies.

While extending the type of companies in our research corpus, we refined our theoretical framework. We now think that we offer our readers a perspective on IT management issues from several viewpoints.

Our basic objective has been to examine whether the much-publicized successes of Japanese companies in product and process technologies is replicated in their use of information technology in the coming global battle for strategic advantage.

We chose to investigate Japanese companies in a range of industrial sectors for a number of reasons. Firstly, we were interested to see whether our initial findings held true for companies operating under different pressures. Secondly, we were keen to discover the differing perspectives that companies use in their approaches to IT management. Thirdly, we wanted to find out if companies handled IT management differently at different periods in their development cycle.

There are a number of reasons why we have written our research in the form of case studies. We are aware that the potential readership of our book is managers who are interested in the management of IT, academics and participants involved in business courses. We feel that case study descriptions make our data accessible and are the best means of illustrating the various issues faced by IT managers. For the academic reader, we felt that each case study would provide an informative snapshot of a number of aspects of current managerial thought in Japanese multinationals.

We believe that our research has produced some interesting findings. Firstly, we have been able to shed some light on the notion that Japanese management is omnipotent. Secondly, we discuss IT management in terms of one of the weapons that is available to companies in the battle for strategic competitive advantage. Thirdly, we have examined some Japanese management practices with a view to evaluating what effects these have on IT management. Additionally, our research from head offices provides a useful insight into a range of issues from the perspective of Japan.

Acknowledgements

We are particularly indebted to the managers and staff in Europe and Japan who invited us into their companies. In spite of their busy schedules, they took time to describe and explain various aspects of their company. A number of managers told us they found our research thought-provoking. We thank them for their kind hospitality. As requested by the majority of our informants, we have refrained from naming individuals.

We especially thank Michael Houser and Shinkai Hirokazu for valuable briefings on Japanese business protocol and for liaison with company head offices in Japan.

We acknowledge the generosity of All Nippon Airways who, in addition to being one of our case studies, also provided support for research in Japan.

Several friends and colleagues read parts of our manuscript at earlier stages. These include John Beaumont, Tim Brady, Steve Brigley, Fiona Cowan, Bill Colwill, Keith Donne, Nigel Dufty, Barbara Farbey, Alan Kemp, Mike Lake, David Madigan, Masashi Nakamura, Nicola Thompson, Ryuta Yasutake, Naoki Yoshigai. We are grateful to them for their many comments and suggestions.

Part One
Setting the Scene

Our main objective is to investigate the coming strategic battles between Western and Japanese organizations. The battleground is Europe, and information technology will be a key weapon in determining the outcome. In particular, the capability of organizations to use IT creatively to transform business and management in *revolutionary* ways is likely to be crucial. How good are Japanese organizations at such radical innovation? Will they be able to create completely new ways of doing things? Or is evolutionary improvement their main skill? – leaving us to conclude that there is nothing new under the (rising) sun?

Part One sets the scene for this investigation.

Chapter 1, **Competition between Japanese and Western organizations,** provides the background. It reviews current thinking on the balance of power and analyses the factors which, historically, seem to have determined success and failure.

Chapter 2, **The strategic role of information technology,** describes how IT has recently become a significant factor in business strategy. It shows how competitive advantage has been won or lost and how IT has played a major part in inducing the transformation of organizations and industries.

Chapter 3, **Japanese culture and Japanese management**, summarizes the distinguishing features of Japanese management style. It highlights areas that are clearly different from Western practices and which, according to some experts, have been decisive factors in strategic business battles.

1
Competition between Japanese and Western organizations

The time? A Friday in September 1968. The scene? The management training centre of a division of one of the UK's major car manufacturers. The occasion? The final afternoon of the company's three-week induction programme for new graduate trainees. The managing director was there to rally the new recruits and provide the 'big finish'.

The course had had its ups and downs. The sessions on work study had been boring but necessary. It was important to know how to determine how many seconds a particular operation such as riveting the front wing to the car should take. Under the piecework system this was the main determinant of the cost of a car and the main trigger for strikes. The most amusing session had come from the chief safety officer, who had recounted the hilarious (or so it seemed) circumstances in which people had suffered injury by disobeying the simplest of safety rules.

All in all, it had been a successful three weeks. We (yes, one of the authors attended) had learned what the motor industry was all about. The trades unions were squeezing as much as possible out of the great golden goose of the British motor industry (in the 1960s British-made cars dominated the UK market and the market share of British-owned manufacturers was around 50 per cent). The role of management, it seemed, was to get as many cars as possible through the gates without costs escalating too much. They did this by making a vain attempt to check the unions, avoid strikes and to keep these costs down.

All this, we heard, was simply the uncontrollable environment in which the company had to operate. True, there were one or two company-specific problems such as the unattractive appearance of most of the cars in the range, but a new styling director had just been appointed from a rival UK manufacturer and the future was viewed with confidence.

Engineering was not a difficulty. Indeed, the company had made several engineering innovations in the last ten years, including transversely mounted engines and a new type of suspension. Great pride was taken in the fact that the class of engine used in most of the product range had first been introduced in 1948 and was still going strong. It had already been adapted to fit many of the models and it was planned to last for many years yet. This was just as well, since to develop another would

4 The Japanese Advantage?

cost a large capital sum and this did not seem to be available either from retained profits or the money markets.

So it was the last afternoon and we had a chance to question the managing director. Question time was not successful – try as we might, we clearly failed to impress. He despatched our enquiries brusquely and with, we thought, contempt for our naivety. For example:

Q: 'What new models are planned?'
A: 'Confidential.'
Q: 'How can graduate trainees move out of the support functions to which we've been allocated and into line management?'
A: 'Not possible and not why we employed you.'

One series of questions and their answers remain in the memory, indelible to this day.

Q: 'What threat do Japanese car manufacturers pose in the UK market?'[1]
A: 'None at all. Everyone knows Japanese cars are piles of rust within two years.'
Q: 'But what about cameras and radios?'[2]
A: 'They're small. The Japanese are only good at making small things.'
Q: 'But what about motorcycles?'[3]
A: 'They're smaller than cars.'

By this stage the questioner could see his vision of a bright future in the company fading rapidly and he did not go on to mention shipbuilding and the iron and steel industry.

It is a matter of record that the next twenty-five years were, to say the least, traumatic for the British motor industry. The indigenous car industry collapsed, imports soared and those of Japanese cars were artificially restricted to agreed market shares. It became clear that the success of Japanese cars in so many world markets stemmed from their quality of build and engineering innovation – in complete contrast to the received wisdom of British management in 1968. By 1978 many British cars had an unenviable reputation for rusting while Japanese manufacturers were offering six-year anti-rust guarantees. By 1988, in a mini-revival of the indigenous British car industry, a major role was being played by Japanese manufacturers. In the 1990s Britain is once again a net exporter of cars but only because foreign manufacturers have built plants in Britain. Intriguingly, British-made Japanese models are exported to, and highly prized in, Japan.

Over these years many lessons have been learned in Britain and the West generally, and certainly nobody refuses to take the Japanese seriously any more, in any market. The faults of British and other Western management are better understood. Complacency, resting on the laurels of out-of-date engineering and a narrow focus on the balance sheet are not regarded as sensible approaches to business. The introspective management methods of 1968, when the customer and international competition were arrogantly dismissed, seem laughable.

The other side of the coin, the question of what has made the Japanese so successful is less well understood, in spite of the profusion of studies, articles and books. Our discussion of these issues is not intended to put forward any new explanations or define a new rationale. We are trying to review, as dispassionately as possible, the main themes as background to some case studies on Japanese organizations and in preparation for developing our own themes around the role of information technology.

Japanese success in the past

There can be no argument that Japanese organizations have been extremely successful. Their dominance of so many world markets has been extensively analysed. So have the reasons for this success but no consensus has emerged. Factors have been proposed, contradicted, resurrected and re-analysed with bewildering speed.

Lower costs

The first Japanese successes originated in lower wages. As long ago as the 1930s the Japanese textile industry had displaced the British industry as the world leader. This advantage was also a major factor in the first two decades after the end of the Second World War but it has long since disappeared. The rising yen has pushed Japanese costs sky-high in spite of their continual and largely successful battles to reduce them. Now, however, as Drucker[4] points out, blue-collar wages have become such a small percentage of overall costs that strategies based on cheap labour or moving production offshore are no longer of major relevance to competitive positioning.

Nevertheless, Japanese companies have relentlessly pursued the elimination of unnecessary costs and have streamlined processes in a quest for continual improvement. They have had to. The rising yen and increasing oil prices have forced them to offset these external cost effects by seeking ever greater internal efficiencies.

Quality

By the late 1970s even the managing directors of British car manufacturers had come to realize that quality was a major issue. The rate at which the quality of Japanese products had improved had been impressive and people in the West were looking for the reasons why. The first realization was that Japanese companies had a clear focus on quality and cared about it. 'Good enough' was not an expression used in Japanese companies.

The oldest anecdote is that of an American customer for Japanese goods who demanded a defective rate of 5 per cent, a high standard in the West at the time. The Japanese supplier could not understand this but the customer insisted and so the supplier sent two shipments. The first was for 95 per cent of the order and the goods were all perfect; the second was for 5 per cent of the order and they were all defective. Apocryphal probably, but it is true that Sir John Egan recounts what he found when taking over at Jaguar Cars. A crucial difference between Jaguar and their German rivals was that the average defective rate for goods received from suppliers by Jaguar was 15 per cent compared to 5 per cent for the German rivals.

By the 1970s a number of Japanese quality techniques were being imported by the West. Quality Circles, in which the whole workforce would meet in groups to discuss how to improve quality, was a favourite. Another, Statistical Quality Control, a method of monitoring quality levels, was a re-import. The idea had originated with Deming[5] and become widely used in Japan before being taken up in the West more recently. In the view of Drucker, however, the West has missed one of the major ingredients of SQC. Although it gives direct benefits in improving quality, its main benefit is indirect and social. SQC links quality information with accountability: the workforce is responsible for its own mistakes. This eliminates many inspectors and fixers, greatly reducing indirect costs. It also increases the feeling of pride in workmanship – another indirect benefit.

Product design

A characteristic of all their areas of success has been the ability of Japanese companies to bring out new, improved products with bewildering speed. The story is always the same – in cameras, hi-fis, televisions, motorcycles, cars, etc. – Japanese companies have made new products quickly and, apparently, in timely anticipation of developing customer requirements. Many Western rivals seem to have manufactured new products with reluctance – slowly and only when they have had to. Emmott[6] draws attention to this capability but adds that this does not signify technological leadership: it reflects a skill in technological implementation.

Japanese companies say their ability to do this reflects their closeness to the customer. 'The customer is king' is a phrase often repeated and sincerely believed. Even in areas where the West has led, such as the design of silicon chips, Japanese organizations have shown themselves able to sense customer needs very clearly and willing to act to satisfy those needs as a first priority.[7]

In the view of Ohmae[8] the customer focus imbues everything that a Japanese company does. In particular, strategy is about customers first, then competition. Japanese companies try to avoid head-on competition and strategic battles. He describes Nintendo's early successes which were achieved without any real competition. Nintendo had made strategic alliances with potential competitors who were involved in the manufacture of the products and therefore had a slice of the profits. As Ohmae says, 'everyone was making too much money to think of competing'. He contradicts the view that Japanese companies have done well only in growth markets. He quotes the example of Yamaha, who devised an innovative strategy based on the creation of new value for their customers in a declining market. Yamaha's success in the piano market was to devise an electronic 'piano player' for use in conjunction with existing pianos. Customers were able to find a new use for wasting assets.

Finance

Some commentators believe that many of the success factors, such as new product design and up-to-date, efficient manufacturing processes are related to the ability of Japanese companies to obtain finance more easily and at lower cost than their Western counterparts. The 'more easily' part of this thesis relates to the *keiretsu*. This expression refers to groupings of companies around a major bank, and held together by cross-shareholdings. The group is mutually supportive and a bank would be expected to give long-term support to members. In return, the members would give their business to the bank. Information is shared to create an atmosphere of trust. *Keiretsu* are the successors of the pre-war *zaibatsu*, which were much tighter groupings around holding companies in which all business, not just financial, was kept within the group. The *zaibatsu* were outlawed by the American post-war administration for a number of reasons, including that they encouraged militarism, damaged free trade and worked against an harmonious society. This history has led to the notion in some Western minds that *keiretsu* are *zaibatsu* in a different guise and that therefore their existence fringes on unfair trade practice.

The 'low-cost' part of the finance has extensive roots in factors such as the Japanese peoples' propensity to save, low inflation, the stock market and government policy. The effect of government policy links the low cost of finance with the *keiretsu* which are promoted and held together under the influence of the government.[9] It is all part of the government's intention that industry should have access to cheap, secure funding.

The easily available cheap finance, together with other factors, has meant that Japanese companies are under much less pressure from shareholders than Western ones. The funding of Japanese companies, whether equity or debt, tends to be in friendly hands, often other members of the *keiretsu*. This implies, it is argued, that Japanese companies are able to take a long-term view of business investment, in contrast to the short-termism of the West.

Finance also includes accounting methods. Writers have pointed to the greater flexibility of Japanese accounting methods. Drucker explains this by saying that Western cost accounting is based on an obsession with direct labour costs, unlike the Japanese system, which is not based on the pre-eminence of direct labour but is linked to strategy. A cynic might say that the difference is that Japan has many fewer accountants compared with America and Britain.[10]

Unfair practices

Whether explicitly or implicitly, some investigations into Japanese success conclude that the Japanese have indulged in unfair practices. Dumping has been one allegation. In particular, there was widespread belief that the success of companies such as Canon in the photocopier market was based on below-cost pricing. The European Community did in fact intervene to protect European rivals. This intervention, however, was nothing short of disastrous – Japanese success continued and European companies were damaged.[11]

The allegations of unfair practice have spread well beyond dumping. Unfair financial support for R&D, led by MITI and focusing on *keiretsu* is another. Unfair import controls and duties are yet another.

The most recent allegations have centred on invisible restrictions. For example, the distribution system in Japan is complex and inefficient. A Western company, lacking the financial muscle to set up its own and needing to use what is already there, faces a difficult task to penetrate the many layers of wholesalers and middlemen. This and other such restrictions have led to the 'Structural Impediments Talks' in which the American and Japanese governments are discussing such issues and seeking ways to break down these alleged barriers and make the market more open.

Domestic competition

At the other end of the scale from the unfair protection suggestions is the idea that Japanese companies, at least in Japan, are not protected at all. The fierce competition between them is a prime reason for their success according to such notable writers as Michael Porter.[12] The argument is that Japanese companies refine their competitive skills in the keen, customer-oriented competition of the Japanese domestic market to the point where taking on Western rivals is relatively easy.

The contrast between these last two factors, protection and competition, illustrates the diverse list of reasons for Japanese success that have been put forward at one time or another: the list is virtually endless. Most of them, at least on the surface, have some validity but the question of which are, in reality, the right explanations must be mainly a matter of opinion.

Emmott emphasizes differences in information flows. In Western companies information may flow from the top down or from the bottom up, depending upon whether the company is centralized or decentralized. The Japanese style is 'middle up and down'. In other words, information flows more freely and is less susceptible to political influence. Emmott cites this as a reason for success in expanding overseas but suggests that the companies need to ensure that their local middle managers adopt non-local attitudes, i.e. Japanese attitudes, and that the companies need to treat them differently – like Japanese middle managers.

Ohmae proposes a counter-intuitive argument. He believes that rich national resources can be a hindrance. Japan has none, therefore its strength must be in its people and in their ability to find, continually, new ways to add value to national and international customers.

This argument is close to the main theme of Oppenheim,[13] who debunks many of the standard arguments. The reasons for success, he says, are not unfair practices, not the low cost of finance, not the role of MITI. Indeed, he suggests that if MITI have had a beneficial influence it is because they have intervened less than their Western counterparts. If the government has done some good it has been in creating an environment in which market forces can succeed.

The reasons for success are, according to Oppenheim, complex and interwoven but he stresses the particular importance of education: 'Those who search for the key to Japan's astonishing post-war economic success could do a great deal worse than settle on her education system' (p. 47). The other factor he emphasizes is the attitude of the people. They are learners and improvers rather than, as the West thinks, copiers and imitators.

Japanese weaknesses – and their failures

The Japanese record, although successful, has not been one of unblemished success. There have been failures and Emmott[14] describes some of them.

In the late 1980s Bridgestone took over the ailing American tyre company Firestone. Bridgestone seemed unsure how to deal with their foreign acquisition, in terms of both strategy and the management of the workforce. The result was disastrous.

Emmott also suggests that Japanese investments in Hollywood have not worked out well. Both Sony and Matsushita purchased film and entertainment companies in Hollywood. The publicity was enormous, mainly along the 'whatever next! – something must be done' lines in America. Emmott, however, sees the purchases as big mistakes rather than symbols of an approaching Japanese dominance over America. He believes the prices paid were too large and that the vast differences in culture between Japanese electrical companies and American film studios presented an insuperable obstacle.

In other areas, too, Japanese ventures, while not outright failures, cannot be described as highly successful. Airlines are an example. Japan Airlines (JAL) has had a number of problems and cannot be classified with the best in the West. Financial services are another example. Japanese banks were at one time thought to be about to conquer the world. It has not happened. Money may cross boundaries with ease but customers do not: relationships are important and financial services companies find it hard to become global. Again, this is an area where Japanese companies are not generally thought of as world leaders and have not enjoyed the success of American rivals.

Emmott also describes Western companies which have beaten the Japanese at their own game. He concludes that there is no magic in Japanese methods. He believes the best in the USA and Europe is better than the best in Japan, but that the average in the USA and Europe is worse than the average in Japan.

Future competition between Japan and the West

Some experts such as Thurow[15] predict an increasingly adversarial pattern of international trade. Jackson[16] characterises the situation to an economic world war in which the major contestants will be the international companies of the United States, Europe and Japan. The battleground will be Europe. Why Europe? Jackson gives three reasons.

1. Europe is a big prize: the biggest market, the biggest economy.
2. Europe's single market has the potential to change the competitive environment and the competitive power relationships.
3. Many US firms rely on European profits, having lost out to Japanese companies on home territory.

The prospect of this world economic battle is a prime reason for this book, and, in particular, for investigating Japanese operations in Europe rather than in other parts of the world.

What will determine success in this battle? Undoubtedly, many factors will be just the same as before: product design, time to get new products to market, the ability to apply and implement technology. In discussing the strengths and weaknesses of the three contestants Jackson mentions Japanese intellect (meaning their capabilities for logical thought and attention to detail) and American inventiveness. Industrial relations are also important and here the United States and Europe are weak, Japan strong. Japan appears to be able to export this: Nissan's productivity in Europe is just as good as in Japan.

Some other factors, while important in the past, will no longer be so in the future. The new view of blue-collar productivity, as articulated by Drucker, is one. The ability to export management methods is another as management methods become increasingly global.

The real question is what the new factors are: those issues which have not had a crucial influence in the past but will do so in the future. A number have been proposed.

More than one eminent writer has suggested that Japan's very recent overseas investments will play a part. These investments, even if they were made primarily because of the high value of the yen and the consequent relative cheapness of overseas assets, can nevertheless bring competitive advantage to Japanese companies. For example, they bring the companies closer to their overseas customers. Japan has invested most heavily in California and the UK. Investments in the UK are around half of Japan's total investments in Europe. They will enable Japanese companies to take on their European rivals on their own ground from inside.

These investments have been the source of much antagonism, particularly in the USA. Emmott[17] compares the situation with the arrival of GIs in the UK in the Second World War: much of the antagonism is irrational. Emmott, too, points to the substantial competitive advantages that these investments will bring: synergy between overseas workers and Japanese senior managers, better understanding of business obstacles and local market competition, the ability to take better advantage of local business opportunities and use of local technology. He also highlights a new factor which may be critical in the future: the pursuit of traditional customers in Japan who have now become global. He adds a warning against overstating this advantage by saying that studies of smaller Japanese companies overseas show them to be, in the main, sweatshops using cheap unskilled labour.

The advantage that overseas investments bring is associated with Emmott's view that a characteristic of long-term successful, global companies will be their ability to become local, i.e. although global companies, they will build complete local operations in their important overseas markets. This idea is in fact summed up in Sony's corporate motto: 'Think global, act local.'

Drucker's[18] key to the future is rather different. He firmly dismisses the importance of productivity, based on old definitions of blue-collar productivity, as no longer being strategically relevant: 'The productivity revolution (in moving and making things) is over in developed countries' (p. 80). He does, however, attach considerable importance to what he calls 'the new productivity challenge'. He points to the poor record of productivity increases in knowledge and service work. Numerous studies[19] have shown that, in contrast to manufacturing productivity, productivity in the office has hardly changed in decades. For Drucker, 'working smarter' is the issue. By this he means that it will be necessary for organizations to redesign, radically, the way they operate. They will have to transform many of their business and management processes, their working practices and their business scope. It will be necessary for all organizations to ask questions such as: What is the task? Why do it? He calls for a 'productivity revolution' in the area of knowledge work.

Ohmae[20] also advocates a similar idea from a Japanese point of view. Just doing more better will not be enough. This can work, as in cases such as Toyota, but mainly it destroys industries, reducing profits to zero. He refers to the traditional Japanese *Kabuki* drama which illustrates companyism – the idea that it is better for all to lose than one. This attitude, he says, is typified in the Japanese reaction to whaling, where reducing the size of the industry, with a few companies losing out, is not an acceptable approach – better all should lose. He sees the need for Japanese companies to change course, in radical ways. Even when the need to change course is recognized, the great skill will be to know when to do it. There will be a need to question values and systems continuously, from the customer's point of view.

Ohmae,[21] however, also cautions us against the whole concept of battles between nations. He introduces the idea of ILE (Interlinked economies) in which he sees the economies of Japan, the United States, Europe and some aggressive Far East economies as inextricably and inevitably bound together. The concept of ILE will, he believes, swallow business, corporations and bureaucrats and, in effect, blur or even eliminate national borders. The extent to which this is happening has already rendered traditional macroeconomics almost meaningless. He gives examples such as the car industry, where it is already impossible to know exactly how much value was added to each product where. Such confusions mean that traditional ideas of, for example, current account surpluses do not carry the meanings they are usually given. The implication for organizations is that global strategic alliances are the way ahead. Organizations will have to find the right global partners and Ohmae suggests that we should work to understand global alliances better.

Conclusion

In looking to the future, a mixed forecast comes from Paul Kennedy,[22] the guru of political, demographic and economic forecasting, in his book about the state of the world in the first quarter of the twenty-first century:

> The overall conclusion...is that....the Japanese are probably the people least likely to be hurt by...the globalization of production....but even such a successful nation as Japan will find it hard to escape the larger repercussions of demographic and technological change.

Wilkinson[23] would seem to come down in favour of Japan: 'Europe is dead, the US is dying.'

Although Emmott, too, is optimistic about Japan's future he admits that Japanese companies will be cautious and incremental rather than move in quantum leaps. This is a relevant thought in the context of the single theme that has been developed strongly by several writers. Drucker, Ohmae and others are advocating the need for more than continual, incremental improvement and to keep doing things better – keys to many past Japanese successes. They are saying that organizations will have to be creative and do revolutionary new things, not just in their products but also in the way they manage and organize themselves and form strategic alliances.

This is also the key issue for us. As the next chapter will demonstrate, organizations are finding that the innovative use of information technology is an essential ingredient of organizational transformation. Hence our question: how good are Japanese companies in the radical, as opposed to careful and incremental, use of information technology?

The evidence so far is that they may not be very good. Certainly the Japanese have become technological leaders in areas such as establishing patents[24] but this is not always the same as pure creative work. It is important to distinguish between information technology as a product or part of a product and information technology as 'the air we breathe' of business processes and management practices. In the remainder of this book we will develop the theme and provide enough evidence to allow a conclusion to be reached.

Notes

1 At the time some Japanese cars such as Datsun (now Nissan) were on the market but their market share was uncountably small.
2 In the late 1960s Japanese cameras had taken over the world market, including defeating the Germans, who had been the market leaders until then. Japanese transistor radios were also dominant across the world.
3 By the mid-1960s the British motorcycle industry had almost disappeared, overcome by Hondas, Yamahas, Suzukis, etc.
4 Drucker, P., *Managing for the Future*, Butterworth-Heinemann (1992). A series of articles discussing international management and competition.
5 W. Edwards Deming is the American who developed the technique but his ideas were largely ignored in the West. Just after the Second World War he was invited to Japan, where his ideas were taken up with enthusiasm.
6 Emmott, W., *Japan's Global Reach*, Century Business (1992).
7 See Oppenheim, P., *The New Masters*, Business Books (1991), pp. 240ff. for a description.
8 Ohmae, K., *Borderless World*, Fontana (1990).
9 MITI (the Ministry of International Trade and Industry) has played a major role in the development of Japanese business. However, there are different schools of thought as to whether their influence has been extensive or not, beneficial or not, unfair or not. This is a complex topic, extensively analysed in most 'Japanese business' books. See, for example, von Wolferen, K., *The Enigma of Japanese Power*, Papermac (1990) for a view which leans towards the 'much influence, beneficial, rather unfair' bloc.
10 In the 1980s around 11 per cent of graduates from British universities went into accounting.
11 See, for example, the thorough analysis in Jackson, T., *Turning Japanese*, HarperCollins (1993).
12 Porter, M., *The Competitive Advantage of Nations*, Macmillan (1990).
13 Oppenheim, *op. cit.*
14 See Emmott, *op. cit.*, Chapter 5 for the Bridgestone story, Chapter 7 for the Hollywood story.
15 Thurow, L. C., *Head to Head: Coming Economic Battles among Japan, Europe and America*, Brearley Publishing (1994).
16 Jackson, *op. cit.*
17 See Chapter 1 of Emmott, *op. cit.* Emmott discusses the recent phenomenon of Japanese overseas investment, at least on the present scale, and analyses the reasons behind it.
18 See Drucker, *op. cit.*, Chapter 13.

14 *The Japanese Advantage?*

19 See, for example, Scott Morton, R. (ed.), *The Corporation of the 1990s*, Oxford University Press (1991).
20 See Ohmae, *op. cit.*, Chapter 4.
21 *Ibid.*, Chapter 9.
22 Kennedy, P., *Preparing for the Twenty-first Century*, HarperCollins (1993), p. 138.
23 Wilkinson, E., *Japan versus the West*, Penguin (1990).
24 Jackson, *op. cit.*, pp. 33–34.

2
The strategic role of information technology

By the instantaneous communication of information between customer, dealer, supplier and manufacturing plant, Toyota can deliver a car manufactured to a customer's exact specifications, in terms of colour, engine size, internal trim, features etc. within days. By 'locking' travel agents into their computerized reservation system, American Airlines significantly increased its market share and, because this system gave the capability to manipulate its fares extremely rapidly, put other airlines out of business. And information systems became the most profitable part of the organization.[1] By linking the personal computers on doctors' desks to their drug information database, a UK pharmaceuticals company increased its market share significantly.

There is no shortage of examples such as these where IT has had a significant, transforming effect on an organization. Since the mid-1980s it has become accepted that IT is strategic, meaning that IT now has the capability to affect the overall direction of an organization and can lead to a major competitive advantage.

The three examples above illustrate the successful achievement of competitive advantage, but 'strategic' does not necessarily equate with such success. Some strategies are defensive, preventing rivals from achieving competitive advantage; others are concerned with the continuing operation and survival of the organization. Of course, the story is not always, or even mostly, associated with a favourable outcome. Some strategic uses of IT have been neutral and some catastrophic. The case of the London Stock Exchange and its abandonment of the Taurus system was a well-publicized failure.[2] However, even when the outcome is not one of success, the impact of IT can still be categorized as strategic.

In the past IT has not generally been strategic. Since the 1960s organizations have applied IT to mechanize and automate support functions such as the payroll and stock control. The purpose of the automation has usually been to increase efficiency: computer systems have taken over basic clerical tasks and thereby reduced staffing and some other costs such as inventory and documentation. The effect of these applications has been localized, being confined to one part of the organization with no major repercussions elsewhere.

With good reason, organizations' major concerns have been whether such automation is being achieved on time and within budget. By and large, responsibility for the management of projects has been in the hands of the IT department. Generally the IT manager has decided, in consultation with functional managers, which functions to automate, how to automate and how to implement before the project is handed over to the user department. At the end of a failed project, senior management has occasionally caused heads to roll but has otherwise had little involvement with IT. This lack of senior management involvement may have been mistaken, and has frequently contributed to failure, but it has been very common.

The situation is now very different. There are four inescapable reasons why today, more than ever, senior and general managers need to be closely involved with IT: four reasons which reinforce the fact that IT is strategic:

- *IT affects competitive issues.* If IT can gain, or lose, competitive advantage and if it can radically alter market share then Chief Executive Officers (CEOs) can hardly regard IT as merely a technical matter.
- *IT is at the core of business processes.* Many organizations could no longer function without IT. A bank which did not offer the customer services that computerization brings would have a poor future. Many business processes have been changed radically by IT – for example, share dealing.
- *IT accounts for large expenditures.* In many organizations IT expenditure regularly runs at 4 per cent of revenue or more. For some banks it is as high as 10 per cent. A recent survey revealed that IT accounts for 50 per cent of new capital expenditure. Even if other strategic arguments are ignored, it is certain that a CEO will pay close attention to such major cost factors.
- *IT failures lose CEOs their jobs* (sometimes). Recent well-publicized IT disasters, such as Taurus, have been characterized by the fact that it was the CEO's head that rolled. CEOs have noted this and are paying close attention.

This rapid change in the role of IT is thought by some to be an 'information revolution' on a par with the Industrial Revolution of 200 years ago. For some organizations this revolution has been taking place since the early 1980s; for others, the IT revolution has not yet occurred but they have seen how quickly it has struck elsewhere and do not want to be left behind by competitors. Whatever the reasons, IT is firmly on the strategic management agenda.

Why has IT's role changed?

Since the mid-1980s IT's role has gradually been redefined. Organizations have been changing their views of IT for two main reasons, as illustrated in Figure 2.1. First, there have been rapid advances in the capabilities of IT, such as increased power and improved linkages and connectivity, combined with substantial reductions in its cost. If, over the

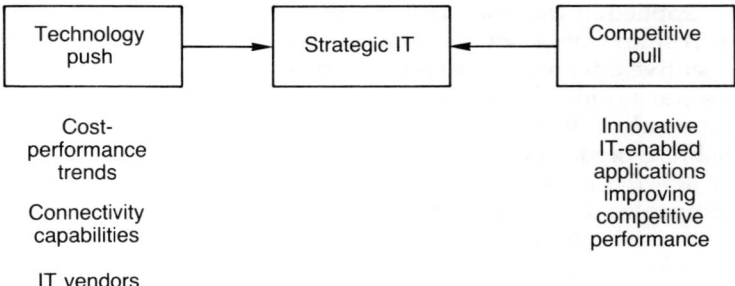

Figure 2.1 Why IT's role has changed (from M. Scott Morton (1991) *The Corporation of the 1990s*)

last thirty or forty years the price of aircraft had decreased at the same rate as IT, the latest jumbo jet could now be purchased for less than the pilot's annual salary. Whether there would be any air space in which to fly it is another matter.

Second, virtually all organizations in both public and private sectors have been subject to severe competitive pressures and turbulence in their spheres of operation. The MIT90s Research Programme[3] described these pressures as organizational turbulence, and highlighted four aspects of the environmental changes affecting organizations:

- *Social*: consumers' heightened expectations of quality, price, delivery and service; environmental issues.
- *Political*: the unification of Germany, the collapse of the USSR; opportunities in Eastern Europe; regulatory changes; the single European market.
- *Economic*: US trade and budget deficits; the strength of Japan; the rise of Far Eastern 'tigers'.
- *Technological*: consistent and rapid developments in product, process and information technology; advances in the biosciences.

These same pressures are also affecting the way organizations are structured and the roles people are expected to play in them. Of course, they are also influencing the whole of society well beyond the confines of the business world.

As a result of technology push and competitive pull, IT now does more than automate *support* processes. IT is increasingly being applied to the *cores* of businesses and transforming industries, organizations, business processes and management methods. 'Core' is difficult to define, but examples are plentiful. Retailers' use of Electronic Point of Sale (EPoS) systems and travel agents' use of computerized booking systems are just two examples of information systems which operate at the core of the businesses and which have transformed the way business is carried out. Developments such as credit cards, and more recently smart cards, depending upon IT for the growth in their use, have added new dimensions and totally new businesses to computer-based organizational activities.

18 *The Japanese Advantage?*

When applied in this way, IT gives benefits much wider than the traditional cost and personnel reductions. The benefits sometimes amount to competitive advantage, usually occurring when IT is associated with business transformation, rather than automation.

IT has also had the effect of seeming to shorten geographical distances and enabling organizations to cross international boundaries. Just as a century ago the development of the telegraph and telephone allowed local companies to become national ones, so modern IT improves communications within an organization and promotes closer alliances between organizations. A European car manufacturer can be linked more closely with offices and agents on other continents and can communicate electronically with suppliers in other European countries. IT helps it to establish joint ventures with other manufacturers. As a result, international trade has been transformed in several industries. In defence and civil engineering, for example, it is now the norm for multinational and national consortia to bid for major contracts.

How strategic is IT for a particular organization?

IT may, in general terms, be strategic but this does not mean that it is of equal importance to all organizations. McFarlan,[4] of the Harvard Business School, suggests the use of a Strategic Grid, as in Figure 2.2, to determine the potential strategic relevance of IT to any particular organization.

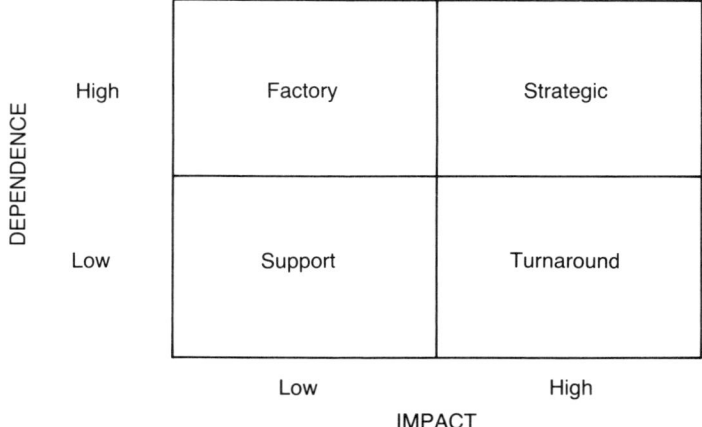

Figure 2.2 The Strategic Grid

The Strategic Grid has two dimensions:
1 *Level of dependence* on existing operating systems.
   • *High dependence* means that reliable functioning of the core systems is essential to the company's well-being. For example, a

UK building society has stated that if its key systems went down for as long as 60 hours it would be out of business.
- *Low dependence* means that unreliable functioning of systems, while frustrating and to some degree costly, does not in any way threaten the survival or overall profitability of the business. Small businesses offering household services may use some technology but they can easily survive without it.

2 *Strategic impact* of planned IT developments.
- *High impact* means that IT is one of a small number of things an organization must get absolutely right if it is to survive and flourish in the future. Car manufacturers are increasingly developing IT applications in all their core business processes: design, manufacturing, delivery, selling and marketing.
- *Low impact* means that IT development, while useful, is not one of the critical activities that the organization must get right. Management consultants use IT but it is not a critical determinant of their success.

McFarlan gives labels to the four boxes of the matrix shown in Figure 2.2:

1 *Strategic* (high impact, high dependence). The organization is critically dependent on IT now and in the future. American Airlines is an example. The IT function is one of the most important in the company, demanding careful attention from senior management.
2 *Turnaround* (high impact, low dependence). Existing technology is not of critical importance but the organization is moving to a situation where IT will have a strategic capability and will be a key determinant of success or failure. Suppliers to large manufacturing organizations in most sectors have moved into this segment. For example, suppliers to retail chains have not traditionally used much technology but moves towards electronic links (EDI – electronic data interchange) and preferred partnerships will make IT critical in the future. Without the right IT capability suppliers will not even get on the short-list of 'preferred partners' to retailers who are seeking to use IT to reduce stocks and, more importantly, stockouts.
3 *Factory* (low impact, high dependence). Reliable operation of existing systems is crucial and may even be the backbone of the business but new developments are not going to alter the competitive environment. Utilities with large billing systems at the core of their business are an example.
4 *Support* (low impact, low dependence). IT has been, and will continue to be, outside the short-list of major determinants of success. Management consultants are an example.

McFarlan suggests six questions that will help an organization to determine its position on the Strategic Grid. The questions concern the use of IT in the context of classical methods of achieving competitive advantage. All 'no' answers mean that the organization is probably on the

Factory–Support side; one or more 'yes' answers suggest a position on the Strategic–Turnaround side:

1 *Are there ways to use technology to create defensible entry barriers*? For example, the cost of building American Airlines' reservation system would prevent smaller airlines from doing the same.
2 *Do we have the opportunity to induce switching costs*? A switching cost is the cost incurred by a customer if he or she decides to move to a new supplier. For example, in the case of the UK pharmaceuticals company mentioned above, it would be costly and disruptive for a doctor to switch to the database system of another company, even if one were available.
3 *Are there opportunities to change the ground rules of competition*? For example, car manufacturers used to offer a narrow range of cars and compete largely on the basis of price, but now customers are demanding a choice from a wide range of options – and expecting to have their choice of car delivered quickly. Information systems allow some manufacturers to offer customers as many as 100 000 variants on a standard model and have their particular choice delivered within a few days.
4 *Can IT change from cost-based competition to competition based on sustainable product differentiation*? For example, computerized banking has led to competition based on financial products such as tailored mortgages, rather than low-cost banking.
5 *Can IT be used to link in suppliers*? For example, retail organizations 'locked in' suppliers by establishing EDI links.
6 *Are there ways to use technology as a product*? For example, American Airlines used their reservation system as a product: they charge other airlines for using the AA system.

The Strategic Grid and the six questions are intended to help managers to develop a greater awareness of the role of strategic IT in their organizations. In the 1970s most organizations were on the Factory–Support side. Now many have moved or are moving across to the Strategic–Turnaround side. For example, professional groups such as architects and law firms were in the support cell but have now moved to 'turnaround'.

The range of IS benefits

The idea that IT is strategic suggests that it must be underpinned by substantial business benefits, benefits which must be wider-ranging than just cost saving. What, then, are the business benefits that underlie the strategic impacts? How can they be categorized, so that they are better understood and so that IT investments have a better chance of achieving all potential benefits?

Many writers have tried to classify them and describe their development over the years in different and imaginative ways. For example, the

Index Group use the matrix in Figure 2.3(a), which shows IT impacting at the level of the individual, the function and the whole organization. It shows benefits of efficiency, effectiveness and transformation. In other words, there are nine different classes of benefit. Each has been given a descriptive name to explain its meaning better.

The Index matrix describes the development of IS applications as falling into three *eras*. This is illustrated in Figures 2.3(b)–(d):

1. *Era 1*. IT was first applied to functional areas bringing efficiency and, later, effectiveness benefits.
   - *Process automation* (function/efficiency cell). For example, automating stock control to reduce warehousing costs.
   - *Functional enhancement* (function/effectiveness cell). For example, automating the sales/ordering process provides better information on the state of an order or invoice, resulting in better customer service.
2. *Era 2*. The next stage was when the impact of IT was on individuals, mainly through the introduction of microcomputers.
   - *Task mechanization* (individual/efficiency cell). For example, word processing mechanizes secretarial activities. The ability to make changes quickly and to store standard letters and documents should reduce staff costs.
   - *Work improvement* (individual/effectiveness cell). For example, desktop publishing not only automates document production but also improves the quality of the end product. This should result in the document being accepted more easily by those to whom it is being sent and, therefore, perhaps faster decision making.
3. *Era 3*. The current era has moved IT into new areas: IT is playing a key part in transformations of various kinds and is also having a significant effect on the whole organization.
   - *Role expansion* (individual/transformation cell). For example, computer networks can transfer documents rapidly backwards and forwards between departments. As a result, they can be handled almost simultaneously by different functions instead of in strict order. This has led to the streamlining of management processes and created a need for the development of team-working and for managers in new coordinating roles.
   - *Functional redefinition* (function/transformation cell). For example, clothing retailers have been able to transform their distribution systems because the availability of information from EPoS gives daily, accurate information on sales. Distribution schedules for each store are prepared overnight in response to the previous day's sales. The traditional method was to forecast and guess, weeks in advance, resulting in unacceptable levels of overstocking and stockouts. The changes have been accompanied by the development of new warehousing and distribution arrangements.
   - *Boundary extension* (organization/efficiency cell). For example, white-goods manufacturers have computer links with many of their suppliers, allowing the manufacturer to specify up-to-the-

22 The Japanese Advantage?

Areas of impact

Benefits		Individual	Function	Organization
	Efficiency	Task mechanization	Process automation	Boundary extension
	Effectiveness	Work improvement	Functional enhancement	Service enhancement
	Transformation	Role expansion	Functional redefinition	Product innovation

(a)

Beneficiary

Benefits		Individual	Function	Organization
	Efficiency		Process automation	
	Effectiveness		Functional enhancement	
	Transformation			

(b)

Figure 2.3 The Index matrix. (a) Benefits and their impact; (b) Era 1; (c) Era 2; (d) Era 3

The strategic role of information technology

Beneficiary

	Individual	Function	Organization
Efficiency	Task mechanization		
Effectiveness	Work improvement		
Transformation			

Benefits

(c)

Beneficiary

	Individual	Function	Organization
Efficiency			Boundary extension
Effectiveness			Service enhancement
Transformation	Role expansion	Functional redefinition	Product innovation

Benefits

(d)

minute distribution and delivery requirements. The manufacturer has extended its boundary to include the supplier in its domain, at least electronically, leading to efficiency benefits.
- *Service enhancement* (organization/effectiveness cell). For example, insurance brokers are linked electronically to most major insurance companies. Brokers take only minutes to search through insurance companies' databases to find the policy best suited to a client's requirements.
- *Product innovation* (organization/transformation cell). For example, American Airlines sell the facilities of their reservation system to other airlines. This is a new product for AA, which has transformed the scope of their business in the sense that they now make a majority of their profits from an area of business in which the airline did not previously operate.

It is important to be clear that the Index matrix is not meant to be a precise classification system. It is intended to create awareness and demonstrate the areas where, potentially, benefits can be found. The titles given to the cells are not, of course, tight definitions. Their purpose is merely to illustrate – to enhance perception of and sensitivity to benefits rather than act in a book-keeping role.

The eras of the Index matrix represent stages in the development of IT within an organization, rather than precise periods of time to which exact dates can be given. Some organizations were in Era 1 in the 1960s; some very large organizations did not move into Era 1 until the mid-1970s with the purchase of their first computer; some small businesses are not yet in Era 1.

Eras 1 and 2 are the traditional, first areas for IT developments. All large organizations and most small ones are now in Eras 1 and 2. Few organizations are firmly in Era 3 although many have had some occasional involvement. Nor is it just large organizations that are operating in Era 3. Many small and medium-size businesses have transformed themselves in some way. Their relatively small size could be an advantage, providing the flexibility to enable them to implement transformation in contrast with large organizations, whose processes, procedures and organizational structures may be firmly entrenched.

Organizations do not, of course, move through the matrix one cell at a time. An organization is likely to be operating in several cells at once and, in particular, organizations that are involved in using IT as an agent of transformation will almost certainly still be heavily involved in Era 1 investments seeking efficiency benefits.

The matrix is like a balance sheet giving a snapshot of the situation at a point in time. Primarily it illustrates where an organization is at a particular time, but it is also able to track progress over months or years. There is no optimal or recommended route for moving through the matrix. The sequence Era 1–Era 2–Era 3 is usually followed, but within each era an organization tends to move along a path which is related to its specific circumstances.

The link between benefits and business transformation

Efficiency benefits were the major reason for introducing computers into businesses from the early days. Effectiveness benefits have also been sought for some time. Over the years, organizations have developed expertise in managing these types of project.

Transformation benefits are more recent and require greater attention, first, simply because they are new and, second, because they are the basis of many of the largest, most significant and riskiest IT projects currently under way. They are also much more difficult to manage simply because IT-induced transformation always involves corresponding changes to other areas of the organization: structure, working practices, lines of communication and authority.

The MIT90s Research Programme suggested that there are five levels of IT-induced business transformation each of which relates a degree of transformation with a range of potential benefits.

Level 1: localized exploitation

Localized exploitation refers to the application of IT to different parts of an organization, in isolation one from another. Separately computerizing accounts, customer records and stock levels, without connecting the three systems in any way, is localized exploitation. It is in effect the traditional mode of IT application. A suitable area for automation is chosen and the IT department develops and implements a project to implement the automation. The level of transformation is low, if not zero, and the range of potential benefits is largely restricted to efficiency gains. Level 1 is in fact more automation than transformation and is shown graphically in Figure 2.4(a). Figure 2.4(b) shows the enablers (the factors prompting applications) and inhibitors (the obstacles restraining applications) of level 1 transformations. These enablers and inhibitors provide a greater understanding of the nature of level 1 applications.

The enablers are both technical and organizational. Technical enablers are the remarkable improvements in the cost/performance ratio for IT equipment and its marketing by IT vendors in determined style. The organizational enablers are that the management tasks of cost justifying the investment are relatively straightforward and that implementing a project in just one part of the organization has negligible impacts in other areas.

The inhibitors are also technical and organizational. Technical inhibitors have the view that the equipment will very soon be obsolete and that later models will, in any case, be cheaper. It always seems preferable to wait. Organizational inhibitors are concerned with a lack of management perception of the value of introducing IT and a lack of drive in pursuing it.

26 The Japanese Advantage?

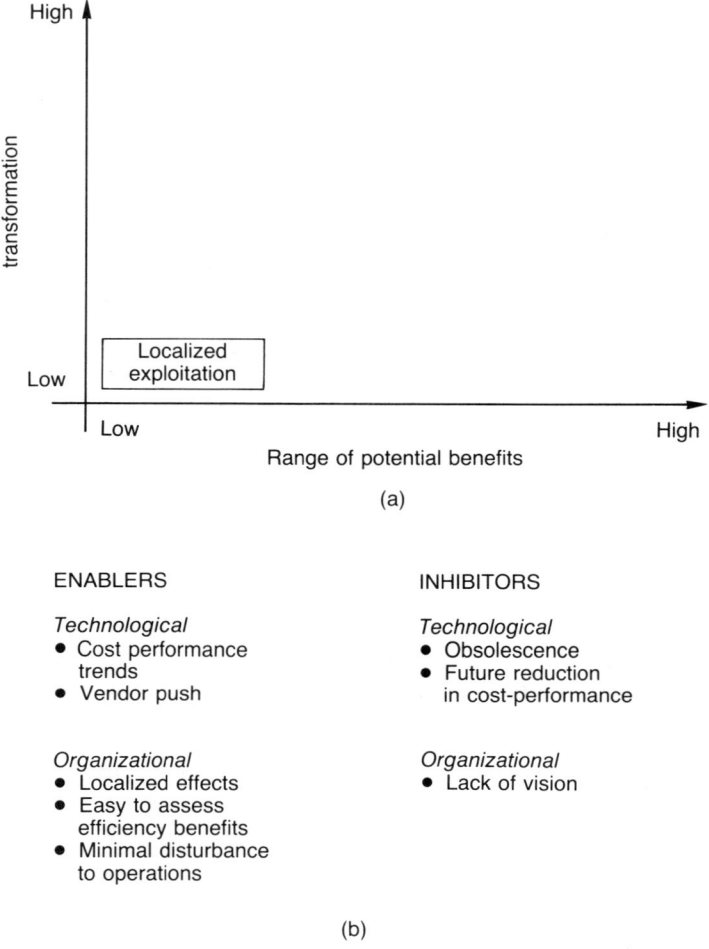

Figure 2.4 (a) Business transformation – level 1; (b) localized exploitation

Level 2: internal integration

Internal integration is the development of IT-based links between different parts of an organization. If accounts, customer records and stock control have been computerized separately, these are level 1 developments. Connecting the three systems together so that a customer can immediately know the status of his or her order or so that a manager can investigate how much a customer has been buying and how good is the customer's payment record is a level 2 development.

The degree of transformation is higher because more will change as a result of this integration. The project must involve the management of

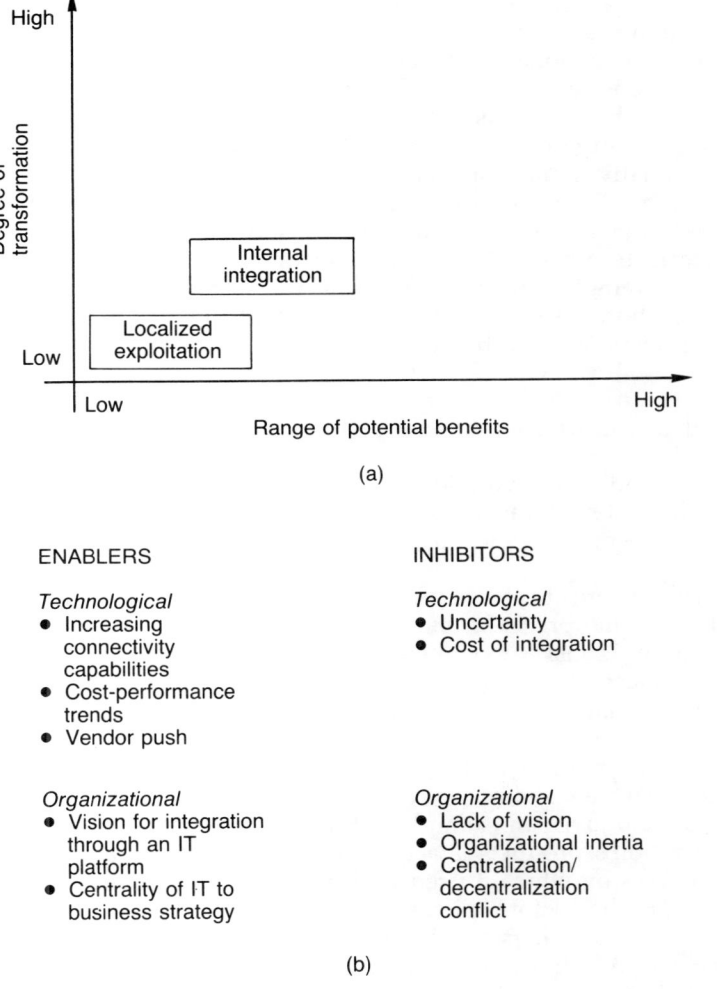

Figure 2.5 (a) Business transformation – level 2; (b) internal integration

different functions, persuading each to change its mode of operation. Equally, the range of potential benefits is higher through more effective management of operations and better customer service. For example, all aspects of a customer's account can be managed together and the customer can find out everything he or she wants to know from just one point of contact. Level 2 transformation is shown graphically in Figure 2.5(a).

The technological enablers of level 2 transformations are the same cost-performance factors as before plus the new and increasing sophistication of IT capabilities for connecting systems together in networks (Figure

2.5(b)). Improvements in connectivity stem from improvements in telecommunications.

The organizational enablers revolve around strategy and vision. As organizations recognize that IT needs to be embedded in their business strategies, they may also see that an IT infrastructure linking different parts of the organization is the necessary platform that will later enable other initiatives and applications.

When an IT project involves many functions within an organization the restraints on progress multiply. This also increases uncertainty, and therefore the possibility of cost overruns. It also raises organizational issues seemingly unrelated to IT: lines of management communication, centralization/decentralization and interfunctional conflict. The low-risk strategy may seem to be: do nothing.

Level 3: business process redesign

Levels 1 and 2 are evolutionary, developing almost naturally over time from the first introduction of IT. Levels 3–5 are revolutionary and do not follow in a smooth logical progression. They are more like creative quantum leaps.

Level 3 relates to the redesign of business processes. A process is difficult to define precisely, but it means the way the organization carries out one of its tasks. Examples of business processes are how a fashion retailer selects the goods it wishes to stock and how an industrial manufacturer manages its cash flow. A process is not the same as a function: it can be one part of a function or cut across several. Nor should a process be confused with a procedure which is a set of rules by which a particular task should be carried out.

Figure 2.6 gives an example of business process redesign. One of this organization's products is a type of industrial manufacturing machine. The process by which it used to deal with its customers is at the top of Figure 2.6, the 'before' picture.

Potential customers would ask for a quote for the supply of a given number of machines built according to a rough specification. A tender would then be submitted. If successful, the organization would work with the customer to develop a final design, after which a final price would be calculated and negotiated. The design would then go to the manufacturing function who would prepare the production layout and then commence production. Finally, the completed machines would be delivered and installed.

All these stages took place in strict sequence like a relay race and each stage had the benefit of its own computer systems to help do the job. The systems were unconnected: this is level 1, localized exploitation. Had the systems been connected then this would have been level 2, internal integration. However, the organization went further and redesigned the whole process, the 'after' picture shown at the bottom of Figure 2.6.

Instead of a number of systems, an infrastructure was the platform upon which all tasks were carried out. The 'team' who dealt with the

The strategic role of information technology 29

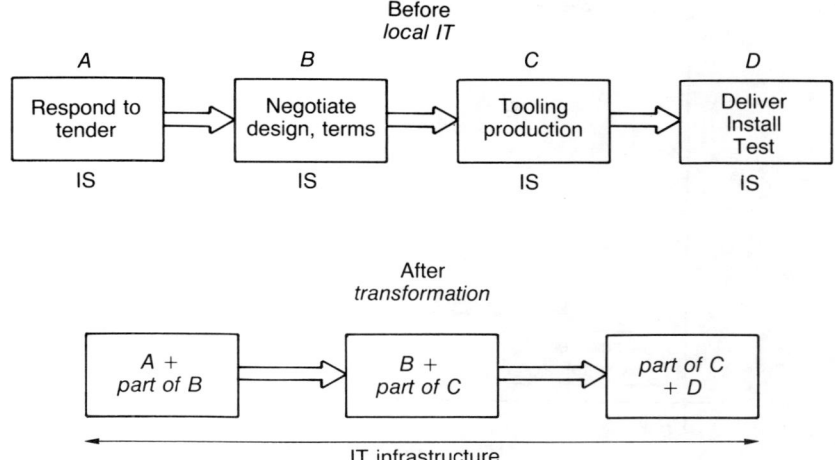

Figure 2.6 Business process redesign for a manufacturer of industrial equipment

customer would be responsible for all the tasks leading up to actual production. The tasks were not carried out simultaneously but they certainly overlapped to a great extent. For example, production plans would be developed at the same time as the final design. Time would be saved but, in addition, both the design and the production plans would be improved because their joint development was able to incorporate a wider range of organizational issues. By balancing the needs of design and production, costs would also be reduced.

The 'after' picture shows a redesigned business process. It allowed the organization to deliver products in 11 weeks rather than 16 and to reduce costs by 25 per cent. At the same time, the infrastructure provides the flexibility to make changes more rapidly and therefore the design of the product was also improved. The organization was able to compete on the basis of cost *and* quality, and customer service was significantly improved.

Figure 2.7(a) shows level 3 on the graph. The degree of transformation involved in level 3 is greater but so are the benefits. To make a transformation such as that described above is not an evolutionary progression; it is revolutionary.

The main new enabler of this level is competitive pressures (Figure 2.7(b)). The organization redesigned its process not because of the cost/performance ratio of IT but because new rivals were entering the market. They were offering better, cheaper products delivered more quickly. It was losing market share and had to respond in a radical way or face the prospect of going out of business.

The main inhibitor is uncertainty, not just of the technology and its costs but also of the impact of organizational change on employees. People

30   *The Japanese Advantage?*

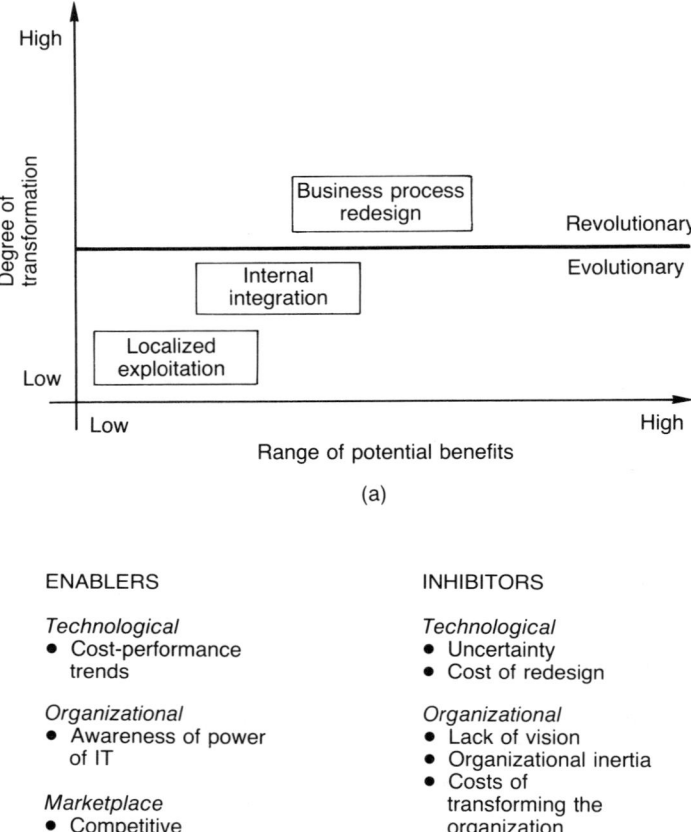

Figure 2.7   (a) Business transformation – level 3; (b) business process redesign

would inevitably feel unsure and threatened by the new plans and their feelings would have to be handled sensitively. The insecurity would be felt at all levels, some fearing job loss, higher levels fearing the decline of their empires. To have the motivation and drive to carry out such radical changes, senior management needs either a clear, firm vision or a serious competitive threat, or both.

Level 4: business network redesign

Whereas level 3 concerned redesign within the organization, level 4 relates to redesign involving other organizations which might be suppliers, customers, services or even competitors. Level 4 refers to a radical change in the nature of the relationships between organizations. The degree of transformation is high because it is likely to have even more widespread and unpredictable effects than level 3 transformations. The good news is that the range of benefits is also likely to be high.

For example, car manufacturers used to design new vehicles in-house. When the design was completed the drawings would be sent to potential suppliers who would be asked to tender for the contracts to supply the individual parts. Once the tenders were received and the favoured suppliers chosen, the new vehicle would move into the production planning phase.

Now, computer links mean that manufacturer and supplier can design jointly. They can work together so that quality is improved (because the expertise of both manufacturer and supplier is used) and costs reduced (because the supplier takes into account the optimal production requirements). The links will probably also extend to the production group within the manufacturer so that they can be involved in the design process and ensure that their requirements are also taken into account. Level 4 transformations are likely to increase in importance as organizations seek to 'outsource' parts of their value chain to 'world-class' collaborators.

Figure 2.8(a) shows the transformation graph for level 4 and Figure 2.8(b) the enablers and inhibitors. The first enabler is technological and without it links cannot be established. If organizations are to be connected through IT then the standards by which the computers can communicate must already exist or be created.

The other two enablers involve management vision. Identifying value-added services means recognizing opportunities for the computer links to do more than just link the organizations. For example, the link might enable the storing and analysing of management information about the costs, difficulties and design weaknesses of previous products, information collected by both manufacturer and supplier.

Clearly, all this implies closer alliances between manufacturers and suppliers than have existed previously. The sharing of sensitive management information means there must be considerable trust. This is why IT developments and particularly interorganizational networks are wrapped up in moves towards 'preferred partnerships'. Manufacturers are reducing the number of their suppliers but are developing much closer relationships with the ones that remain. Supply contracts tend not to be based solely on short-term issues such as price but on long-term benefits resulting from organizations working closely together and having a good understanding of each other's business. For organizations to move in this direction there must be a recognition of mutual benefits.

The inhibitors focus on a lack of the above enablers: a lack of standards and of the vision and understanding which are required if relationships between organizations are to change. It is important to stress that establishing IT links is not in itself enough: these links are just part of a series of organizational and other changes which will allow the partnerships to work smoothly. Organizations are often concerned that these closer relationships will result in an erosion of their market positions, i.e. having

32 The Japanese Advantage?

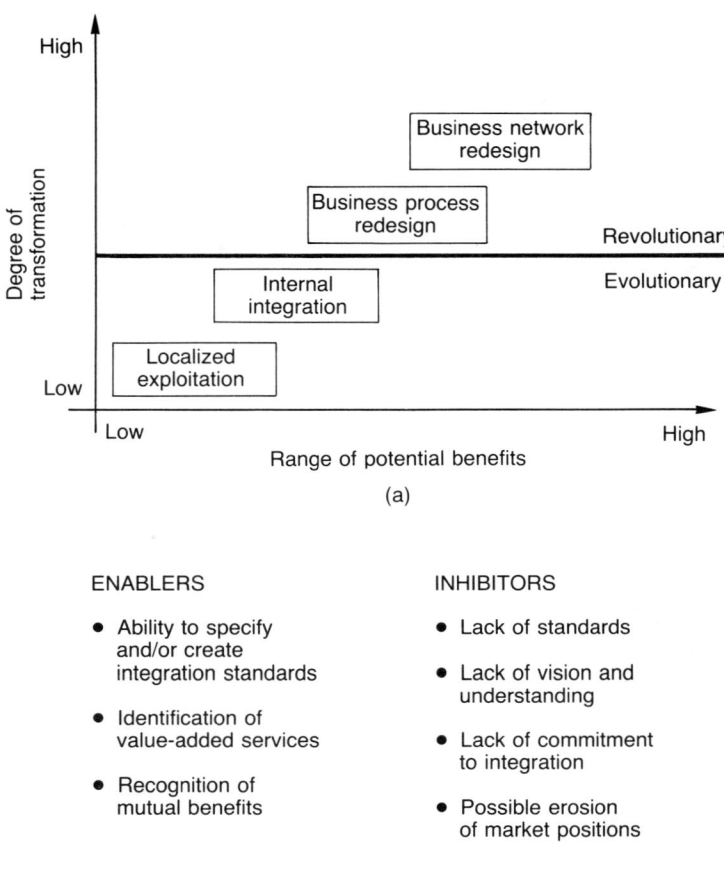

Figure 2.8 (a) Business transformation – level 4; (b) business network redesign

set up a close partnership they worry that their partners will steal their secrets and expertise and move to other partners or even set up their own internal functions to do the job.

Level 5: business scope redefinition

Figure 2.9 illustrates a level 5 transformation which is an extension to an organization's range of business. The degree of transformation is high, as is the range of potential benefits. Level 5 refers to the use of IT as the basis for a new information-based product, and not to its use in enhancing

The strategic role of information technology 33

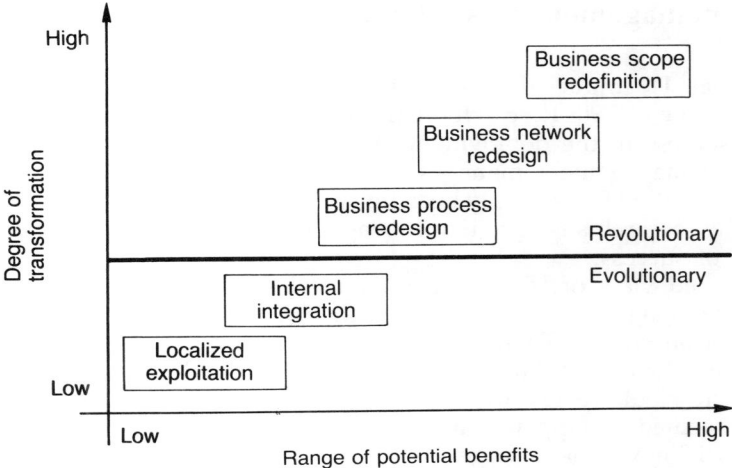

Figure 2.9 Business transformation level 5

existing products. The case of American Airlines, charging for other airlines' usage of their reservation system, is an example.

The level of transformation is high because level 5 is about major new businesses, not marginal ones. American Airlines is reported to make more profit from its information systems than from air transport.

Like level 4, level 5 goes outside the organization and involves strategic thinking. The enablers and inhibitors are similar to those for level 4, being associated with strategic vision and recognition of new types of benefits, or lack of such vision.

A number of aspects of the transformation graph need to be emphasized. The first is the distinction between the evolutionary changes implied by levels 1 and 2 and the revolutionary changes implied by levels 3 to 5. Levels 1 and 2 developments can take place through logical thought and implementation; levels 3 to 5 need creative and lateral thinking.

The second is that although the levels have been presented in the order 1 to 5, this does not necessarily mean that an organization has to start at level 1 and move in the strict sequence 1–2–3–4–5. It is likely that any organization will start at level 1 and then move on to level 2, but after that there is no generally preferred order. American Airlines, for example, moved straight from level 2 to level 5.

The third point is that the transformation graph, like the Index matrix, is similar to a balance sheet giving a snapshot of where an organization is at a particular point in time. An organization's progress can be monitored over time as its strategic position changes.

Organizations can also move down as well as up the graph. For example, although American Airlines was once at level 5 when it started selling its reservation system services, it is no longer at this level since the 'new product' is now firmly established.

The management of strategic IT

'Strategic IT' implies that IT must be on the senior management agenda. Indeed, the MIT90s Research Programme and other research demonstrates that success in the deployment of strategic IT depends upon the way general management manages this resource. This is not easy because until recently IT has simply been delegated to the IT manager. In particular, the research suggests that management's *view* of IT is a prime indicator of success.

The old view of IT was of a technical support function. The job of senior management was to appoint the right IT manager and let him or her get on with it. There would be no need for senior management involvement unless things went badly wrong, in which case senior management would reorganize the IT department and/or sack the IT manager. Both seemed to happen rather frequently. However, the key characteristics of IT have now changed.

Characteristic		Emerging view
Focus	IT platform	*Not* Isolated systems
Investment vision	Business transformation	*Not* Technological sophistication
Investment criteria	Business criteria	*Not* Cost-benefit criteria alone
Scope of impact	Business domain	*Not* IT/IS domains
Executive responsibility	Strategic (line) manager	*Not* IT manager
Guiding principle	Strategy–IT alignment	*Not* IT for implementation

Figure 2.10 The emerging view of the IT infrastructure

These changes are inherent in all the aspects of strategic IT discussed in the chapter so far. Figure 2.10[5] draws them together and summarizes them. The *focus* is no longer on isolated systems (level 1 of the transformation graph). It is on the idea of an IT infrastructure which can support transformations of level 3 and above. The *investment vision* has changed from seeking the goal of technological sophistication to attempting to transform the business, its internal processes and inter-organizational networks. *Investment criteria* have moved on from efficiency criteria, i.e. spending money to reduce costs and using Return on Investment techniques to measure them. Investment criteria now focus on business criteria such as whether the system improves the competitiveness of the organization or, in the case of public sector organizations, helps them achieve their objectives significantly more effectively. The *scope of impact* was formerly limited mainly to the IT domain of the organization but now it has significant impacts throughout the business domain. As we have mentioned frequently, *executive responsibility* has broadened from the IT manager to include strategic, senior line managers. The overall *guiding principle* used to be the application of IT to automate functions and procedures. Now thinking should be led by strategic concerns and, in particular, the necessity of aligning IT strategy with corporate strategy.

The implication of these changes must be that, in the future, organizations' views of IT will have to be different. In many organizations IT operated (and often still does) *independently* of the main business. Senior management attended to strategic matters such as improving competitiveness, increasing profits and extending market share. Meanwhile, IT managers would search the organization for opportunities to automate functions. They would do this with only the briefest reference, or even no reference at all, to the strategic activities.

As the view of IT as a strategic resource has gained ground, some organizations have moved to a *dependent* role for IT. After the corporate strategy has been developed and finalized, the IT manager is asked to develop an IT strategy which is essentially the objectives and projects which demonstrate how IT can contribute to the achievement of the corporate strategy.

The implications of strategic IT, however, require more. The organization should view IT as *interdependent* with the strategic management of the organization. There should be an interaction between the creation of corporate strategy and of an IT strategy. Both will feed off each other, resulting in an IT strategy deeply embedded in, if not indistinguishable from, the corporate strategy.

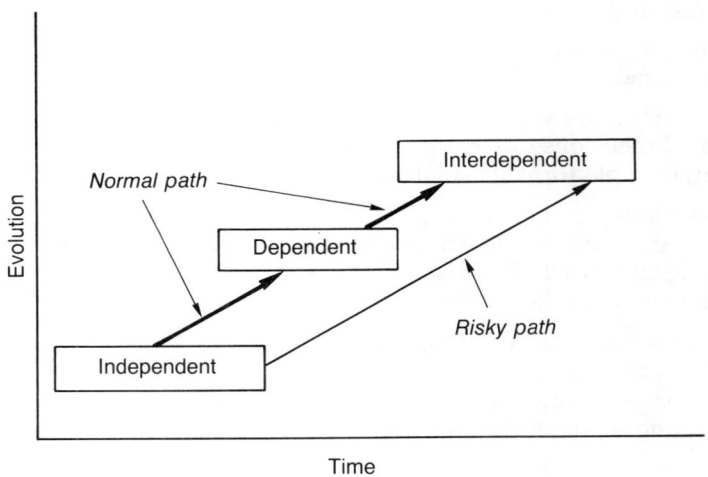

Figure 2.11 The organization's vision of IT

These organizational views of IT are summarized in Figure 2.11. The implication is that organizations should move towards an interdependent view of IT. For an organization at the independent level, the normal move will take it through the dependent view first. However, it is possible to move directly to the interdependent view, but it could be risky to do this too quickly because the move requires radical changes in modes of thinking and management skills.

Conclusions

If we accept, as we surely must, that IT is a strategic resource and one of the key factors in determining competitive positioning in the next century, then IT must also be a key factor (not, of course, the only factor) in determining the winners and losers of competitive battles. This must be particularly true in terms of global companies and global competition since one of IT's biggest impacts is its effect in breaking down barriers, whether organizational or geographical, permitting organizations to move more easily into wider international areas.

The next logical step is therefore to ask what part IT will play in deciding the outcome of any future competitive battles between Japanese and Western companies. Kenichi Imai believes that it will be a significant part:

> There is no doubt that information technology is fundamentally changing the structure of the world economy and that information-related industries are actually becoming the core of new industrial development. New business contexts have been created in the 1980s by information technology...In the 1990s a total restructuring of world industry and business will proceed on a fully-fledged scale...
>
> Information technology will contribute to new growth in the Japanese economy and is thus the major driving force of structural change.[6]

It is difficult to assess and analyse the strategic contribution of IT but the four dimensions described in this chapter do provide something in the way of a platform for analysis: i.e.

- How strategic IT is for a particular organization
- What the business benefits of strategic IT are
- The extent to which IT is being used to induce transformation
- The view of IT held by the senior management of an organization

When the case studies of Japanese companies have been presented in Part Two of this book we will have extensive data with which to carry out an analysis. The case study data will be used to analyse the companies along these four dimensions. The results will be presented in Part Three.

Notes

1 In the American computer magazine *Computer Weekly*, Robert Crandall, Chairman of American Airlines, is quoted as saying 'If you told me I had to sell either the airline or the system, I'd probably sell the airline'.

2   The Taurus system had the strategic aim of allowing the London Stock Exchange to leapfrog its European rivals in terms of efficiency and customer service. Its abandonment wasted anything from £200 million to £500 million and beyond (according to the many, and wildly different, estimates) and put London at a competitive disadvantage. See reports in the *Financial Times, The Times, The Independent* on 11–12 March 1993 for details.
3   The MIT90s Research Programme took place between 1985 and 1990 and was led by the Massachussetts Institute of Technology. It involved around twelve sponsoring organizations from the United States and Europe, each of whom contributed $500 000. It addressed the question: How will IT influence organizations and their ability to survive and prosper in the 1990s and beyond? The research is summarized in Scott Morton, M. (ed.), *The Corporation of the 1990s*, Oxford University Press (1991).
4   McFarlan, F. W., 'IT changes the way you compete', *Harvard Business Review*, **62**(3), 1984.
5   Figure 2.10 is adapted from one developed in the MIT90s research programme and presented in Scott Morton (ed.), *op. cit.* Likewise Figure 2.11.
6   Imai, K. in Soesastro, H. and Pangestu, M., *Technological Challange in the Asia Pacific Economy*, Allen and Unwin (Australia) (1990).

3
Japanese culture and Japanese management

In their book the *Art of Japanese Management*, Pascale and Athos suggest: '...Managerial reality is not an absolute; rather it is socially and culturally determined.'[1] Managers, of any nationality, do not make decisions in a vacuum. Much of the way in which managers think, behave and make decisions is influenced by countless factors determined by cultural background. Management styles tend to reflect cultural norms; those of society at large and the more specific culture of a particular organization.

An organization's culture is the product of the organization's history tempered by current employees; and work practices. New recruits learn an organization's culture through induction courses, their own errors, day-to-day work practices, examples, suggestions, and comments of peers and superiors. Some employees, especially those who have a high profile, may exert a greater influence on an organization's culture.

A closer look at the customs and etiquette of Japanese society will provide a framework for our later discussions of Japanese management concerns and priorities.

Isolation and insularity

Like all nations, Japan's geography, history, climate and the relative paucity of its natural resources have combined to give the Japanese a distinctive worldview. Japan is a group of mountainous, volcanic islands extending some 3000 kilometres from north to south with a total land area of roughly one and a half times the size of the UK, or the extent of the Eastern seaboard of the United States from the Canada–US border to northern Florida.[2]

Unfortunately, most of Japan is unsuitable for either agriculture or habitation. Fifteen per cent of the land area is given over to agriculture and the population (currently about 124 million) is cramped into less than 10 per cent of the total land area; the majority inhabiting the relatively flat strips of land along the coast.[3] Predictably, Japan has some of the highest population densities in the world. In urban Tokyo approximately 11 500 people inhabit each square kilometre, and this falls to 332 people per square kilometre in Japan as a whole.

For most of their history, the Japanese have been inward-looking. Apart from Portuguese missionaries and a settlement of Dutch traders (who lived in segregation on an island off Nagasaki), Japan was isolated from Western influences for over 200 years from 1638. The first contact with the West was in 1853, when America's Commodore Perry and his flotilla of 'black ships' forced the Shogunate of Edo (as Tokyo was then called) to open up the country to foreign trade.

Japan enjoys a temperate climate, with summers which are hot and humid. Rainfall is more than adequate with monsoon rains during the summer months. The winter months are mild by some European and North American standards, although the northern island of Honshu experiences heavy snow. Apart from this, the relatively mild climate provides a growing season of around 250 days. This climate and the shortage of quality farmland mean that Japanese farmers farm their land intensively.

Japan has very few natural resources and needs to import most of its raw materials, including domestic energy requirements. The country's most valuable natural asset is a highly educated population.

Japanese perceptions of reality

Historical, political and geographical factors have contributed to Japanese isolation. The Japanese have not been refugees from their homeland, nor have they admitted large numbers of foreigners.[4] In Japan's entire history, foreigners have attempted to invade twice.[5]

The net result of all these factors is a closely knit, homogeneous society which sees itself as a cohesive group. In sociological terms, this gives rise to a 'high-context' society where members do not need to explain their terms of reference and where mutual understanding is a forgone conclusion. Recognizing this, the Japanese frequently prefix opinions with 'we Japanese' (*'ware ware Nihonjin'*).

Inside and outside

To the Japanese the world consists of two kinds of people: the Japanese and everyone else. *Uchi* (inside) and *soto* (outside) are two words used by the Japanese to classify themselves and others. All Japanese are insiders, everyone else is an outsider. Being inside means being part of the group, be it local community, school or university, workplace and, ultimately, Japan. As one writer notes:

> To be Japanese means to bear one of the names in the official register of Japanese names; to celebrate the yearly Festival of the Dead, when the spirits of all the other Japanese who have ever existed return to their native places. It means to be for ever an inside man – inside a family, inside a village, inside a company, inside the Japanese islands surrounded by sea.[6]

Insiders are treated differently from outsiders. Foreigners (*gaijin*, literally = outside person) are given respect, according to rank or status, including being treated as an honoured guest. However, by definition, outsiders may never become insiders; even those who live in Japan for long periods and who marry Japanese citizens. In the words of one writer: 'The only way to win acceptance by the Japanese is to be born into their tribe.'[7] Another author writes: 'To a Japanese, being Japanese is a primary fact of life.'[8] One Japanese businessman is quoted as saying 'We Japanese are a hundred million brothers.'[9]

This concept of 'us and the rest' endorses for the Japanese the view that they are different; a trait that some politicians have not been slow to exploit when justifying import restrictions on foreign goods.[10]

Harmony, conformity and consensus

Japanese society has one overriding concern – sustaining harmony (*wa*). Group well-being takes precedence over individual happiness. Shuji Hayashi, author of *Culture and Management in Japan*, states: 'In Japanese society, individual rights were always equated with private interests, which are always inferior to public interests.'[11] In Japan, individuality is not admired, as it detracts from the well-being of the group. For the same reason, spontaneity, whether of thought or action, is discouraged. Group solidarity is paramount. Hayashi continues: '...The dominant perception in Japan is that the whole is more than the sum of the parts.'[12] Within the group, a smooth surface appearance is to be preserved at all costs, even if individual members feel inner turmoil. A Japanese will avoid giving criticism or opinions which conflict with the group, as these cause disharmony and loss of face to group members. It is more important to express empathy (*omoiyari*) with the feelings of others. In this way, obstacles can be overcome by combined effort.

The price paid for group support is a sense of obligation for favours carried out. The words *kashi* (lending) and *kari* (indebtedness) refer to the expectation from the giver to the receiver of a personal favour. The individual shoulders this responsibility until the debt of gratitude is repaid. In Japanese the words *arigato* and *sumimasen* are different ways of saying 'thank you'. However, *sumimasen* literally means 'not yet finished'; with the implied meaning of acknowledging that a kind deed incurs an obligation which must be returned.

Front and back

Japanese culture accepts two realities: an idealized version and one which may be less than ideal. Both realities co-exist and are regarded as opposite sides of the same coin. For the Japanese, a sign of intellectual maturity is the mental agility to acknowledge both versions simultaneously, especially when they conflict.

The concepts of *tatemae* (external appearances, general principles) and *honne* (the true self, internal feelings and thoughts) give more subtle dimensions to Japanese multi-layered perceptions of reality. Preserving flawless external appearances (*tatemae*) is paramount. On most occasions, Japanese people are adept at keeping these two aspects of their daily lives separate and admire foreigners with the sophistication, and good manners, to do likewise.

Individuals avoid saying or doing anything to disturb the tranquillity of the group. Personal feelings and opinions are compromised in the interests of group solidarity. Hayashi captures this succinctly:

> In Japanese society the organization is more important than its members. The group is the source of ultimate values, the loci of moral obligation.[13]

Innermost feelings, including dissent, occupy an inner reality (*honne*). Heartfelt feelings are seldom, if ever, discussed except possibly between very close friends. It would be impolite and a sign of poor character to express personal feelings publicly. An individual who does so risks being the 'nail that sticks out' which, according to a Japanese proverb, 'gets hammered down'.

Associated with collective and personal comfort and peace of mind is the notion of 'face'. In Western societies, this concept is somewhat vague. Although we have the English expressions 'to save face' or 'to lose face', these phrases may have entered the language from our understanding of other, mainly Asian, cultures which place a higher importance on position and status than is usually the norm in Western societies. To the Japanese, 'face' (*kao*) is an important part of an individual's psyche and affects a person's inner feelings and sense of well-being. Losing face brings great shame.

In personal interaction the Japanese are careful to avoid giving offence to others. Consideration for the feelings of others includes not doing or saying anything that would cause someone to 'lose face'. Criticism and anger directed at another person, particularly from a younger person to an older, more senior person, are strenuously avoided. It would be particularly hurtful to cause someone to 'lose face' in front of others, and especially in the presence of a foreigner.

Appearance has two related concepts, *omote* and *ura*. These refer to the surface or front side of an object (*omote*) and its reverse side (*ura*), corresponding to the public and private sides of life. *Omote* refers to the projected outward appearances, including public ceremony; while *ura* relates to activities carried out 'behind the scenes', including the conduct of everyday life. These words have a number of everyday uses: *Ura Nihon* (the back part of Japan) refers to the part of Japan away from the industrial metropolis on the Pacific coast; main roads in cities and towns are called *omote-dori*, narrow lanes and backstreets are called *ura-dori*.[14]

The Japanese value modesty (*kenson*) and a person will instinctively understate their achievements in order to avoid being the 'nail that sticks out'. Complimentary personal remarks induce a smile and a self-deprecating phrase; gifts given to family, friends and colleagues are dismissed by the donor as 'nothing special'. Similarly, individuals are reluctant to appear pushy. Offers of help will repeatedly be refused until a person feels they have shown an appropriate degree of reserve (*enryo*). Patience (*nintai, shinbo*) is another virtue that is appreciated. 'Patience is the first virtue' (*Nanigoto mo shinbo ga daiichi*) is a well-known Japanese proverb.

An important aspect of Japanese life is recognizing tradition and social conventions and being seen to do the correct thing at the right time. This is demonstrated in all aspects of daily life, from gift giving (where the wrapping is often more elaborate than the gift it contains), the conduct of social routines and human interaction, personal appearance and demeanour, to the high importance of ritual and ceremony in the Japanese social calendar.

Rank and status

Japan is a hierarchical society, an attribute it shares with most, if not all, other Asian countries. Age and seniority are respected and there is a direct correlation between age and wisdom. The Japanese language has special words and postures for addressing people who are older or younger than oneself. Respect for an older person is shown by the words chosen when speaking and by giving a lower, and thus more deferential, bow than received.

Awareness of rank and one's social position relative to other people is one of the lubricants of Japanese society at all levels. It guides behaviour in all human contact and pervades all aspects of society. Rank and status determine social etiquette, including which words and gestures are appropriate between people, the form of greetings (younger and junior people use more polite salutations, bow first and give a lower bow to older and senior people); the appropriate place for a person to sit at a meeting (the senior person sits farthest away from the door); who leaves meetings first (the most senior leaves first).

The duties and social implications of rank, in terms of who is senior (*senpai*) and junior (*kohai*), follow an individual from cradle to grave. Awareness training begins in childhood and continues throughout formal education and into the workplace. An unspoken bond cements *senpai–kohai* relationships. Juniors afford seniors the respect warranted by their rank; in turn, seniors act as mentors to juniors. This relationship is especially strong if both follow each other into the same company after graduating from the same university. In this situation, the senior person will initiate the junior into company ways.

The corporate family

A Japanese person joining a company as a *salariman* (white-collar worker) joins a corporate family. In return for loyalty, diligence and hard work the company acts like a surrogate family. The company maintains a paternalistic attitude towards employees, in a relationship that has been called 'welfare corporatism'. It is therefore not surprising that reversing the Japanese characters for corporation (*kaisha*) make the word 'society' (*shakai*).

However, the relationship has obligations for each side. The company provides individuals and their families with security and welfare during and after their working lives. The much-publicized benefits include the 'four treasures' of Japanese corporate life: lifetime employment, promotion and salary based on seniority, consensus decision making, and enterprise unions.

Additional advantages include company housing, on-the-job training, pension and other benefits, and sports and recreational facilities. In return, the company expects loyalty and commitment from the individual. In this respect the company can be a stern taskmaster – a fact of life that the employee accepts as part of the work ethic. The habit of Japanese employees to work long hours, followed by late evening socializing sessions with the boss has been much reported. (However, there are signs that this may be changing, especially with the younger generation of employees who wish to spend more time with their family.) It is not unknown for companies to transfer employees to another job away from home at short notice.

Lifetime employment

Lifetime employment is a corollary of the long-term commitment which the company expects from its employees and of the continuous on-the-job training that companies give to employees, especially the management cadre. Managers who are life members of the same corporate family are more likely to generate a sincere commitment to their own and their company's development.

In fact, lifetime employment was introduced as recently as 1955 and is still only offered by the larger corporations, and then only to specific members of the organization who constitute an inner core of management. These are mainly males recruited directly from university who are destined for promotion up the corporate hierarchy. This cadre may constitute 30–40 per cent of a company's total workforce.

The system of lifetime employment does not usually extend to contract workers, females or employees at affiliated companies. In times of economic adversity, companies will reduce the numbers of employees who do not hold lifetime positions, while keeping sacrosanct the inner core of management. Smaller domestic companies cannot afford the luxury of offering employees lifetime employment. Besides, as one Japanese author has suggested, lifetime employment is an ideal:

> ...Lifetime employment as practised in Japan is no more than a general guiding principle. It is by no means a guarantee.[15]

Even those managers who benefit from lifetime employment may find that their companies restrict employment at head office only up to the age of 50–55, at which time retirement becomes obligatory. Even before this time, some managers, especially those who have not made senior management grade, may be transferred to serve out their remaining time with affiliated companies, suppliers, or subcontractors. However, companies, and Japanese society in general, are rethinking lifetime employment.[16]

Job rotation

Potential managers are recruited into a large company as generalists rather than specialists. Once new recruits have served a period of two years, it is conventional practice to rotate them between a series of jobs. There are a number of reasons for this.

First, it allows the generalist manager to gain experience in a number of departments and functions; in effect, transforming generalist managers into specialist generalists. Second, it allows managers the opportunity to extend their network – a factor which will ease later cross-department cooperation and decision making. A third reason is that managers who rotate between various functions within the company gain a larger picture of the company's operations. Fourth, job rotation allows candidates for promotion to senior positions to be monitored and assessed by other managers. Getting on with people is a prerequisite for advancement into senior management ranks. Companies seek to promote team players to comply with Japanese concepts of leadership in which leaders are merely representatives of the group.

Corporate hierarchy

Japanese companies divide the workforce into senior management and everyone else. One commentator explains:

> ...The critical dividing line is drawn between top management and all other employees. In the Japanese case, to be in top management clearly equates with being a member of the board of directors. Except for this elite group everyone is simply an employee.[17]

To Western minds, Japanese job titles and the duties which accompany them, appear flexible. However, Japanese society and corporate life are more at ease than the West with flexibility and ambiguity. One writer argues that the acceptance of ambiguity (*ma*) gives Japanese managers 'a dual frame of reference – recognizing the clear and the ambiguous...in certain situations ambiguity may serve better than absolute clarity'.[18]

Job titles exist but, for several reasons, managers' duties tend to overlap. Job descriptions are rare: the employee interprets broad guidelines for policy and objectives. Responsibility is shared and work tasks are done in teams. Decision making is by consensus and, unlike in Western companies, is less likely to be constrained by job boundaries. On-the-job training encourages expertise in diverse functions. Employers regard flexibility as a valuable asset.

Table 3.1 shows the principal corporate ranks in a Japanese company. The concept of seniority is also demonstrated in a system whereby senior members of the organization are responsible for training a junior colleague. The senior person (*senpai*) may be a former university senior of the junior colleague (*kohai*). The relationship will continue throughout each person's time with the company and will encompass both professional and social matters. This system also generates close ties between individuals within the company as each *senpai* is simultaneously someone's *kohai*.

Table 3.1 Japanese corporate ranks[19]

Position	Title	Translation	Age (approx.)
	Top management (*Keiei shoku* = board members)		
Top management	*Keiei kanbu*	Executives	Early 50s–late 60s or 70s
	Kaicho	Chairman	
	Shacho	President	
	Fuku shacho	Vice president	
	Senmu torishimariyaku	Senior managing director	
	Jomu torishimariyaku	Managing directors	
	Torishimariyaku	Directors	
	Employees (*Kaishain* = company members)		
Middle management	*Kanrisha/midoru manejimento*	Middle management	Mid-40s
	Bucho	Department chief/head	Mid-/late 30s–early 40s
	Chukan kanrishoku, Kacho	Section chief/head	
Junior management	*Kakaricho*	Sub-section chief	Early–mid-30s
	Hancho	Group leader	
	Shunin	Person in charge	
	Daichisen kantokusha[a]	First-line supervisors	
	Shokucho[a]	Foreman	
	Uribasekininsha[b]	Floor manager	
	Tencho[b]	Person in charge (store chief)	

[a] Job titles in a factory.
[b] Job titles in a department store.

Promotion by seniority

Conventionally, promotion in a Japanese company is by length of service. Length of service rather than job grade denotes salary increases. As an employee gains experience in a number of company departments through job rotation, so he or she is considered able to accept greater responsibility. Personal expertise or merit are secondary considerations. However, even managers who show promise and potential need to conform to age requirements. This keeps everyone who graduated at the same time in lockstep and slows down the progression of younger 'high fliers' up the management hierarchy. This ensures that no-one in the same group of graduates feels left behind and diffuses any feelings of jealousy or bitterness that may build up and have an adverse effect on work. In a large Japanese company promotion of relatively young managers on grounds of merit would be unusual, if not downright eccentric. One British manager is reported as saying 'the Japanese simply like grey hair'.[20]

As the corporate pinnacle becomes narrower, managers who are no longer regarded as senior management potential are relegated to sections and departments away from the main business functions. Here, underemployed and with little responsibility, they become members of 'the window-gazing tribe' (*madogiwa-zoku*). Such employees occupy desks around the periphery of the office where they are well placed to spend their working day looking out of the window. To all intents and purposes, further career advancement is precluded. Such managers would be tempted to resign from the company, were it not for the feeling of belonging, however tenuously, to the group.

Not surprisingly, most senior management positions in subsidiary companies are held by Japanese managers, usually on five-year assignments.[21] The promotion of a non-Japanese to senior management rank is newsworthy.[22]

Task sharing and team work

One acknowledged attribute of successful Japanese management is the natural ability of the Japanese to organize themselves into working groups. Shuji Hayashi, the author of *Culture and Management in Japan*, cited earlier, writes: 'Groupism sets the tone of Japanese-style management and organization behaviour.'[23]

In the offices of large Japanese companies, the close proximity and physical layout of desks encourage team working and constant communication between staff and section heads. Desks are arranged so that work teams in a department are next to and facing each other. At the head of the section, and facing down the two rows of desks, sits the section head. This layout ensures rapid two-way communication. Everyone in the particular section knows what is happening in the section and section heads can maintain constant touch with section members.

At the beginning of each working day the section heads talk to their sections and outline the work priorities for the day. They also allocate work to their sections, usually to be shared between teams of several members so that no individual has the burden of responsibility for the work. This routine also promotes egalitarianism.

Japanese companies are said to be astute at 'getting things done through people'. David Lu, author of *Inside Corporate Japan*, suggests: 'The key to Japanese success has been dedication to team-work and desire to promote human resources (*jinzai*).'[24] Conceivably, the close working environment and the propensity of Japanese workers to work as a combined effort are contributory.

Decision making

Perhaps the most quoted difference between Japanese and Western management styles relates to the concept of Japanese consensus decision making, in which middle management has the opportunity to inform senior decision making, and the contrasting 'top-down' decision making in Western companies.

Nemawashi, a phrase taken from Japanese horticulture, literally means the process of separating and binding plant roots to prevent damage while replanting. In a business context *nemawashi* is usually translated to mean consensus decision making.[25] Lobbying is a similar procedure in Western management.

In business practice all relevant parties who will be affected by a decision are alerted in advance. This is not solely restricted to members of the company. In addition to department heads and section managers, it is not unknown for government bureaucrats, bank officials, suppliers and customers to be involved in decision making. Subsequently, when feelings and ideas can be converted into a written proposal, a document (*ringisho*) is prepared by a middle-level manager and circulated to colleagues. Individuals signify agreement by stamping a personal seal (*hanko*) on the *ringisho* document.[26]

However, *nemawashi* does not mean that middle-level managers make the final decision, rather that they have the opportunity to put their viewpoint to their superiors. In practical terms, *nemawashi* means that middle-level managers keep their superiors informed and avoid any unexpected surprises. In fact, the system requires more subtlety. As one Japanese senior executive is reported as saying:

> To be truthful, probably 60 per cent of the decisions I make are my decisions. but I keep my intentions secret. In discussions with subordinates, I ask questions, I pursue facts, and try to nudge them in my direction without disclosing my position as a result of the dialogue. But whatever the outcome, they feel part of the decision. Their involvement in the decision also increases their experience as managers.[27]

Basically, *nemawashi* is verbal lobbying which ensures that managers at similar seniority levels can communicate with each other, while having an input into the decision-making process. An additional advantage of *nemawashi* is that when proposals are discussed between a number of departments managers contribute ideas for development, improvement and sharing resources.

The system of preparing a written *ringisho* document allows managers at lower levels to inform their superiors of 'grassroots' feeling. When used in conjunction, the *nemawashi* and *ringi* systems ensure that corporate management at both horizontal and vertical levels are kept fully informed. However, when this style of management decision making is imported into a subsidiary, its success depends on the sensitivity of the Japanese senior management and on the willingness of local managers to adopt the system.

In Japanese subsidiaries in the UK, British and Japanese managers, particularly those in middle-management positions, experience frustrations with the *nemawashi* system. In particular, it can be frustrating for British managers and Japanese middle managers who feel excluded from the centre of decision making and who believe that such a system slows down the decision-making process. Some managers noted an inner and outer circle of decision involvement and bemoaned their exclusion from an 'inner circle' of decision makers. Some middle-level local and Japanese managers complain that they make a token contribution to decision making. 'Senior management decisions', some said, 'are a forgone conclusion.' However, shrewd managers influence decisions by channelling suggestions and proposals by lobbying a senior Japanese colleague. For their part, Japanese managers note a tendency for their non-Japanese colleagues to want quick decisions from one senior person, and to become impatient with the time needed to reach decisions acceptable to all interested parties.

A sceptic might suggest that consensus decision making is one of the Japanese management myths, and that in practice decisions made from the corporate pinnacle are passed downwards for implementation. This argument misunderstands the nature of *nemawashi*, which is more a way for senior managers to keep informed of 'grassroots' opinion. Senior management makes actual business decisions, taking into consideration the opinions of middle management.

Pareto effect

Reference is frequently made in management literature to the Pareto effect, sometimes called the 80:20 rule. When applied to Japanese and Western decision making, the Pareto effect highlights one of the basic differences.[28] This refers to the way in which the different cultures use available time.

According to the 80:20 rule, Western management uses 20 per cent of the time allocated for a particular project for decision making; the remaining 80 per cent of the time is spent working on the project. This 80 per cent will include 'fine tuning' to adjust the project in the light of unexpected problems. Japanese management practice decrees that 80 per cent of the allotted time is spent deciding every aspect of the project and ensuring that everyone involved in the project has a chance to contribute

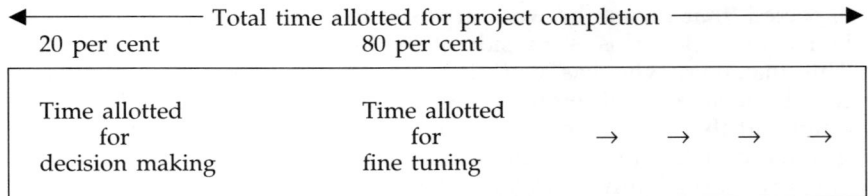

Figure 3.1 Western use of project time

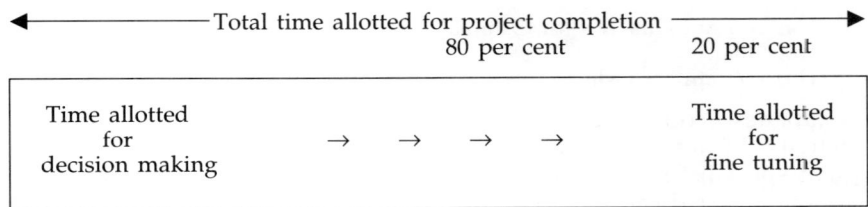

Figure 3.2 Japanese use of project time

their ideas and opinions; the remaining 20 per cent of the time is used to complete the project according to consensus; and there are no unexpected problems. Figures 3.1 and 3.2 illustrate how Japanese and Western managements use allotted project time.

A slightly different version of the Pareto effect notes that over a one-year project Western organizations spend three months deciding what to do, nine months putting the decision into practice and a *further* twelve months getting it right. In contrast, a Japanese organization spends nine months deciding what to do, three months putting the decision into practice...and it is right.[29]

Employees of Japanese companies frequently complain of the slowness with which Japanese managers make decisions. Employees in Western companies, used to decisions made 'on the hoof' by one senior manager, have little sympathy for collective decision-making procedures. Their frustration is exacerbated when head office in Tokyo takes months or even years to make decisions. For example, one company in London waited patiently for two years for a decision to be made on the most suitable mainframe computer to purchase. Another company waited a similar length of time for its Tokyo head office to prepare an item of purpose-designed software.

Decision-making boundaries

One Japanese manager related an incident in his former company when he helpfully made a decision on behalf of a colleague. Instead of an expected 'thank you', he was surprised to receive a stern reprimand by being told: 'Hey, this is my side of the fence; you're not in Japan now.' This manager, who has worked in Western and Japanese companies, noted one striking difference between the organization of a British company and that of a Japanese one. The former has a clear separation into groups according to corporate responsibilities, e.g. management functions and operational functions. Boundaries are vertical (defining decision-making responsibilities) and horizontal (to denote separate functional responsibilities).

The lack of functional boundaries is demonstrated by the Japanese company name preceding name or job title during introductions:

'This is/I am Hitachi's Mr Oshima'
rather than
'This is/I am Mr Oshima, from Hitachi'

Japanese companies tend to have looser distinctions of functional activity. In Japan, company recruitment exercises seek generalist rather than specialist skills. Once recruited by a company, an employee may follow a varied career path, which requires him (less frequently, her) to serve in a variety of functions. Graduate engineers and similar specialists are sometimes, although not invariably, exceptions.

Culture in a Japanese subsidiary

In the workplace, various factors affect the cultural arena of the work environment. In a Japanese subsidiary, some factors promote or moderate Japanese management styles and practices. Factors such as the length of time that a company has conducted business in the UK; the number of Japanese managers as percentage of the total workforce; the degree of deliberate effort on the part of senior Japanese management to introduce Japanese management styles. These factors in combination influence, consciously or otherwise, management styles within a company.

A predominant influence on the degree to which Japanese management styles are part of company culture is the attitude of senior Japanese management. Company behaviour is determined by the disposition of the senior Japanese director and his fellow directors. Directors who have had previous overseas assignments in an English-speaking environment dilute the company's 'Japaneseness'. A Japanese manager who feels familiar with a non-Japanese working environment is less likely to insist on Japanese work procedures and more likely to promote a 'neutral' working atmosphere. Such managers are also more likely to work successfully in the cultural landscape in the workplace.

In a subsidiary company, one attribute of a successful Japanese manager is an ability to switch, where appropriate, between the two cultures: for example, maintaining Japanese protocols when dealing with colleagues in head office while continuing to meet the local managers' cultural expectations. Conversely, a manager who relies solely on a Japanese style of management runs the risk of generating ill feelings from local colleagues, who may feel uncomfortable with unfamiliar practices. When this occurs, local staff may distance themselves from the manager concerned and give a less than full contribution to the team effort. Such a situation could lead to friction on both sides and the Japanese manager excluding local expertise from his management team.

Subtle clues indicate a company's cultural background. For example, some companies subscribe to Japanese newspapers and magazines and place these for the convenience of their customers in their reception area along with *The Times* and *Financial Times*. Others have glass display cabinets containing Japanese artifacts (models of *samurai* warriors are popular). Where the subsidiary has been commended by head office, the award certificate written in Japanese will be framed and proudly displayed.[30] Trading rooms at Japanese securities houses have certain computer screens which display financial markets information in Japanese. In one company numerous *salarimen*, members of a inspection team from head office, congregated in the reception area.

As they have become acclimatized to the UK market, Japanese companies have broadened their customer base. From solely serving other Japanese companies, subsidiaries have developed to serving British and now European companies. This has reduced the need for Japanese middle managers, who can be replaced by other nationals familiar with new markets. Some financial services companies employ various European and Middle Eastern securities trading staff to deal with newly instigated financial markets.

Aversion to conflict and risk

Respondents from a variety of Japanese companies describe Japanese management as exceedingly cautious in their business decision making. This feature is compounded in certain industries, e.g. banking and financial services, where prudence is a way of life. However, Japanese managers are said to be averse to conflict rather than risk.

Uncertainty and risk avoidance is not a cultural trait restricted to the Japanese.[31] Countries as seemingly diverse as Argentina, Spain and Israel display similar uncertainty-avoidance tendencies.[32] The Japanese themselves seem to be aware of this cultural characteristic. A Japanese manager told the following joke at the beginning of a presentation to a mainly British audience:

> A Japanese *salariman* is shipwrecked on a desert island. While walking around to explore he meets an attractive woman who is also a castaway. After polite introductions, including proffering his *meishi*,[33] the man uses his mobile phone (which he had made sure to rescue) to call his superior to ask 'What do I do now, boss?'

Some decisions, for example those which relate to IT, may foster a cautious approach. This may be amplified by unfamiliarity with the topic and an inclination to prevent loss of face by making an unsuitable, and potentially costly, decision. A high profile decision would be readily apparent to end users and most other employees. Several managers told us that when faced with uncertainty, Japanese management would most likely take a 'wait and see' approach.

Summary

Cultural upbringing and background guides managers' decisions regardless of their nationality. Japanese managers are the product of a society in which geography, history, climate and the relative paucity of its natural resources have combined to produce a distinctive, and in many ways unique, view of the world. Tempered by periods of natural and political isolation, the Japanese inhabit a society which is closely knit and homogeneous. In such a 'high-context' environment, mutual understanding between members is a forgone conclusion.

Harmony, conformity and consensus are strong guidelines in Japanese life, be it social or corporate. Japan is a hierarchical society where an awareness of rank and status and one's place in the hierarchy are of paramount important in the conduct of human relations. In the workplace, the duties and social implications of rank are reflected in the strong relationships between seniors and juniors.

Recruitment into a large Japanese company means 'joining the corporate family'; a paternalistic relationship that has been called 'welfare corporatism'. Obligations for each side oblige the company to provide security and welfare, including the 'four treasures' of Japanese corporate life: lifetime employment, promotion and salary based on seniority, consensus decision making, and enterprise unions. Loyalty and commitment are expected in return.

Job rotation, continual on-the-job training and team building ensure that managers become specialist generalists. Promotion by length of service, rather than merit of service means that managers make their slow but steady progress up the corporate hierarchy.

A close working environment, combined work effort and consensus decision making contribute to efficient communication. However, the Japanese system of consensus decision making can be frustrating for British managers and Japanese middle managers, who feel excluded from the centre of decision making and who believe that such a system slows down the decision-making process.

Applying the Pareto effect (the '80:20 rule') to this management technique demonstrates that time is gained in the long term as the lengthy 'thinking time' obviates future problems that may be overlooked when only 20 per cent of allotted time is devoted to thinking and planning.

The expertise of Japanese senior management shows itself in both cultural sensitivity (usually to matters involving human resources) and IT sensitivity (an awareness of IT issues). Japanese managers who have previously worked overseas, preferably in English-speaking environments, are more likely to be culturally sensitive. With such a person at the head of a company, reporting procedures (including Japanese styles) are likely to be more informal and dealings with a head office in Tokyo are less likely to be conducted deferentially.

Notes

1. Pascale, R. T. and Athos, A. G., *The Art of Japanese Management*, Simon and Schuster (1981), p. 22.
2. Japan consists of the four main islands of Hokkaido, Honshu, Shikoko and Kyushu and another 6850 smaller islands.
3. Approximately 75 per cent of the land is covered by mountains and volcanoes (of which 60 are active). Agriculture occupies plots of land between unsuitable land.
4. Currently, 900 000 foreigners live in Japan (approximately 0.75 per cent of the total population). Eighty per cent are Koreans who, except the few who have been naturalized, are classed as resident aliens.
5. In 1281 a Mongol invading fleet was thwarted by a hurricane which the Japanese called *kamikazi* (divine wind). From 1946 to 1952 the Allied powers occupied Japan.
6. Tasker, P., *Inside Japan*, Sidgwick and Jackson (1987).
7. Christopher, R. C., *The Japanese Mind*, Charles E. Tuttle (1983) p. 49.
8. Tasker, *op. cit.*
9. Christopher, *op. cit.*, p. 51.
10. Some of the reported examples are that Japanese snow is unsuitable for foreign-made skis; and that Japanese stomachs are unable to digest imported beef.
11. Hayashi, S., *Culture and Management in Japan*, University of Tokyo Press (1988).
12. *Ibid.*
13. *Ibid.*
14. Tasker, *op. cit.*
15. Hasegawa, K., *Japanese Style Management; An Insider's View*, Kodansha Press (1986). Quoted in Whitehill (1991) (see note 17).
16. See, for example, the following discussions: 'The sun sets on Japan's lifers', *Management Today*, September 1993; 'Sitting by the window, looking at the sack', *Daily Telegraph* 11 October 1993.
17. Whitehill, A. M., *Japanese Management – Tradition and Transition*, Routledge (1991), p. 112.
18. For an interesting discussion of ambiguity see Pascale, R. T., 'Zen and the art of management', *Harvard Business Review*, March–April 1978; 'Communication and decision making across cultures: Japanese and American Comparisons', *Administrative Science Quarterly*, March 1978.
19. The table is an amalgam from the following three sources, each of which contains an interesting discussion of the importance of rank and job title in Japanese corporate life. Handy, C. (ed.), *Making*

Managers, Pitman (1988); Whitehill, *op. cit.* Jones, S., *Working for the Japanese*, Macmillan (1991).
20 Quoted in Jones, *ibid.*, p. 96.
21 Jones, *ibid.*, p. 250, gives much higher figures on the basis of a larger sample size.
22 See, for example, *Financial Times*, 4 October 1989, 'American to head Nomura US offshoot'.
23 Hayashi, *op. cit.*
24 Lu, D. J., *Inside Corporate Japan*, Charles E. Tuttle (1989) p. 27.
25 Several sources contain more detailed descriptions of *nemawashi*. For example: Oppenheim, *op. cit.*, p. 123; Jones, *op. cit.*, pp. 71–72, 77, 82, 217; Reischauer, E. O., *The Japanese Today*, The Belknap Press of Harvard University Press (1977, 1988), pp. 321–22.
26 Examples of *ringi* in practice are contained in Jones, *op. cit.*, pp. 69–85. See also Lu, *op. cit.*, pp. 42–43; Reischauer, *op. cit.*, pp. 321–22; Tasker, *op. cit.*, pp. 55–6, 79; and Oppenheim, *op. cit.*, p. 123.
27 Quoted by Pascale, in 'Zen and the art of management'.
28 See, for example, Whitehill, *op. cit.*, pp. 161–162.
29 For a similar anecdote see Harvey-Jones, J., *Making It Happen*, Fontana (1988), pp. 75–76.
30 Examples of further facets of 'Japaneseness' can be found in White, M. and Trevor, M., *Under Japanese Management*, Heinemann (1983), pp. 54ff.
31 See Hofstede, G., *Culture's Consequences, International Differences in Work-related Values*, Sage Publications (1980), particularly Chapter 4.
32 Hofstede, G., *Cultures and Organizations*, McGraw-Hill (1991), Figure 5.2. See also pp. 113–115, 122, 126.
33 *Meishi* = namecard. Exchanging namecards is the opening ritual in Japanese business meetings as it alerts people to the status of the other participants.

Part Two
Case Studies

This part contains case studies from ten subsidiaries of Japanese companies. These companies, who are recognized as leaders in their fields, represent a variety of industry sectors. They include travel and tourism, financial services and a distributor of information systems. A number of manufacturers are represented in the case studies including steel, semiconductors, consumer electronic products and motor vehicles.

Specifically, this part contains cases studies of IT in the following companies:

- *All Nippon Airways Ltd (ANA)*, the largest airline in Japan, is actively pursuing its expansion plans. ANA's IT systems are a vital element in the company's operations as not only do they control booking and reservation procedures but they also provide ANA's business development, marketing and planning departments with crucial commercial data.
- *Daiwa Europe Ltd (DEL)*, is a securities house based in the City of London. A subsidiary of Daiwa Securities Co. Ltd, DEL's main business is underwriting, brokering and dealing in the capital markets. In an industry where the timely and accurate transmission of information is vital to commercial success, DEL relies heavily on its IT systems.
- One of the largest and most diversified Japanese companies in the UK, *Hitachi Europe Ltd (HEL)* was established in 1982 to sell Hitachi products and expand the company's market share throughout the EC. HEL is a market leader in semiconductor manufacturing, and uses IT to provide its customers with a high standard of service.
- *Japan Travel Bureau (JTB)* is an international travel company with a network of 300 branches and 602 agencies in Japan and over 50 offices worldwide. JTB uses IT to manage bookings on airlines, trains and ships and offer travel-related services including hotel reservations, car hire and tours for 1.8 million travellers annually.
- *JVC (UK) Ltd* markets and distributes JVC-branded consumer electronic products in the UK. From its head office in north London, JVC (UK) manages a sales network of dealers. IT is used to provide sales teams and their customers with up-to-the-minute information about available products, orders, deliveries, prices and discounts.
- From offices in London, *Kobe Steel Europe Ltd (KSE)* uses IT to provide procurement services for head office in Kobe, Japan.
- *Nissan Motor (GB) Ltd (NMGB)* is responsible for the marketing and sales of Nissan products in the UK. A relative newcomer into the British motor industry, NMGB has had to start trading almost from scratch. The company

uses IT systems to manage an extensive dealership network and to provide analytical and logistical services for dealers and NMGB sales teams.
- *Nissan Motor Manufacturing (UK) Ltd (NMUK)* manufactures the Nissan Micra and Primera models at its site in Sunderland, UK. Apart from using IT to facilitate manufacturing processes, NMUK has developed IT systems to manage procurement, production and finished product shipment.
- *Sony (UK) Ltd (SUK)* is the division of Sony Corporation responsible for sales and distribution of Sony products in the UK. SUK uses IT systems for three main purposes: communicating with head office and manufacturing sites in Japan: communicating with Sony sites in the UK: giving an efficient service to UK dealers.
- *Toshiba Information Systems (UK) Ltd (TIU)* distributes electrical and electronic products manufactured by companies in the Toshiba group for the UK market. TIU uses IT for a number of reasons, including warehouse and distribution systems, management information systems (MIS) and an executive information system (EIS).

For ease of reference and accessibility we have organized each of the case studies in the same way. The *case profile* at the beginning of each case study describes why each company uses IT and outlines other essential facts. This is followed by *company background*, which describes the history of the company. This section also gives some information about the particular industry or marketplace in which the company operates.

The section headed *business impact* of IT describes the effects that IT has on the company and its business activities. *Managing IT* describes how the company manages its IT resource.

4
All Nippon Airways Ltd

Case profile

Information management is crucial to ANA, especially as the airline seeks to expand its operations and increase the number of passengers it carries. In common with other modern airlines, ANA relies on its computer reservation systems (CRS) to manage the volume of passenger bookings. ANA uses its CRS for three purposes: to maximize passenger yield; to attract new passengers; and to create business opportunities by managing existing data.

Flight bookings are managed through *able-D* (domestic) and *able-I* (international). The *able* CRS allows ANA to gain access to any other airline's CRS. In the interests of saving time and cost, ANA bought existing CRS software from another airline in preference to in-house development. In conjunction with *Infini*, a 'one-stop' computer system designed for travel agency services such as hotel accommodation, rail reservations and car hire, *able* allows ANA to maintain links with the main outlets for airline ticket bookings. It is axiomatic to say that the interests of both ANA and travel agents are best served if flight information is displayed clearly and accurately and passenger booking information is transmitted quickly to ANA. Rapid transmission of accurate information is vital.

Zeus, a yield control system which shows the breakdown of fares on each flight, was installed in London office in January 1993. A link between *Zeus* and *able* will help ANA to increase profitability from tour group bookings.

ANA's ticketing and reservations department produces and collates passenger information for sales and marketing purposes. The vast majority of ANA's current international passenger base is Japanese who travel to and from foreign capital cities from ANA's hub in Tokyo.

When analysed historically, airline travel data, supplemented by current business intelligence, can reveal useful information about increased or decreased passenger volumes. These data help ANA's marketing department to target business opportunities, possibly in collaboration with a local travel agency. For example, the data may reveal that certain flights on certain days carry a load capacity that could be improved by offering group discounts.

Company background

All Nippon Airways (ANA) was founded in 1952 as a purely domestic carrier in Japan. ANA prospered in the wake of the expansion in the Japanese domestic aviation market. In 1986 the Japanese government implemented policy changes relating to domestic aviation, in order to stimulate a competitive environment.[1] Operational restrictions of JAL (Japan Airlines Limited) were eased and the airline was allowed to fly between domestic destinations. ANA was allowed to fly internationally and expanded its activities into areas prohibited to JAL.[2]

Since its inception, ANA has grown to be the largest airline in Japan[3] and the eighth largest in the world. ANA holds just over 50 per cent of the Japanese domestic market (See Figure 4.1).

ANA became an international airline in 1986 and now flies to eighteen international destinations on four continents. ANA currently carries approximately 34 million passengers a year on over ninety-five scheduled routes. The most recent scheduled destinations on ANA's international routing are Los Angeles, Sydney, Honolulu, Paris, New York, Frankfurt and Shanghai (Figure 4.2).

With its fleet of 129 aircraft and orders placed with Boeing for their latest models, including the Boeing 777 twin-jet, the airline is well placed to benefit from Japan's three airport-construction projects.[4]

ANA's business goal is to maximize revenue from the finite number of seats on each flight. This is done by first selling the high-yield, most expensive seating in first and business class.

Airline profitability

Airline profitability is predominantly linked to yield, which is the return on the transportation of passengers after operating costs have been covered. Direct operating costs include landing fees, fuel and catering; indirect costs include administration, marketing, salaries and aircraft pay-back. These costs are 'built into' each aircraft departure in order to calculate the breakeven figure.

An average payback period for a commercial aircraft is approximately ten years, and airlines tend to depreciate their fleet over this period. While certain airlines market themselves as a young fleet and reduce their payback period to less than the industry norm, some operate with a payback period extended to twenty years.

Within the commercial aviation industry the convention is to lease aircraft and to depreciate them as a fixed asset over a ten-year period. ANA's policy has been to buy an aircraft outright, over a maximum period of one year, but it is currently considering introducing more leased aircraft.

Fare pricing

The market price of an airline fare depends on several factors. These include the time of day (a.m. or p.m.) of the departure; whether the flight

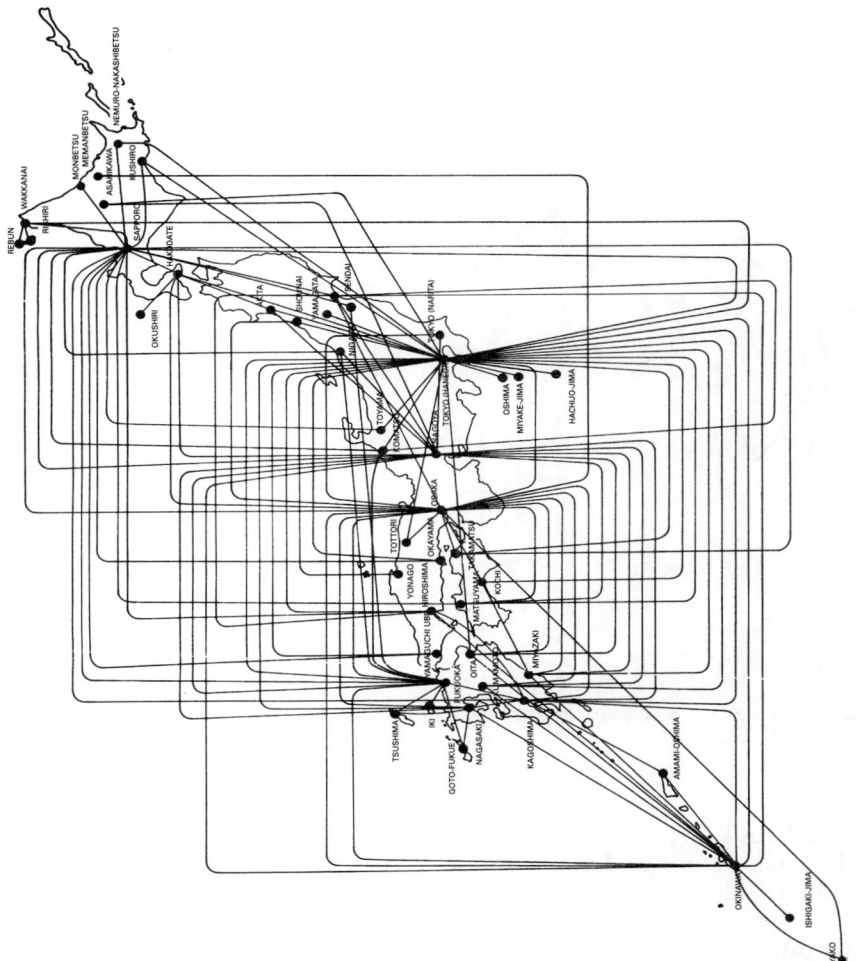

Figure 4.1 ANA's scheduled domestic routes network. (*Source*: All Nippon Airways)

60 The Japanese Advantage?

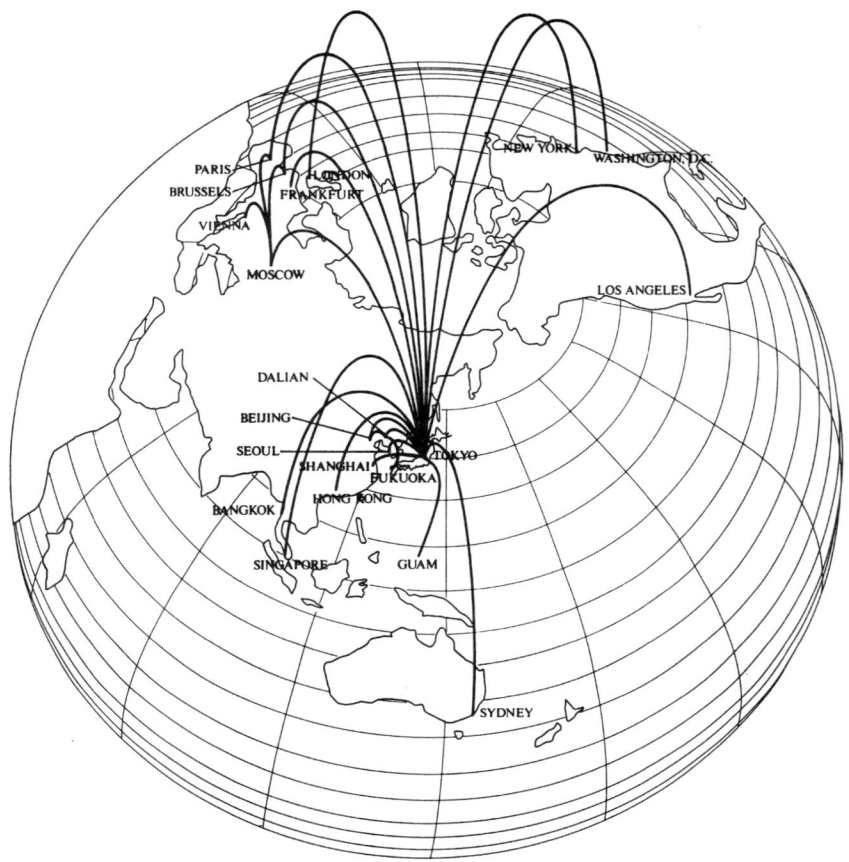

Figure 4.2 ANA's scheduled international routes network. (*Source*: All Nippon Airways)

is short-haul (e.g. from Tokyo to Hong Kong) or long-haul (e.g. from Tokyo to London); and the season of travel. The published price remains constant, although it is seasonal.

Fare share is the responsibility of SITA, an international airline communication company. There is no group fare data and travel agents do not input fare data manually. There is one group fare per day and the market price of a fare changes daily. ANA's international passenger marketing department uses database information and aims to increase passenger volumes and improve customer loyalty.

Airlines apply for permission to fly a route to the two governments in whose countries the route destinations are located. In the UK, once gaining permission to fly the route, the airline applies to the Civil Aviation Authority (CAA) for a route fare. Most countries employ a double-approval regulation. In Japan the Japan Civil Aviation Board (JCAB) is the government agency empowered to authorize route fares. Each of the two authorities approves the fare level for the newly requested route. After approval, the fare is registered with IATA.[5] In practice, the aviation authorities' liaison procedures are inefficient and airlines themselves inevitably assume responsibility for registration of their fare with IATA.

ANA's international relations department is responsible for the advance logistical planning before the airline decides to elect for a new route. Part of the marketing department, this department analyses competitors' current activity on the route, potential passenger volumes and profit viability before plans to operate a new route are made firm.

Yield factor

Airlines' loads are increasing, as are the numbers of flights and passengers; at the same time, airlines' revenue is decreasing. This paradox is explained by the yield factor.

Yield is broken down into the three major seating classes; first, business (C), and economy (Y). Y represents full-fare economy; further gradations are indicated by B, Q, V and other letters of the alphabet. Passengers who pay less than the full IATA fare (for example, by booking in advance with certain restrictions) are seated in a random order in the economy cabin. Seating classes are not readily identifiable and passengers in adjacent seats may have paid greatly differing fares.

Airlines offer numerous fares according to travellers' individual needs and circumstances. Fare tariffs correspond to destination, length of stay, maximum stay and a traveller's willingness to travel on a particular flight. Further fare reductions are possible for a traveller who agrees to return on a fixed date on a ticket which cannot be changed. Each element of flexibility that the intending traveller is willing to forgo within various restrictions enables an airline to reduce the standard IATA fare for that destination.

First- and business-class seating occupies approximately 30 per cent of an aircraft's seating capacity. For an airline, business class generates most profit per head per flight (calculated by the number of occupied business-class seats multiplied by the full fare paid). First- and business-class tickets are unrestricted and passengers gain the flexibility to change flight dates; some passengers even change their reservation to another airline. Economy tickets vary from fully flexible (at the standard IATA price) to wholly restrictive (at the lowest discounted price).

Prorated fares

On the frequent occasions where a passenger uses more than one airline to reach the destination, the system known as 'proration' is used. This permits each of the airlines contributing to the journey to receive a proportional share of the total fare tariff. The fare system is calculated on the basis of travel from point to point. Journeys requiring multiple landing *en route* are referred to as multi-sector flights. A journey from point to point with the same airline is known as 'on-line'. In this instance a single airline collects the entire revenue paid for the whole journey. A journey which requires a passenger to change airline at an airport mid-journey and continue to the destination with a different airline is called 'inter-line'.[6] On such occasions, the airlines involved apportion the total fare according to the flight mileage.

Airline tickets between two destinations can be sold and issued anywhere in the world. Fares are quoted in the country of origin of the journey and converted at the Bankers Selling Rate at the time of ticket issue. When flights originate in London the fare basis is always shown in sterling (although the traveller may pay in any currency). Consequently, the actual revenue received by the airline may vary according to where the ticket is purchased.

Although ticket prices are credited to the airline at the exchange rate ruling on the day of the transaction, an airline's revenue accounting system needs to cope with exchange rate fluctuations.

Business impact of IT

ANA makes weekly revenue and booking forecasts for a two-month period up to the departure of the flight. A variety of reasons make accurate predictions more difficult, not least of which is passengers' increasing sophistication. Travel books, magazines and brochures allow current passengers to be better informed than their predecessors. One effect of the ready availability of travel-related information is to reduce customer loyalty to any one carrier, making revenue prediction uncertain. The trend for passengers to book later for psychological or financial reasons exacerbates the situation.

Forecasting is carried out in two ways: by using the Zeus system and by attempting to spot trends by making comparisons of earlier booking details. In either case predicting actual numbers of travellers is most difficult as names are only available thirty days before the flight departure. Travel agents can give the airline weekly figures. This is not lost on travel agents, who realize that they, and not passengers, are the airlines' customers.

In Japan government legislation sets airline fares. ANA negotiates discounts with travel agents. Travel agents are a key factor in ANA's home market as they provide a range of services to customers, including passport and visa services, hotel and car-hire bookings via their CRS. Travel agents realize their power in the marketplace. ANA's city sales offices cover specific territories for their sales and reservations activities and maintain relationships with between ten and fifteen travel agents through daily contact (for example, to explain promotional issues).

Computer reservation systems (CRS)

In the mid-1980s CRS developed from being purely airline reservation systems. CRS were introduced into travel agencies, who preferred to make airline bookings themselves rather than telephone the airline. American Airlines' decision to place terminals in travel agencies brought the airline an increased competitive edge.[7] Additionally, by providing computer terminals to travel agencies airlines discovered that they could reduce the number of their own booking staff.

ANA's computer reservation system for both internal use and travel agents in Japan was originally founded in 1978 totally for ANA's domestic operations. At that time, ANA was planning to renew completely its domestic reservations system into a comprehensive airline system including registration, ticketing, check-in, boarding and, finally, accounting. Simultaneously, while planning to expand its international operations, it also desired to adopt IBM hardware which had almost become the standard reservation system in the world.

ANA's in-house CRS is called *able* and had two formats: *able-D* (for domestic flight bookings) and *able-I* (for international flight bookings). Other early CRS were Apollo (United Airlines), SABRE (American Airlines) and System One (Eastern Airlines and Continental Airlines).

When ANA realized that it needed its own proprietary computer reservation system it had to choose between developing its own CRS or buying an existing system which could be adapted to its own purposes. After careful consideration, and recognizing that designing a new system would be lengthy, difficult and costly, the company bought existing CRS software from another airline.

As the core CRS, *able* allows ANA to gain access to any other airline's CRS. Reservation systems similar to *able* are common to all airlines. Some airlines operate a second CRS to service travel agencies and allow them to sell the airlines' products without needing to telephone the airline.

ANA also uses Infini,[8] a system which was created to serve the needs of travel agencies. Infini is a 'one-stop' computer system which allows travel agencies to sell additional travel-related products, e.g. hotel room accommodation, railway travel reservations, car-hire facilities, as well as reservations on other airlines.

CRS are updated on a regular basis as end-users (airline booking staff) constantly request improvements to the system. Future computer reservation systems are likely to have a wider range of enhanced functions to simplify the job of reservations staff.

CRS distribution directly influences sales volume. This is known as the halo effect where, for example, a fourfold increase in the number of CRS terminals leads to a fivefold increase in the number of customer bookings. Over time, this ratio of CRS terminals to bookings can increase further.

For this reason, CRS have fought to deploy their terminals in travel agencies. This has resulted in travel agents' complaints about 'computer terminal jam'. CRS have been obliged to concede to requests from travel agents that access to CRS be via their PCs. This overcomes the problem of limited space while giving the increased convenience of allowing the travel agents access to various CRS displays.

ANA repositioned its CRS terminals over a period of two and a half years. In 1989 ANA had 700 terminals which used Infini. By late 1991 these had extended to more than 3000 terminals. Development work is done by ANA with Infini. When ANA staff develop the system the benefits of the development are solely for use by ANA and Infini users and will not be sold or leased onto a third party.

The relationship between CRS in operation throughout the world is shown in Figure 4.3.

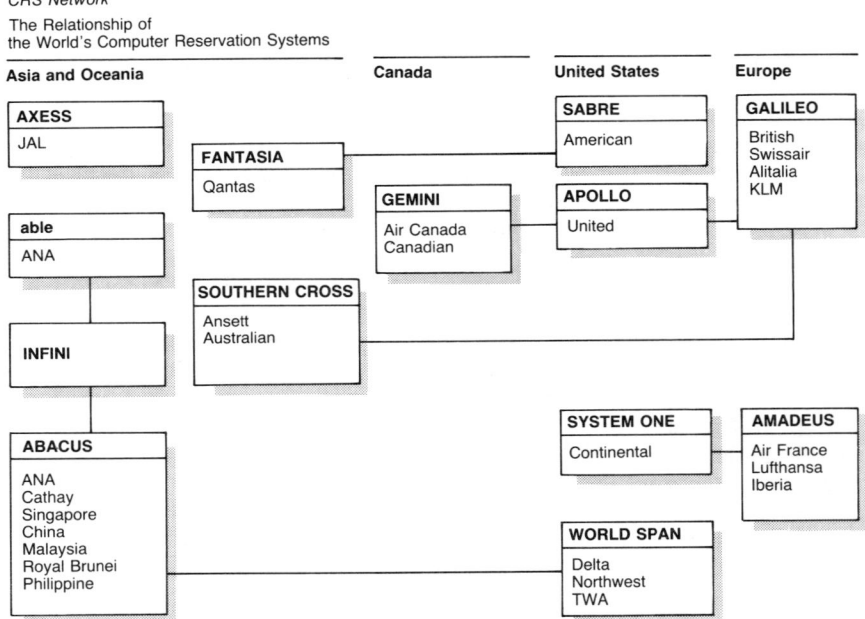

Figure 4.3 The world's computer reservation systems. (*Source*: All Nippon Airways)

ANA's priority is for a CRS system that displays information clearly and accurately so that the agent can readily identify the prices of available seating on which ANA flights. The information from the travel agency should then be transmitted as quickly as possible to ANA's system. ANA would like the facility to input marketing information into the travel agencies' systems, so that travel agencies are informed immediately of any ANA sales campaign. Speed in both directions is the essence.

Transmitting passenger information

Details of all advanced loads are printed on a monthly basis from computers by the space control and yield management department in head office. ANA offices worldwide receive hard copies of these data. The printouts record current and previous historical data for the same trading periods in earlier years. Additional figures indicate 'boarded' passengers, i.e. the number of passengers on board a flight in relation to the number of available seats. These figures are expressed as a percentage to give the load factor. The figure for ANA's international routes for fiscal year 1992 is 66.3 per cent, down five points from fiscal year 1991.

London office also produces its own information from the various sources of data generated by its flight bookings and reservations. The information from head office and London office are passed to the sales and marketing departments. Close investigation of the data reveals specific business opportunities ripe for targeting. The load capacity of certain flights on certain days reveals scope for augmenting existing loads by offering reduced fares to bulk groups.

PNRs (passenger name records) or travel agents' data helps ANA to identify passenger loyalty. Regular passengers appreciate being recognized by ANA ground staff and flight attendants and PNRs can help to alert ground staff to passengers' previous flights with ANA.

ANA has an automated distribution policy that it should participate in all major worldwide CRS at considerably high link levels, and most of these linkages have been implemented. This means that ANA flight availabilities are shown on all major CRS on a real-time basis.

How IT helps airline profitability

Airlines sometimes cooperate in a 'pool agreement', where two airlines operate one aircraft on a route-sharing basis. The costs of operating the route (e.g. maintenance, airport landing charges) are shared, as is operating profit. Airlines prefer to share such arrangements with other airlines who are not direct competitors and whose product enhances rather than detracts from their own.

Such an agreement is in force between ANA and some European airlines: Austrian Airlines on the route to Tokyo from Vienna and Sabena from Brussels to Tokyo. However, some national airlines in Europe would pose a serious competitive threat if they were ANA's pool agreement partner. Each of these 'pool' airlines has a completely different product from that offered by ANA.

When ANA became an international carrier the company began using a CRS called Access. This was JAL's secondary system and was originally developed to imitate Galileo and used by travel agencies. Such systems are called 'third-party' computer systems. To comply with legal requirements, the Access system was intended to be unbiased. However, as Access was accessed through a JAL host computer, the 11 000 travel agencies in which it was installed found that the system favoured JAL flight bookings and that a further entry needed to be made to book flights on other airlines.

ANA wanted to leave Access and introduce its own dedicated system for two reasons: first, to protect sensitive commercial data (e.g. yield, the number of seats available at the lowest available fare, the number of seats held for last-minute business travellers)[9] and second, to avoid paying JAL, a competitor, a participating fee.

Airline marketing

One of the functions of the ticketing and reservations department is to generate customer information for the purposes of the sales and marketing departments. For example, the CRS may identify travel agencies in a certain area who have booked passengers on a particular flight. This information is passed to the marketing department, who can compare records for the same flight over different historical periods.

Arguably the biggest target of CRS is 'database marketing' which enables travel agents to sell their accumulated valuable information concerning airline bookings and ticketings. After all, CRS have achieved their role as distribution tools, the next important stage is how best to present airlines' marketing information to achieve optimum sales. One of the most recent developments is marketing information data tape (MIDT), which contains all necessary information relating to detailed data of booking and ticketing for each participating airline. However, while booking and ticketing information is relayed in real time, it can take up to two months for a participating airline to receive marketing and sales-related information.

The marketing department will try to ascertain reasons for the increase, or decline, in the number of passengers on the flight. This may be because a new Japanese manufacturing plant has established itself in the area. Alternatively, a local travel agency may be encouraging customers to try original holiday destinations. The information will be passed to the sales department so that a sales 'push', perhaps by making presentations in Japanese companies, can be made to develop this business opportunity.

An additional function of the ticketing and reservations department is to anticipate fluctuations in the demand for products and to alert the sales and marketing departments of impending business opportunities. The ticketing and reservations department would receive such items of business intelligence through its direct contact with travel agencies and other airlines, e.g. through informal and social interaction with JAL staff. The airline industry is a tightly knit community and insiders have few secrets, with the exception of nett fares which remain confidential to each airline.

In the airline industry in general it is extremely difficult to gain new passengers. Airlines tend to believe that, once attracted to an airline, passengers tend to remain loyal. Japanese passengers (who comprise 85 per cent of ANA's customers) are especially loyal. Passengers remain loyal until something goes wrong, after which loyalty, once lost, is difficult to regain.

Airlines spend vast amounts of budget marketing their product in order to generate the initial interest of potential passengers. It is equally important to spend resources on keeping existing passengers satisfied.

Managing IT

ANA's London office takes 5000 telephone calls per month from customers checking flight details, confirming reservations, and from travel agencies accessing the *able* system. Calls are routed automatically to reservations agents who wear headphones so that both hands are free to operate a computer keyboard.

In addition to UK-based calls, the reservations staff also receive 0800 toll-free calls from mainland Europe. When the reservations agent accepts the waiting call a display on the telephone shows where the call originates and the language of the call (e.g. GB (English), JP (Japanese)). All Japanese calls are directed to the Japanese-speaking staff. Calls from mainland Europe, mainly in French or German, are directed to the pool of speakers of these languages.

The reservations system is managed by British Telecom and SITA,[1] an international airline communications company. All airlines who are SITA members have a seven-letter SITA address; ANA's London address is LONRRNH. This address allows instant worldwide communication between airlines.

Apart from inter-airline messages, the SITA lines carry the permanent signal from the mainframe *able* system in Tokyo to ANA's terminals around the world. SITA lines transport the messages and signals internationally. Once on British shores, the lines are transferred to the BT telephone system.

The ticketing and reservations department has four possibilities and other systems can be brought in as back-up if one system breaks down. The telephone system is a sophisticated BT product that allows programmable switching of calls to any group of reservations agents in the department. Priority can be given to any individual agents. This is helpful when new employees are being trained, as arrangements can be made to direct fewer calls to them.

Identifying new IT systems

From the viewpoint of ANA's London office, identifying new IT systems is restricted to the level of what PCs the office would like. The London office generates its own back-office systems, including business intelligence databases. The office makes regular requests to head office for new systems.

In January 1993 a Zeus system was installed in London office. This is the culmination of a request submitted three years ago. The lead time from request to installation has been unavoidable because the system was developed 'from scratch' by systems engineers in Tokyo.

Zeus will show the breakdown of fares on each flight, in terms of the proportion of fare levels. This information will be available instantly and will support the efforts of sales and marketing departments. The Zeus system is fed automatically from *able*; both systems operate from mainframes situated in Tokyo. *Able* can speak to Zeus and exchange information and the ticketing and reservations department can extract that information for their own use or redirect it to the sales department.

Once fully operational, the Zeus–*able* link will be available to ANA offices worldwide. This network will better enable ANA to offer discounted fares for block bookings from tour groups. One area of business which is gathering momentum is the transport of large cultural groups such as symphony orchestras, operatic groups and similar ensembles together with their equipment. The volume of business is sufficient justification for ANA to reduce drastically the fares for such groups, who provide publicity in their official programme.

At head office in Tokyo ANA maintains a small team of programmers whose function is to enhance the systems. End-users suggest additions to existing system at CRS development meetings which are held annually, in February. The new development is usually in place prior to the next development meeting the following February, although some proposals take a little longer.[11]

Notes

1. These government initiatives were designed to encourage JAL to expand into routes as a means of protecting the national airline from competition from other international airlines, particularly those in East Asia. For more details of the effects of JAL's privatization see *Flight International*, 15–21 May 1991.
2. Although JAL is the national 'flag carrier' it is no longer government owned; its 34.5 per cent share was privatized in 1987. Its shares are now held by large corporations and the government can exert pressure through its own shareholdings in these corporations. However, government interference is minimal and JAL needs to show an annual operating profit.
3. This is calculated by the number of passengers carried.
4. Narita, Tokyo's international airport, is to be expanded from one runway to three; Osaka is to have a brand-new airport called Kansai (due for completion in September 1994); Haneda, Tokyo's domestic airport, is also due for expansion. See *Flight International*, 15–21 May 1991.
5. The International Air Transport Association, the body with whom airlines are obliged to register their scheduled flights and which determines fare levels for journeys between agreed destinations.
6. For example, a passenger may travel from Tokyo to Rome via London. ANA does not currently fly to Rome so the passenger would change planes in London for a BA flight to Rome. ANA and BA divide the total revenue in proportion to flight mileage.
7. For a discussion of how American Airlines benefited from the Sabre system see Hopper, M. D., 'Rattling Sabre – new ways to compete on information', *Harvard Business Review*, May–June 1990. This also

appears in *Revolution in Real Time*, Harvard Business Review Press (1991), pp. 113–127.
8 Infini (the sole CRS in South-East Asia) is owned jointly by ANA (60 per cent) and ABACUS (40 per cent). Infini solely covers the territory of Japan, and there are no plans to expand its use into other areas.
9 Although air fares are controlled by the International Air Transport Association (IATA), competitors could gain competitive advantage from knowing how a rival airline maximizes its trading profits within the IATA-imposed ceilings.
10 Since it was founded in 1949 by a group of eleven airlines, SITA (Société Internationale Telecommunications Aérienne) has grown into an international organization serving 440 member companies in 187 countries and territories, making it the world's largest specialized telecommunications network. The SITA network includes 120 000 terminals and printers in 31 000 airlines and travel-related offices, with over 62 000 VDUs linked to 100 host computers.
11 One suggestion was that at the end of a booking transaction, details were filed and simultaneously displayed on the operator's VDU monitor. This would allow the operator to confirm the transaction with the customer and to make additional entries to the transaction where necessary. Filing details of the transaction on completion is standard practice, although the booking is 'logged off'. The new proposal suggested that the display continue to appear on the operator's screen so that further work could be performed. This procedure took over a year to develop and is now used by booking staff.

5
Daiwa Europe Ltd

Case profile

Survival in the highly competitive financial services and securities trading industry depends on efficient management of current market information and delivering this quickly and accurately to financial market traders. Success depends on identifying market opportunities ahead of competitors and aligning IT systems to exploit these opportunities for profit.

In today's global financial arena, international communications connect the various financial centres. As a global financial services company, Daiwa depends for its continued success on high-speed and secure international communications systems. Daiwa has a private communications network to ensure security of its business communications. Called the Global Communications Network, this forms two triangles linking Tokyo, New York and London (major financial markets in their respective time zones); and Osaka, Chicago and Paris (important centres for futures and options trading). Most Daiwa regional offices are connected to these twin high-speed digital global communications networks, which facilitate 24-hour global securities trading.

As a major securities brokering house, Daiwa Europe Ltd (DEL) considers that its principal business is the marketing and selling of financial securities, not communications engineering. Consequently, company policy says that IT systems should be outsourced to suppliers as much as possible. For example, DEL rents, on a 'per extension' basis, a fibre-optic delivery system using high-speed voice communications; an arrangement which DEL believes gives advantages of lower cost and flexibility. Managing IT systems on a pan-European basis would involve increased staffing levels to provide the required expertise.

In continental Europe, most of DEL's offices are relatively small and do not include staff with specialist computer engineering knowledge. Sophisticated computer skills are available at DEL in London. When a new IT system is to be installed in an office in continental Europe, DEL sends over appropriate experts to organize planning, connectivity, installation and suppliers. Once a new system has been installed, local staff (possibly with assistance from DEL) assume responsibility for its day-to-day maintenance. London-based staff are transferred permanently to the European office when specialized expertise is required.

Company background

Daiwa Securities[1] was founded on 1 May 1902. It is the second largest securities company in Japan and one of the largest in the world.[2] Daiwa has 127 domestic offices and a global network of ten representative offices, thirty-two overseas subsidiaries, including one affiliate office. Worldwide, Daiwa Securities employs some 11 000 people.

Daiwa regards itself as an innovator in capital markets and maintains that this gives a competitive advantage over other securities houses, in both Japan and the rest of the world. Since April 1990 Daiwa Securities Co. Ltd has been listed on seven major European stock exchanges: London, Paris, Zurich, Frankfurt, Amsterdam, Brussels and Luxembourg; the first Japanese company to attain all seven listings simultaneously. The company's presence in Europe began in 1964 with a small office in the City of London.

Daiwa is proud of its active role in promoting and developing good relations between Britain and Japan. In 1988 Daiwa Securities Co. Ltd endowed the Daiwa Anglo-Japanese Foundation to further this aim. Based in London, the Daiwa Anglo-Japanese Foundation, aims to promote mutual understanding and cooperation between Britain and Japan. Its main means of achieving these goals is by awarding scholarships and grants in the fields of culture, history, science, business and education. The Foundation's figurehead and prime instigator was Mr Yoshitoki Chino, Daiwa's former chairman.[3] In 1992, in recognition of his active leadership of the Foundation and his support for its philosophy, Mr Yoshitoki was made an Honorary Knight Commander of the British Empire (KBE).[4]

Daiwa Europe Ltd

Daiwa Europe Ltd (DEL), a subsidiary of Daiwa Securities, is a securities house whose main business is underwriting, brokering and dealing in the international capital markets. Departments in DEL include those responsible for bond trading and equities trading. DEL has grown extensively over the last five years. In October 1987, feeling constrained by lack of space in its current location, the company moved to offices in King William Street in the City of London. Relocation promised scope for further growth and expansion.

In March 1992 a separate company called the Daiwa Institute of Research (Europe) Ltd (DIREL) was established. Responsibility for systems planning as a company function was transferred from DEL to DIREL. Other functions for which DIREL is responsible include: mainframe computer development; providing service and support for front-office trading activities; and providing support for DEL's PCs. Formerly these activities were carried out by the Daiwa Computer Centre (DCC), now part of DIREL. This reorganization had three effects: it separated the company's support operations from its trading activities; it initiated a facilities management approach to back-office support services; and it streamlined the company's European operations.

Part of DIREL's present function is to advise on systems implementation in Daiwa's European branches.[5] For example, DIREL management now has the responsibility to scrutinize current operations in any of Daiwa's European branches and to recommend the most appropriate computer software for both internal and external use. The Director of DIREL has responsibility for mainframe applications and development in London and Europe. The Director of DIREL and DEL's Executive Director liaise constantly with each other as they do with senior management in head office in Tokyo.

Since October 1987 the downturn in global financial markets has been a fact of life. Financial trading companies have sought to increase profitability with an asset base which, at best, remained constant or, at worst, declined. Rationalization and cost sensitivity have become common factors in the financial sector.

DEL has introduced cost-cutting initiatives. Quarterly operating cost systems have led to greatly reduced technology costs per trading desk. New systems are currently being evaluated. Further expansion plans have been deferred pending favourable market conditions. A proposed move of all Daiwa companies in London into a prestigious European headquarters building has been deferred until economic conditions are more favourable.

IT in the financial services industry

Financial securities are variable products whose prices vary according to market conditions, so it is essential for any financial services company to be able constantly to monitor the movements of financial markets. Milliseconds distinguish the difference between high profit and loss, so it is vital for a financial services company to process market information accurately and quickly. In such crucial circumstances the importance of reliability, security and confidentiality cannot be overemphasized.

In the financial services industry, competitive advantage depends on the way in which standard data are 'delivered'. This can be through a PC, a vendor (e.g. a piece of hardware) or a combination of both (e.g. consolidated in the computer room). These represent increasingly sophisticated levels of IT integration. In their constant quest for timely market information, financial services companies increasingly rely on market information systems (MIS) such as Reuter's Telerate, the Stock Exchange Datastream and similar proprietary monitoring systems.

Software houses sited in and around the City of London develop and market packages for financial trading. Standard financial software products are readily available, 'off the shelf'. However, financial services companies feel that the standard products need a degree of customization to provide a competitive edge.

Some financial houses buy standard software products and customize these in-house. This ensures that such systems are wholly proprietary for a company's IS requirements. Alternatively, a financial services company can sign an exclusive contract with a software house for the development of purpose-built software.

It is usually cheaper to buy a standard package and develop the system in-house from the beginning; although not as cheap as buying and using a standard software package. In-house systems development ensures systems security and that systems are proprietary for a company's IS requirements.

Business impact of IT

DEL's business strategy

Head office in Tokyo sets overall corporate policy. This includes strategic business direction and new business initiatives such as Daiwa's 'Golden '90s'.[6] However, Daiwa's corporate culture encourages each local branch to make business decisions relating to its own market environment.[7] In this way, DEL can respond very quickly to new business opportunities in local markets. This is an asset in turbulent market conditions where market movements can be volatile. It is particularly advantageous in the currently liberalizing markets of some of the former 'Eastern bloc' countries, where DEL's expertise is strong.

DEL's Management Committee is responsible for identifying emerging market opportunities. The Management Committee meets monthly and consists of London board members: the president, chairman, managing directors and directors of the different business functions in the company. This committee comprises Japanese delegates[8] and local senior managers. The Business Committee consults head office as a matter of policy and practice. Constant interaction between senior managers in Tokyo and London ensure that decisions are mutually beneficial.

IT strategy

Daiwa's IT decisions take into account systems in use in other parts of the company. However, the size and global spread of the company's activities preclude any single IT delivery system throughout the organization's worldwide network. Additionally, the quest for commonality of IT systems is impeded by different levels of technology available throughout the world (e.g. fibre-optic technology, high-speed information services).

The efficient delivery of information via MIS systems is critical to DEL's trading activities. DEL is currently building highly sophisticated financial software systems for its market traders. DEL considers itself 'at par' for its selection and use of IT systems in terms of its financial trading support systems.

Twelve directors of the company are also department heads of specific financial market sectors, e.g. fixed-income securities, equities and derivatives. Such members of DEL's senior management team are 'on the trading floor' and, as a matter of course, receive current market information on their desktop PCs. In this way, high-echelon operational staff have access to networked information.

The Executive Director of DIREL's Systems Planning Department is responsible for developing IT strategy. This covers IT systems in DEL's offices in those European countries where Daiwa has a stock exchange listing.[9] The Executive Director of DIREL's Systems Planning Department is also Executive Director of DEL where he is responsible for strategic systems planning and budgeting.

DIREL's Executive Director receives a budget subsidy from head office in Tokyo. This is intended to cover purchases of hardware and marketing information services, and to maintain DIREL's operational facility. DIREL's Executive Director in London makes IT investment decisions, although he naturally consults regularly with local senior managers and with managers in head office.

Equipment maintenance, capital purchase and capital maintenance are paid for by DEL. Revenues from end-user departments, who pay a standing charge for MIS services, supplement DEL's annual IT budget.[10] DEL and DIREL liaise on systems requirements and jointly prepare expenditure and budget proposals for board approval.

Managing IT

Systems Planning Department

As a result of the reorganization in March 1992, the Systems Planning Department changed its area of responsibility. This now includes: the IT communication systems inside DEL; the provision of MIS services for front-office trading activities; and the procurement and maintenance of PCs.[11] The department is also responsible for identifying problems. Two particular areas are: reducing the number of network failures and decreasing the time taken to identify problems in the system. As a back-up for its own expertise DEL uses an external maintenance contractor to service the network and maintain PCs on a routine basis.

The department has twenty-five staff, including a five-person software development group. The department tends to be reactive rather than proactive in that it responds to calls for help from end-user departments. There is a 'help-desk' function and users who are in trouble can dial an internal extension number to request assistance.

When a senior person on the trading floor identifies a position risk with respect to profit and loss, the Systems Planning Department acts to solve the problem as quickly as possible. In such a situation a working group is elected to investigate the claims and identify possible solutions.

The working group includes personnel with a range of functions and expertise. The London Board of Directors makes the final decision.

The Systems Planning Department constantly seeks to upgrade or replace existing systems within the organization, and to refine the topology[12] of current systems. A constant goal is cost reduction matched with an associated cost benefit from IT investment in a particular system.

IT in DEL's offices in continental Europe

Most of DEL's offices in continental Europe are relatively small enterprises. Consequently, these offices are not staffed with computer engineering specialists (e.g. experts in fibre-optics and information delivery).[13] When needed, such skills are on hand in the company's London offices where departments have been developed to deal with IT issues. From its London base this body of expertise is readily available to tackle IT systems throughout DEL's European operations.

When a European office needs a new IT system the relevant IT experts in London organize planning, connectivity, installation and suppliers. Once 'up and running', the day-to-day maintenance of the new system devolves to the local staff with assistance from London. When specialized expertise is required, London-based staff are transferred permanently to the European office.

International communications

In 1991 Daiwa Computer Centre (DCC) merged with DIREL, and the amalgamated institute is located in London's Docklands. DIREL is responsible for DEL's mainframe computers and for its international communications. Daiwa's continuing success as a global financial services company depends on high-speed and secure international communications.

DIREL acts as the European 'hub' for communications between Tokyo and New York, and is also responsible for maintaining communication links between mainframe computers in Tokyo and New York. The mainframes rely solely on the collection and input of data from computer centres. Daiwa's private network ensures that communications are secure.

Global Communications Network

Daiwa's Global Communications Network consists of two triangular pathways. The first triangle links the three largest financial centres of Tokyo–New York–London. A second triangle links Osaka–Chicago–Paris; important centres for futures and options trading. Costing Y100 billion to start up in 1991,[14] these twin high-speed digital global communications networks allow global securities trading on a 24-hour basis. They are connected through an apex to most regional offices and can be accessed by almost all other offices.

Office systems

In a financial services house front-office systems support financial trading. These systems consist of computer systems and compatible software packages designed to facilitate speedy and efficient trading by financial traders. In 1988, following relocation to its current premises, DEL took the opportunity to invest in state-of-the-art computer hardware and related software systems. DEL purchased and installed Micronosis, an MIS service which is transmitted over a fibre-optic network using IBM proprietary hardware. DEL also uses Invision. Back-office systems provide the administrative support for the company's trading operations.

The company's relocation in 1988 represented a watershed in the company's operations and eased the transition from manual towards electronic working routines. The physical relocation, together with the installation of new technology, gave employees a feeling that the organization for which they worked was rapidly changing.

In the interests of cost savings, it is company policy that IT systems are outsourced to suppliers as much as possible. As DEL is now responsible for European-wide IT, the alternative to outsourcing would bring about vast increases, particularly in staffing levels. DEL regards itself primarily as a financial services house not a communications engineering company.[15]

Global communications companies maintain staffing 24 hours a day, 365 days a year. DEL and similar subsidiary companies would find self-management of such services on this scale prohibitively expensive. Senior management at DEL believe that the quarterly network management fee paid to the outsourcing agency represents a small fraction of the cost that would be incurred if DEL decided to maintain its own communications systems.

DEL was one of the first Japanese companies in London to use Centrex. This is a fibre-optic delivery system using high-speed voice communications designed by Mercury Communications. DEL rents the whole system on a 'per extension' basis and is an outpost of the Mercury telecommunications network. The system's necessary hardware and software is situated on Mercury's premises. This gives DEL a flexibility over its own office premises, as the communications system does not have to be transported should the company need to relocate.

Since the financial market adversities in October 1987 financial services companies have been cost-conscious. DEL has introduced cost-cutting initiatives. Quarterly operating cost systems have led to greatly reduced technology costs per trading desk. New systems are currently being evaluated.

Notes

1 The name Daiwa means 'great harmony'.
2 Daiwa Securities is one of the world's largest financial institutions with total assets of US$39 billion (1990 figure). Major shareholders of

the parent company include Sumitomo Trust, Sumitomo Bank, Industrial Bank of Japan, Yasuda Trust, Fuji Bank and Nippon Life.
3   He served as Chairman from 1982 to 1991 and was made Honorary Chairman on his retirement.
4   Two other Japanese businessmen have received this honour. In 1992 Mr Akio Morita, Head of Sony Corporation, received the honour in 'recognition of his contribution to British industry and exports as well as to Anglo-Japanese relations' (*The Times*, 5 October 1992). Mr Takashi Ishihara, Chairman of Nissan Motor Manufacturing UK (MNUK), was awarded an honorary knighthood by prime minister Margaret Thatcher.
5   From April 1992, DIREL assumed former head office prerogatives in IT-related matters in DEL's European network of offices.
6   Daiwa's statement of its corporate principles for the decade to the year 2000. These are: a world-class financial leader; a community member in work and play; an organization that serves worthy goals. (Source: President's message in Daiwa's annual reports 1990 and 1991.)
7   Some companies refer to similar policies as 'local globalization'.
8   Expatriate Japanese managers on work assignments in the UK are known as delegate staff.
9   Amsterdam, Brussels, Frankfurt, London, Luxembourg, Paris and Zurich.
10 This is calculated by the use of computer hardware time.
11 Control and monitoring of IT systems also form part of the function of the Systems Planning Department.
12 The form of interconnectiveness between the various points in a communications system.
13 Such sophisticated computer expertise is an expensive addition to the payroll.
14 Daiwa's annual report for the financial year ended 31 March 1991 quoted an exchange rate of Y140.95 = US$1.
15 As a securities brokering house, Daiwa considers that its business is the marketing and selling of securities.

6
Hitachi Europe Ltd

Case profile

Since 1990, when the head office of Hitachi Europe Ltd (HEL) relocated from London to Maidenhead, IT has become a more mainstream corporate activity. HEL has used IT to improve back-office support services and administrative and support functions which have reduced staff numbers and maximized work output.

IT plays a strong role in the semiconductor market where customer service requirements lead IT developments. HEL gains competitive advantage over rivals by allowing customers to access in-house design facilities. Performance capabilities of semiconductors can be demonstrated to customers using computer-aided simulations. In semiconductor sales and marketing, HEL has introduced its Product Marketing Information System (PMIS), which collates information about what companies want to buy and enables HEL's Marketing Department to build up a picture of changing requirements in the semiconductor marketplace.

IT systems aid manufacturing and sales functions in a number of ways, facilitated by Hitachi's proprietary IT platform between manufacturing sites. For example, HEL's sales division in Maidenhead and Hitachi's manufacturing plant in Germany electronically exchange procurement information (including forecasted requirements, purchase orders, order shipments data and invoicing documents). This information enables Hitachi to plan manufacturing processes more effectively and predict product shipment dates with greater accuracy.

HEL sees the capability to react swiftly both to customer needs and to technological changes as a source of competitive advantage. HEL is keen to provide a high-quality service to its customers and distributors, and sees IT as part of achieving this.

Company background

Hitachi was founded by Namihei Odaira in 1910 and incorporated in 1920. From humble beginnings as an electrical repair shop, Hitachi (the name means sunrise) has grown into an international conglomerate employing 310 000 people. Now, with 172 offices in 34 countries, the company produces over 20 000 different products with annual sales surpassing US$58 billion[1] and, in terms of sales, ranks twelfth among global companies.[2]

Worldwide, Hitachi employs 16 000 people in Research and Development, investing almost US$14 million every working day (equivalent to over 6 per cent of total sales revenue).[3] R&D concentrates predominantly, but not exclusively, on three areas: electronics, energy and materials.

HEL's own Design Groups in Düsseldorf and Milan, in collaboration with design houses in Germany, Italy and the UK, continuously analyse design trends. As a result of its research efforts, Hitachi has over 85 000 industrial property rights worldwide.

Hitachi Ltd has six manufacturing plants in Europe: at Landshut and two sites at Landsberg in Germany; Barcelona (Spain); Orleans (France); and Hirwaun (Wales). The factory at Landshut, Germany, assembles and tests semiconductor products. More recently, its facilities have been extended to cover wafer fabrication and it is now moving into the production of fully integrated devices. The plant in Orleans, France, manufactures large-scale magnetic disk drives (for mass data storage) which are sold mainly to the European market.

Consumer products (colour televisions, video recorders and microwave ovens) are produced at manufacturing plants at Hirwaun, South Wales, and Landsberg, Germany. The Landsberg plant will shortly also be producing frequency inverters and programmable controllers.

Hitachi Europe Ltd

Hitachi Europe Ltd (HEL) was established in 1982 to sell Hitachi products and to expand market share in the UK and Europe. In 1988, HEL amalgamated with the Electronic Component Division (ECD). In 1990, the head office relocated from Hammersmith to a 6-acre site situated on the River Thames at Maidenhead. HEL's Support Computer Centre continues to be situated in Hammersmith.

In addition to the headquarters at Maidenhead, main offices are located in Düsseldorf and Munich. Branch offices can be found in the City of London, Hammersmith, Paris, Madrid, Milan and Stockholm. Liaison offices are located in Copenhagen, Helsinki, Oslo, Rome and Stuttgart.

HEL is now one of the largest and most diversified Japanese companies in the UK. Its product range includes information systems and equipment; power and industrial systems and equipment; and electronic components.

Business strategy

HEL perceives the high-quality customer support services as one of its major competitive strengths and directs a variety of endeavours towards making sustained improvements in customer service. This reflects Hitachi's stated business strategy:

Every Hitachi product is developed to meet two specific requirements. It must be customer driven, accurately reflecting the real needs of the market; and it must exhibit the highest levels of quality, in terms of design and long term reliability.[4]

HEL deals directly with its major customers. In the semiconductor market its customer base is some 150–200 companies. Fifteen European franchised distributors service the remaining customers for semiconductor products.

Distributors are not exclusively franchised to HEL. As a result, the business relationship is complex and, at times, 'cut-throat'. Distributors have their own customer network for whom they wish to obtain the 'best deal'. Distributors are not exclusive distributors of HEL products and 'shopping around' is routine. For much the same reason, distributors trade with HEL's competitors, with whom they are in regular contact. In this way they can obtain the best deal for their customers.

Among its Japanese competitors, Hitachi is viewed as a conservative company – after all, it has been in existence since 1910. Its main Japanese competitors in the semiconductor market are NEC, Sony and Toshiba. These competitors may have more sophisticated IT systems with, for example, their distributors and also in their factories. (Table 6.1 shows the relative positions of HEL and its competitors.)

Table 6.1 Survey of major Japanese electronics suppliers

Quality	Price/performance	Technical support	Delivery
NEC	NEC	NEC	Toshiba
Toshiba	Toshiba	Toshiba	NEC
Sony	**Hitachi**	**Hitachi**	**Hitachi**
Hitachi	Fujitsu	Fujitsu	Sony
Fujitsu	Mitsubishi	Sony	Fujitsu
Mitsubishi	Sony	Matsushita	Sharp
Matsushita	Matsushita	Mitsubishi	Mitsubishi
OKI	OKI	Sharp	Matsushita
Sharp	Sharp	OKI	OKI
Sanyo	Sanyo	Sanyo	Sanyo

Source: *Electronics World News*, September 1991 (based on a survey conducted June–August 1991).

In its pursuit of higher quality in its customer service, the Electronic Components Division of Hitachi Europe Ltd (HEL-ECD) is actively seeking registration for ISO 9000. ISO 9000 is linked to HEL-ECD's Quality Policy and the statement on its most recent five-year corporate plan to 'become number 1 Japanese supplier in Europe'. Approval for ISO 9000 is expected following a company-wide registration audit in November 1992.

IT product development at HEL is market-driven. This 'pull' is exerted by customer intelligence gathered from frequent customer contact by salespeople and their support teams. At the same time, the company's position as a market leader ensures a constant 'push' from within the organization.

In the strategic sense over the long term, HEL is customer-driven. This means that HEL product development managers learn what basic technology customers want by talking to the marketplace.

Unfortunately, in the semiconductor industry product development is not so straightforward. Semiconductor production has an element of unpredictability; partly because the output from similar batches of raw material cannot be accurately forecasted. Therefore, in tactical terms, e.g. over a twelve-month period, HEL has to market what manufacturing units produce. Production output is decided at senior management level in Japan. As one division of a large multinational corporation, HEL is at the end of the company's long value chain. Taking a geographical viewpoint may be somewhat simplistic and not in the best interests of Hitachi as a whole. When making its own business plans HEL needs to be aware of corporate planning and the manufacturing situation in Japan.

However, there is evidence that senior management considers such an approach to be oversimplistic in today's business environment. Increasingly, HEL makes suggestions about what products should be made, based on customer feedback. The MIS manager describes the situation:

> We're not in the baked bean business where we can advertise our brand new baked beans and hope to find a market place. At HEL we need to understand our customers and the direction they want to go in, what they want to do and what sort of things they are looking for...we've got to understand what they want to do . . . Speed is vital; if we don't get that information back to our Planning Department early enough we're not going to have the products our customers want – and the chances are our competitors will.

The Support Computer Centre at Hammersmith provides a number of services for HEL's customers. These services help HEL to respond to perceived customer needs and to tailor products accordingly. The range of services provided by the Support Computer Centre is as follows:

- A client disaster recovery and back-up service
- A range of training and education programmes
- Frequent seminars
- Technical enquiry 'hot' lines
- A 'data desk' with a wide range of data sources
- Product development in cooperation with customers.

A newly introduced on-line service, the Hitachi On-Line Information System (HOLIS), gives customers access to product information. The HOLIS database contains descriptions of Hitachi's latest products. Customers use a desktop PC, a telephone and a modem to scan the HOLIS database. They can also make requests for further data and log comments on the products.

HEL undertakes a number of joint venture research projects, although this is not the most common way in which the company tries to get closer to its customers. More usually the procedure is to create a deeper relationship with customers. The account management team of the Sales and Marketing Department is responsible for managing communication between HEL-ECD and its customers. Specialist marketing teams support sales personnel when a customer requests a specific product requirement. A marketing team helps customers to identify specific needs, which are used to refine and direct HEL's research and design efforts.

HEL-ECD helps the customer to design a purpose-built microchip, 'tailor-made' to the customer's exact job requirements. Designing an application-specific integrated circuit allows HEL-ECD to develop a stronger relationship with their customer. However, this requires flexibility and clear communication systems on the part of HEL-ECD to ensure that its servicing capability is customer-reactive.

HEL-ECD welcomes customer involvement at all stages of product design and manufacture. Interaction between representatives of the customer's organization and HEL-ECD depends on the stage in the customer's product cycle. At the initial stages design engineers from each company liaise with each other; they are followed by staff responsible for specifications; who, in turn, are followed by procurement specialists.

A majority of HEL-ECD's customers operate vendor-appraisal schemes, covering aspects of the full life cycle of the product from design through delivery to post-sales service. Most vendor-appraisal systems have a weighted points score, as different customers afford weight scores according to their particular circumstances (e.g. business style and what is important at a particular time). Some aspects on which HEL-ECD is assessed on vendor appraisal documents are:

Product-related aspects
- Range of products
- Design capabilities
- Quality of product

Service-related aspects
- Ability to deliver on time
- Speed of answering telephone
- Dealing with technical enquiries
- EDI capability

The service-related aspect of delivery on time is considered by HEL-ECD's customers as one of the most important. However, the definition of 'on time' depends on the particular customer, as different customers have differing degrees of rigidity or flexibility concerning time. For example, one customer may allow leeway of plus or minus two days, while another customer may issue a more precise schedule and penalize any deviation from it. In most cases customers stipulate an avoidance of premature delivery, although one or two days late are usually acceptable. In a broad sense, HEL-ECD accommodates customers' Just- In- Time (JIT) requirements although this is an informal, rather than a formal contractual, arrangement.

Business impact of IT

Electronic Data Interchange (EDI) is an area where the company's IT products and policies have been stimulated and directed by customers' needs. Customers' businesses needs and concerns have dictated HEL's strategies for EDI development.

HEL-ECD has tried to build closer ties with distributors through a number of schemes mainly involving buffer stock held by the distributor. However, electronic data information flow relating to such stock held by distributors has not been as useful as hoped. Current developments in EDI systems are being tried again in this marketplace.

Electronic data interchange (EDI)

HEL first became involved in EDI in 1986. At this time presentations were made to a small number of interested customers but no strategic plan evolved, either nationally or internationally.

Manufacturers' speed of response on EDI-related matters proved to be slower than expected. Customers throughout the industry expressed keen interest in EDI but there was no concerted effort to produce EDI systems to match proclaimed intentions. It is now felt that EDI is a criterion for winning customer orders. Consequently, neither HEL nor any of its competitors would admit to a customer 'No, sorry, but we can't do EDI'.

Distributors develop their own IT strategies and want EDI to help them manage their own suppliers, including HEL-ECD, in their own way. Accordingly, distributors have resisted overtures from HEL-ECD, and other suppliers, requesting them to accept computer terminals for order entry. Suppliers believe that this would result in their premises being inundated with computer terminals.

Conforming to customers' EDI requirements is a source of competitive advantage. HEL is conscious that potential competitive disadvantage would result from *not* being customer-driven. Future competitive disadvantage is reduced by satisfying customers EDI needs.

The MIS manager at HEL contrasts being led by the marketplace and being led by customers. In the latter, customers and *their* marketing strategy provide the stimulus for EDI development. He adds, 'IT is a support factor for the users of our products, rather than a component of strategy'.

At the current time, it is highly unlikely for one of HEL's customers to stipulate IT as a reason for doing business. Customers tend to ask whether Hitachi can transmit a particular type of message in a particular format. Customer acceptance of HEL depends on a 'Yes'/'No' answer to the EDI question, although in practice things are less simple.

The IT systems which allow HEL to provide customer service are noted by its customers. Many customers operate vendor-appraisal systems in which IT is assessed as an element in being a good vendor. However, apart from EDI, which is now an important item in a vendor appraisal, IT is a minor part of vendor-appraisal schemes.

One exception would possibly be in the design of customized semiconductors, where customers are allowed access to design facilities. This allows HEL to demonstrate through simulations that the microchip will actually perform its intended task. HEL acknowledges that an element of competitive advantage is gained by allowing customers access to such facilities. However, provided that the HEL research is 'heading in the general direction', IT is seen as a bonus.

Most vendor-appraisal exercises are conducted on a quarterly basis. At quarterly review meetings targets are set for the following quarter. Targets may relate to the attainment of an overall score or may concentrate on specific areas of the vendor–customer relationship. There may be leeway for appraisal performance to be discussed but this depends on the individual customer. Customers inform HEL-ECD

- How the appraisal will be scored
- The weighting of the various aspects
- What score they have been awarded
- How their score compares with their competitors.

Customers compare vendors' scores by publishing a list showing HEL-ECD's position in a ranked order with other (anonymous) vendors.

Hitachi's performance on a customer's appraisal scheme can vary significantly from highly praised to low. When scores are on the low scale, managers use these to give a push to their departments. HEL-ECD is prepared to dispute a customer's appraisal scores if they feel that they have been unfairly appraised in their performance as a vendor. However, HEL-ECD believes that 'the customer is king' and this philosophy pervades all their customer relationships.

Time from design to market

There has been a tendency for cycles of development in the mass market for main-memory silicon chips. HEL were market leaders in 256k D-RAM, which enabled the company to gain a very large market share in 1983–1984. In spite of this, competitors decided to stay in this market, but devoted their resources to the next 'generation' of chip. In fact, a manufacturer has little option but to remain in a particular market. Manufacturers seldom, if ever, 'leapfrog' in the face of a swifter, more successful competitor for a variety of reasons. On the one hand, each 'generation' of silicon chip production represents a learning curve for design engineers with the next generation of chip invariably a development of the previous model. On the other, electing not to manufacture a product because a competitor has reached the marketplace first would inevitably exclude a customer and risk the loss of that customer permanently. Experience teaches that when customers buy from a competitor, they seldom return to the original supplier.

An actual time frame is difficult to quantify because each product requires a different manufacturing process; lead time can be anything between 6 and 18 weeks. This lead time is gradually reducing, although some parts of the process cannot be compressed.

Elements of the process that can be reduced are in three areas. Forecasting information can be relayed more swiftly to the factory; planning the manufacturing process can be done more effectively; and when the product will be ready can be more accurately identified so that the process of shipment to the customer can be effected without delay.

Hitachi's divisionalization makes the manufacturing function almost like a separate company. In this environment, IT is seen as a support service. That said, the MIS manager believes that IT should be a support service for the organization – as long as HEL can react efficiently to the customers and the marketplace. A competitive disadvantage would prevail if the IT function was 'not there when we need it'. The MIS manager strongly believes that:

> IT will not get the company market share in this industry. Market share is gained by the products we develop, the way we work with our customers and the overall service we give our customers.

Procurement

HEL manages its own procurement activities. This entails setting future plans which match allocated budget and personnel estimates with proposals for investment in hardware and software. Future plans take into account the needs of end-users from proposed systems.

In the first instance, HEL's managing director at Maidenhead must approve a procurement exercise. The managing director of the International Procurement Department in Dusseldorf must also obtain approval from the managing director in Maidenhead for procurement for his division.

HEL's managing director visits Tokyo twice a year for discussions relating to the following six months' budget and to gain approval for his budgetary requirements. Senior board members from head office in Tokyo visit HEL at Maidenhead for discussions on strategy at regular intervals (up to four times per year).

Hitachi's manufacturing experience in Japan has enabled the company to establish a 'home-grown' IT platform throughout its manufacturing sites. Electronic communication networks facilitate the transmission of procurement information between Maidenhead and Landshut. The kinds of information transmitted via these networks are as follows:

Transmissions from Maidenhead to Landshut
- Forecasted requirements
- Purchase orders.

Transmissions from Landshut to Maidenhead
- Information about predicted order shipments
- Actual shipment information
- Invoicing documentation.

At the current time computer operators at either end of the link need to manipulate transmitted information.

HEL's sales forecasts are increasingly used by head office for strategic planning purposes. Sales forecasts and production planning documents are compared to ensure that they are not contradictory. Negotiation between sales and production departments attempts to rectify misalignments.

Managing IT

In 1990 HEL head office relocated to a 6-acre site on a bank of the River Thames at Maidenhead. Since then, IT has been seen as a more mainstream corporate activity. HEL takes pride in being a flexible organization, capable of responding rapidly to rapidly changing conditions in a market susceptible to swift technological change. For HEL, the capability to react swiftly to customer needs is perceived as a source of competitive advantage.

The Corporate MIS manager is on an assignment from head office in Japan. His main task is to monitor IT strategic planning, particularly when this involves the international networks. He is responsible for long-range EDP planning; developing EDP systems; liaising with head office on IT policy and systems; ensuring compatibility of pan-European IT systems; and problem solving throughout Europe. The Corporate MIS manager at HEL reports daily to the Overseas Systems Department in Tokyo.[5] In this way, he can alert head office to the ideas and suggestions from local staff and influence head office to heed these suggestions.

There is no line management function between the Corporate MIS manager and the MIS manager. The MIS manager has line management responsibilities for MIS in the UK and northern Europe. There are separate line management roles in Munich and Düsseldorf, where Hitachi has its main offices.

Including the MIS manager, the MIS department has eighteen members of staff. This may appear small compared with MIS departments in other multinational organizations. However, perceived from the viewpoint of satisfaction within the company, the department produces a high standard of work output. This is attributable to the department's expertise together with its planning capabilities. The MIS department makes regular checks on its work through analysing the number of objectives that have been met and any project failures.

At present, there are no Japanese staff in the department, although young members of staff from the head office Overseas Systems Department have in the past been sent on short project assignments.

IT development

In terms of IT development, where mutual compatibility is an issue, HEL are obliged to follow the lead given by head office. Each of Hitachi's trading zones has a level of internal autonomy, although they are obliged to maintain a dialogue with head office in Japan.

IT project ideas proposed by the MIS Department at HEL are invariably accepted. The MIS department works within budget and staff quota parameters allocated by head office and this determines work capacity.

In the first instance, the MIS manager decides which projects his department accepts. Senior management and interested parties in other departments are notified of his decisions. Plans which conflict with other departments are resolved by consultation and rescheduling or by reprioritizing one or more proposed projects.

IT decision making

A prime factor which shapes IT decision making is the organizational structure of HEL and its relationship with Hitachi in Japan. Until 1989, Hitachi was organized into autonomous functional divisions (Semiconductor Division, Computer Division, etc.). Each functional division made its own decisions about overseas organization, including choice of computer systems. In early 1989, following a management reorganization in Japan, it was decided to reorganize the company from a functional to a geographical basis. The most recent formation of HEL was one consequence of that reorganization.

From an MIS viewpoint, this organizational change meant that the new company inherited a number of disparate computer systems on different platforms. For example, for historical reasons[6] the semiconductor manufacturing operation was based on IBM mainframe computers and IBM operating systems, while other parts of the organization used UNIX machines and systems.

In the wake of the reorganization, effort was needed to ensure that these diverse systems could communicate with each other and to 'customize' non-business systems for the purposes of specific departments. This was done to prevent end-users from inheriting platforms unsuitable for their department's job requirements.

HEL sees IT as a means of improving administrative and support functions; for example, by reducing staffing levels and by maximizing work output. This use of IT is seen as an effective way of realizing optimum cost-benefit in back-office support services. In the semiconductor market, IT is led by customer service requirements.

The IT Department competes with other departments for its share of budget allocation, although historically there have been few problems in securing sufficient funding for its various projects.

IT and consensus decision making

In common with other Japanese-managed companies, HEL practises a system of consensus decision making. This means that all relevant parties in an IT decision have the opportunity (and obligation) to inform others of their thoughts on particular matters.

In general, Japanese managers do not like to appear autocratic, nor do they like to be surprised by unexpected decisions made by managers at lower levels in the company hierarchy. Most IT-related decisions involve a financial aspect, which is controlled by funding from head office. Japanese managers on overseas assignment make financial decisions at HEL. For these reasons, local managers at HEL have adapted the Japanese system of decision making.

A *ringisho* document lists the people who have assented to the proposal. This group consensus document is passed to the managing director who uses it, together with his own opinions, to inform head office in Tokyo of local thoughts and ideas.

Identifying IT systems

IT systems are identified in a variety of ways. A Marketing Systems Coordinator attends a customer-liaison meeting where various problems are discussed. MIS development staff are involved in consultations to develop appropriate systems which attempt to resolve the perceived problems. Some systems evolve through responding to customers' stated problems. In this way HEL-ECD improved its warehousing and storage systems and in-house documentation and bar coding facilities.

Improvements in the warehousing system enabled warehouse staff to record more precise shipment information. A computer check when boxes of product are selected off the shelf for shipment reduces the possibility of human error. The installation of barcode scanning equipment will shortly reduce this possibility still further. Alternative 'drivers' for HEL's IT systems are regulations introduced by the government and, more recently, by the European Commission (e.g. anti-dumping legislation).

Product Marketing Information System (PMIS)

The Product Marketing Information System (PMIS) enables HEL to coordinate and formalize all the information that various sales staff had noted by various means (e.g. on paper and in personal organizers). This information is about not only existing customers and their potential plans but also *potential* customers and *their potential plans*. Most information of this nature is gained from talking to potential companies about their businesses. Hitachi customers in other parts of the world, particularly head offices in the United States, may be a source of market intelligence about their European subsidiaries. PMIS collates information about what companies want to buy, and enables HEL's Marketing Department to build up a picture of changing requirements in the semiconductor marketplace.

Notes

1 Net sales for year ended 31 March 1992 were Y7 765 545 million (US$58 387 556 000). Gross profit for the trading period was Y2 276 807

million (US$17 118 850 000). Exchange rate at Y133 = US$1, at 31 March 1992. Source: Annual Report dated 31 March 1992.
2 At year ended 31 March 1990. Hitachi Fact Sheet (1991).
3 Company report 31 March 1992, p. 18.
4 Hitachi Europe Ltd, corporate literature, undated.
5 The Systems Department at Tokyo head office has between seventy and eighty staff. Of these, five develop IT systems for overseas operations.
6 In the early 1980s there were only four semiconductor centres in the world. These were California, Germany, Hong Kong and the UK. Hitachi's own 'plug-compatible' systems were not as prevalent as they have since become. The company bought from IBM in the interests of standardization.

7
Japan Travel Bureau (Europe) Ltd

Case profile

For Japan Travel Bureau (JTB), information is 'the lifeblood of the travel industry'. IT helps JTB 'gather and disseminate travel-related information and manage customer data more effectively'. JTBE management seeks to balance the need for enhanced customer service supported by effective IT systems with IT investment expenditure. Members of JTBE's senior management team have given enthusiastic support to the IT department and new IT projects.

Each of JTBE's nine European travel offices is supported by a host computer and over 200 on-line terminals. JTBE's purpose-built travel and booking system is called JETS. JETS replaced previously separate systems and allows each office to combine customer quotations, holiday bookings and tour operations. JTBE sales staff use JETS to design customer-specific travel itineraries.

Development of JETS I began in 1985 and by April 1989 the system was being used by all sections of JTBE. JTBE's management and operations staff feel that JETS I has been a success. Processing faxes and documents and accessing information are carried out faster than before, and JTBE management feels that the system is superior to those used by competitors.

However, the only access to JETS within the JTB's domestic operation in Japan is through the European Travel Centre (ETC). ETC, located in Japan, coordinates enquiries and bookings for European holidays via JETS. An interface between TRIPS V (the Travel Reservation and Information Planning System used in JTBE's domestic operations) and JETS is planned for the next phase of IT development. A project team has begun work on an upgraded model, JETS II, due for completion in August 1994. JETS II will be an on-line fully integrated system giving instantaneous access to transmitted data.

JTBE sought approval and funding from Japan for its pan-European accounting System (POP). Inaugurated in April 1991, POP includes accounting procedures for each of the JTBE's nine European countries and standardizes JTBE's Europe-wide accounting procedures. The system helps JTBE sales offices to generate invoices and ensures that JTBE pays promptly for goods and services from its suppliers. POP also generates data from JTBE's European offices for use by various departments at JTBE's London headquarters.

Company background

Japan Travel Bureau, Inc. (JTB) was originally established on 12 March 1912 as Japan Tourist Bureau to manage the itineraries of incoming tourists to Japan. During the 1950s JTB expanded its operations in the United States, opening offices in New York (1952); San Francisco (1953); and Los Angeles (1957). An office was opened in Sydney in 1962 while in the following year the first European office was opened in Paris.

In 1964, the year of the Tokyo Olympic Games, the government of Japan liberalized overseas travel for Japanese citizens, allowing those who could afford it one overseas trip per year for pleasure purposes. That same year, Japan Travel Bureau International Inc. was established in the United States. The first wholesale package tour for visitors to Japan was also started in 1964.

In 1972 JTB opened offices in London, Geneva and Rome and in the early 1980s further offices were opened in Frankfurt and Beijing (both in 1982); Chicago and Vancouver (1983) and Düsseldorf and Newport Beach, Long Island (1984). These were followed by New Jersey (1985); Vienna, Aukland and Melbourne (1986).

Madrid, Singapore, Toronto, the Gold Coast and Christchurch all opened in time for the company's 75th jubilee celebrations in 1987. Additional European offices were established in Barcelona (1988); Munich and Zurich (1989). Offices in the Strand, London, and Athens (both opened in 1990) complete the current network of 300 branches and 602 agencies in Japan and approximately 50 locations worldwide.

The JTB Group consists of 114 organizations which include 111 companies, two foundations and a professional school. In total, JTB operates 313 offices in Japan and 55 offices overseas. The number of employees worldwide is 9640[1] augmented in each country by locally employed staff. JTB regards itself as the undisputed market leader of the Japanese travel industry, for which it acts as 'an informal industry-wide quality controller'.[2] It supplies a range of quality products, which competitors try to emulate.

Product range

JTB's business operations consist of four principal areas of activity: domestic travel; overseas travel; inbound travel; publishing. Table 7.1 shows JTB's various business interests.

One of the company's core strengths is its expertise in hotel management. It has a joint venture with the US-based ITT Sheraton Corporation to manage the newly constructed 300-room Kobe Bay Sheraton Hotel and Towers, which is situated in Kobe, Honshu (the largest of the four main Japanese islands).

Table 7.1 Diversified businesses of Japan Travel Bureau. (*Source*: JTB corporate literature (1991))

Business area	Number of companies	Principal business
Hotels and resort development	17	Quality hotels in cities and resorts, hotel management consulting company
Real estate	2	Purchase, sale, rental, and development of buildings, houses and land
Travel, trading and service business	53	General and special-interest travel agencies, trading, advertising, insurance, events and conventions, wedding-related services, credit card services
Printing and other services	8	General printing (including computerized composition), commercial photo renting, sale of books
Education and health care	3	Schools for travel, tourism and culture studies, and a health-care foundation
Transport and rent-a-car	6	Air cargo, land transportation, delivery service, car rental
Restaurants	3	Restaurants and catering

In the printing and publishing field JTB is the principal source of travel-related literature in Japan. Its output includes timetables, maps, guidebooks, dictionaries and videotapes. In addition to producing its own corporate literature, JTB publishes commercially several best-selling travel magazines. *Tabi* and *Rurubu*, two such monthly magazines, recently celebrated their 750th and 200th issues, respectively.

JTB divides package tours into one of three niche sectors. 'Look JTB' tours cater for the discerning client who seeks a tailored, exclusive holiday regardless of cost. Also in this category are 'Royal Road' tours, which feature super-de-luxe accommodation and travel arrangements. Palette tours are designed for holidaymakers in the middle-price range; Navi tours are economically priced for travellers on a limited budget who prefer low-cost holidays. The JTB 'Nice' coupons are a popular form of financial service by which customers can pay for travel, shopping and dining.

In the late 1980s, in anticipation of higher industry standards, JTB instigated a company-wide revitalization programme. This was aimed at assessing the relevance of its corporate philosophy to forecasted market needs. Accordingly, JTB realigned its corporate identity to meet what it perceived as market expectations and needs.

In 1992 JTB celebrated its 80th anniversary by introducing 'Go JTB 21', a strategic plan to take the company into the twenty-first century. Total Tour Management (TTM) System is the contribution by the IT Department at Tokyo headquarters. Under this project the IT Department will identify and propose new systems. As part of 'Go JTB 21' the Group proposes to double annual revenues to Y5 trillion.

Business environment

In contrast to popular belief, the large majority of Japanese are not great overseas travellers; of the Japanese population of approximately 124 million fewer than 10 per cent possess a passport. However, international and domestic economic conditions in recent years have encouraged an increasing number of Japanese nationals, particularly young people, to travel overseas for business and leisure purposes.

The number of Japanese travelling abroad in 1991 exceeded 10 million. This figure represents a near-doubling in four years from the 5.5 million Japanese who travelled overseas in 1986. This figure is expected to double yet again by the year 2000. Predictably, Asia was the most popular destination, being visited by over 5 million people. Nearly 4 million Japanese travelled to the Americas, including almost 1.5 million to Hawaii. Europe had 1.2 million Japanese visitors.[3] JTB counts as its customers some 1.8 million Japanese travellers.

As the number of Japanese who desire to travel overseas increases, so has the number of companies participating in the flourishing travel industry. To remain ahead of its competitors JTB has diversified into a range of activities which support its core travel service activities.

Business impact of IT

JTB's stated corporate philosophy is 'We strive always to be the world's number one travel organization contributing to the interchange of people at home and abroad and to the realization of an enriched quality of life for all'.[4] This statement, together with a five-point list of 'commitments', comprises the corporate philosophy:

Commitments
1   'We will constantly maintain the principle of "customer first" at all levels and in all functions of our company.'
2   'We will strive to establish a free, magnanimous and innovative corporate climate wherein each one of us is encouraged to demonstrate his or her potential to the fullest extent.'

3 'We will maintain and increase our competitive advantages, while contributing to the development of the industry as a whole.'
4 'We will forge ahead with the development of travel-related businesses to revitalize the entire JTB group.'
5 'We will build closer and broader ties and grow together with our business partners.'

JTB believes that the keys to commercial success in the 1990s depend on continued careful targeting of its products and services and sustained diversification of activities within the travel sector to provide a broad range of revenue sources. JTB's president recognizes that the rapid growth of the travel industry both in Japan and worldwide has created a mature industry where clients' tastes and expectations are becoming ever more sophisticated. Travellers' increased sophistication includes their preference for products and services tailored to their individual tastes and requirements.

JTB plans to increase the number of retail outlets; both those offering packaged tours and those specializing in other travel services. Also recognized as paramount are strengthened trading links with primary suppliers of accommodation and transport services.

In 1969 JTB inaugurated TRIPS (Travel Reservation and Information Planning System), an on-line computer reservation system. The system is used in the Japanese domestic market and allows JTB to make airline, hotel, car rental and amusement park reservations. Since its inception, the system has been continually updated.

TRIPS IV, the current model, has 4000 terminals, and is used in JTB's domestic market to make approximately 200 000 seat reservations per day on aircraft, trains, buses and other types of transportation. In Japan, over 4500 inns and hotels are linked to the system giving access to 60 000 rooms nationwide. The system is linked with international computer reservation systems, such as American Airlines' Sabre system, so that international reservations can be made.

In Japan, 1100 sales outlets have access via the TRIPS IV computer system to the JTB Data Retrieval system. This database contains 130 000 leisure and travel-related topics. Overseas branches and offices can also access this system. JTB plans to link the Data Retrieval system to Point-of-Sale (POS) terminals. TRIPS-International is an on-line system that links sales booking offices in Japan with European regional offices. This system is used to check tour availability and to make immediate bookings for 'Look' and 'Palette' tours.

Television Oceania is a joint venture between JTB and various organizations. This satellite TV station broadcasts Japanese-language news programmes to Australia, which is an increasingly popular holiday destination for Japanese tourists as well as a preferred retirement place for large numbers of elderly Japanese people.

Also available in Australia is Tourtalk, which broadcasts, in a variety of languages, travel-related news and information on a radio receiver no larger than a business card. This novel concept is marketed by Tourtalk International Pty, Ltd, a subsidiary of JTB.

Managing IT

IT in Japan Travel Bureau Europe (JTBE)

JTB recognizes that information is 'the lifeblood of the travel industry'.[5] JTB's published corporate IT policy is to 'help us gather and disseminate travel-related information and manage customer data more effectively'.[6] Japan Travel Bureau Europe (JTBE) consists of nine regions, each of which has its own host computer and over 200 on-line terminals. A specially designed software program handles all travel functions from a customers' initial enquiry to the final invoice for the holiday package.

While being well aware that leadership in the travel industry is dependent on efficient service supported by effective IT systems, JTBE management is also conscious of a balance between expenditure and income generated. From this point of view, new IT systems are invariably assessed in terms of the income they are likely to generate which is compared with the cost of the investment needed to develop and implement the system. IT systems allow an increased volume of work to be produced by the same, or reduced, number of staff.

The managing director from 1987 to 1992 was an enthusiastic supporter of IT projects and constantly 'pushed' the IT department to explore new IT project areas.

The deputy general manager responsible for Corporate Planning reports to the managing director whose responsibilities include IT systems and projects. The IT department has six members of staff and occupies the same level in the corporate hierarchy as the Operations Department whose head also reports to the managing director.

Through the Japanese decision-making procedure called *nemawashi* the Deputy General Manager for Corporate Planning is able to confer with his opposite number in the Operations Department and to clarify proposals before approaching the managing director for a decision.

JTB Europe *Tehai* System (JETS)

JTBE's purpose-built system is called JETS (JTB Europe *Tehai* System; in Japanese *Tehai* means handling). Prior to the implementation of JETS, JTBE operated separate systems for customer quotations, holiday bookings and tour operations. European management requested JTB head office in Tokyo to investigate the possibility of an improved system.

The introduction of JETS allows JTBE to combine all these activities in one system. JETS enables JTBE offices in the European network to input separate holiday components (hotels, car hire, excursion tours, restaurants). JETS thus allows JTBE sales personnel to design itineraries which cater specifically for customers' individual requirements.

In Japan the European Travel Centre (ETC) coordinates enquiries and bookings for European holidays via JETS. This is the only access to JETS within the Japanese domestic operation. The company's next phase of IT development will see the interface between TRIPS V and JETS.

JETS I

In 1985 JTBE began development of JETS I as an in-house project, led by the Deputy General Manager, Corporate Planning, whose UK work assignment was specifically to organize JETS. Some members of his project team were familiar with IBM systems and guided the project from this technological viewpoint. The projected pan-Europe start date was to be January 1989.

The IT department and a small project team invited a range of tenders from interested companies. With a vision of the current and future possibilities for the system, and with a stipulated pan-European requirement, the team eventually awarded the contract to a company which, in addition to IT technical competence, had experience and expertise in Europe.

The system was designed to specification on schedule and, in June 1988, six months before the projected start date, the project team organized familiarization training for relevant staff members. This began from the top down, beginning with General Managers. Tour Managers (i.e. heads of departments) and Project Managers (heads of particular tour categories) also received familiarization training.

At this stage of training, the project team noticed that tour operations staff (who were to be the end users of the JETS I system) seemed to be resistant to the introduction of the system. 'Look JTB', which deals with exclusive package holidays and which accounts for more than 50 per cent of JTB's business, requested its involvement in JETS to be postponed for several months. Two main reasons were offered for the postponement request: 'the system does not contain enough capacity for our range of data'; and 'we need more time to master input of our data'. 'Look JTB' made its case clearly and effectively and refrained from connecting with the system until April 1989, when it felt ready to join its sister sections, who by now were using the JETS I system.

Informal feedback from management and operations staff and the speed with which faxes and documents can now be processed indicate that JETS I has been a success. Management has access to relevant information in a faster time than previously. The system allows JTBE to outperform competitors and has created effective entry barriers for potential competitors.

JETS II

The selected project team have now made proposals for an upgraded JETS II system. JETS I transmits data via a 'mailbox' which may mean delays of up to several hours before data are received. JETS II will be an on-line fully integrated system which will give instantaneous access to transmitted data. The scheduled project completion date for JETS II is August 1994. As with JETS I, the proposals have received official support from the managing director who has written to all divisions of the organization proclaiming his enthusiasm.

With the benefit of past experience, the IT project team are devoting sustained effort to training at an early stage of the project and to publicizing and promoting JETS II. Even at the current design stage, members of the selected project team, which includes personnel from JTBE's European offices, receive pre-training in the advantages and improvements of JETS II over JETS I. Such pre-education was missing from the JETS I project.

The JTBE Newsletter, which is distributed to all staff on a monthly basis, now contains regular sections on the benefits of the system to both organization and end users. Operations staff, the system's end users, are involved earlier in the system and a higher profile has been given to 'pre-education' of relevant personnel.

The IT manager and the Chief of the Data Processing Department both acknowledge the importance of personalities of the people selected by project managers for involvement in the project. As the project is pan-European, colleagues from JTBE offices in mainland Europe are selected by their managers to visit the UK and assist in aspects of training for the project. National and cultural traits are evident from attitudes towards cooperation with the team by representatives from the various European offices.

Through their particular training inputs for JETS II, individuals' personal temperament affects the shape and scope of the new system. The project team would like to be able to select for membership of their team 'ideal' candidates whose personal attributes include openness to new ideas and receptiveness to change. However, the realistic overriding factors for project team selection are previous experience and current availability.

Each office in the European network has evolved its own styles of working. The JETS system, imposed from European headquarters, represents an intrusion into current working routines. Consequently, a large element of training and project promotion is devoted to explaining the corporate benefits of a single system.

The 'outward-bound' IT project

While the JETS system is an acknowledged success, not all proposed IT systems have been successful. In 1989, JTBE began work on a project directed towards outward-bound tours. This would provide a travel service for European destinations for low-budget 'off-the-street' customers. Various software houses were asked to propose off-the-shelf software packages. JTBE conducted exploratory negotiations and appraised a number of proposals. However, none of the proposed systems quite matched the expectations of JTBE management and the systems were, for the most part, incompatible with those currently in operation at JTBE.

JTBE's current structure has operational sections for each of the different travel services. Under the proposed systems JTBE's tour operations staff would have a new role of travel consultants. Their work routines would change in that they would have one booking with many types of service (travel, accommodation, car hire) which they could offer to customers.

The project team felt that JTBE should evolve towards this way of working as this would reduce the work between the different sections and give sales staff increased job satisfaction. However, management felt such a change to be inappropriate at this time and the project did not progress any further.

JTBE Accounting System (POP)

At the request of several senior managers in Europe, the board of directors in Japan agreed to fund a pan-European accounting system. Such a system would cope satisfactorily with accounting practices in any of the European countries where JTBE maintained an office, as well as standardizing accounting procedures throughout JTBE's European network.

The JTBE Accounting System (POP), inaugurated in April 1991, is programmed to include country-specific accounting procedures. This is a full accounting system which includes the efficient production of invoices by JTBE sales offices in the various countries and the prompt payment of primary suppliers for goods and services, as JTBE head office can be alerted to funds that are required by local offices to enable them to pay their suppliers for goods and services. An additional advantage is that useful statistical information generated by the various European offices is now available to JTBE's London headquarters.

IT in JTBE's Personnel Department

IT Departments and Personnel Departments are motivated by different visions of the organization. Personnel Departments consider data protection and the security and integrity of private personal information to be of paramount importance in an IT system.

JTBE's Personnel Department has an extensive database relating to the company's human resources, including recruitment details, salary scales and attendance records. Some information is held in duplicate if, for example, it has been used by both JTB Tokyo headquarters and by JTBE head office in London. JTBE needs to use these data in different ways, for example: holding a database of potential job candidates; monitoring recruitment; planning for staff promotion; recording generic competencies of staff members; overtime details; and job-evaluation projects. However, manually intensive accessing routines are restrictive in terms of time and effort.

The IT requirements of the Personnel Department are fourfold, all of which are equally important. First, as a service department, the Personnel function serves the needs of diverse managers in the organization. Thus there is a need to provide managers with on-line information (for example, payroll, pension and personnel data) from the extensive database. One of the weaknesses of the current system is the need to wait until month's end before such data can be collated.

Second, Personnel Department staff need ready access to on-line information (for example, relating to overtime and salaries) and to the facilities for conducting sophisticated analysis of the existing data. Third, once released from manually intensive routines, staff would be free to work more closely with new trainees. Finally, there is the need for a career-planning facility so that staff development and training programmes can be coordinated with staffing requirements, particularly for locally employed staff. Additionally, the Personnel Department's daily routines would be better served by computer.

The ideal Management Information System for the Personnel Department would include all these functions in a professional planning module. In addition, personnel staff need to manipulate data according to prevailing needs and the facility to enhance written data with graphics.

In reaching their system specifications, members of the department considered 'What do we need today? 'What will we need tomorrow and in ten years' time?' Increased speed and improved accessibility were predominant 'drivers' for developing new computer systems for the administrative function. The Research Officer to the Personnel Manager believes that an ideal software package would enable JTBE to gain more effective benefit from the partnerships within the European network.

Some software houses were unable to offer a computer system meeting JTBE's need for a pan-European network. Other software houses had insufficient expertise in Europe.

General training has already been provided to end users, through the use of on-screen tutorial activities. This training demonstrated the features of the new system. However, specific training is currently being held in abeyance because the new system has had no data input, as yet. The installation of data will provide the opportunity for training with 'live' screens and avoid abstract concepts which obscure training aims for both trainers and those receiving training.

The Personnel Department derives benefit from the new system, most importantly because staff can produce reports of a more sophisticated nature from the enhanced information from the database. Additionally, work which was previously done manually by Personnel Department staff is now done automatically.

Members of staff feel that progress on the new system has so far progressed smoothly, as a new system has been identified, funding has been allocated and a company has agreed to manage the network. Minor technical problems, mainly relating to the interfaces, have been rectified.

Sources

JTB *Employee Handbook*, September 1991.
JTB Annual Report for financial year ended 30 March 1990.
JTB Annual Report for financial year ended 31 March 1991.
JTB Europe Corporate brochure, undated.

Notes

1 As at September 1991.
2 JTB Annual Report, year ended 30 March 1990, p. 3.
3 The exact figures are: Asia 5 246 000; Americas 3 902 000 (Hawaii 1 440 000); Europe 1 219 000; Oceania 535 000; other destinations 95 000.
4 JTB corporate documents.
5 Annual Report 1990, p. 8.
6 President's message, Annual Report, March 1991, p. 2.

8
JVC (UK) Ltd

Case profile

The computer facility for JVC (UK) is situated in the company's head office in JVC House, JVC Business Park, north London. Called the Computer Room, it is responsible for maintaining communications between JVC's on-site facilities and its offices and warehouses in Leeds and Dublin.

Apart from supporting sales activities, JVC (UK) Ltd uses IT to provide services to the company's network of dealerships throughout the UK. These include spare parts ordering, EDI links and laptop computers for JVC sales teams. When ordering spare parts, dealers dial into JVC's computer system using a monitor and modem. After appropriate security checks dealers can order spare parts and enquire about part availability. Dealers say that the system makes spare parts ordering quick and easy with reduced communications costs. Since 1991 a common European spare parts ordering system has been introduced into European subsidiaries.

In response to dealers' requests, JVC has established EDI links with dealers and the larger High Street retail outlets. Computer Room staff decided that laptop computers would be a valuable asset for the company's twenty-three-person sales team and in 1991 laptop computers were issued to each of them. Sales teams use their laptops to give JVC dealers more accurate information in a faster time. Not only are these computers invaluable for sales teams, they can also be used by JVC dealers to check JVC's available stock, their own orders outstanding and forecasted deliveries. By stimulating more orders, the laptops have brought added business benefits to JVC.

Company background

JVC (UK) Ltd is responsible for marketing, sales and distribution of JVC-branded consumer electronic products in the UK and Eire. JVC House, the head office of JVC (UK) Limited, is located at the JVC Business Park in north London, as are some of the company's warehousing and distribution facilities.[1] JVC has also established sales companies in Austria, Belgium, France, Germany, Italy, the Netherlands, Norway, Spain and Sweden.

JVC Corporation has fifteen factories in Japan. In addition, the company has factories in Germany, France, Belgium, Scotland, Singapore, Malaysia and the United States. Each factory more or less specializes in one product line. The factory in Germany produces video recorders; France, in-car entertainment and CDs; televisions are manufactured in East Kilbride, Scotland; audio equipment is produced in Singapore; and video equipment in Malaysia.

Warehouses in JVC Business Park stock the whole range of JVC products and are the distribution centre for JVC dealers and other retail outlets in south-east England. JVC products for the north of England and Ireland are distributed from JVC (UK)'s warehouses in Leeds and Dublin.

National accounts department manages relationships with the well-known High Street retailers (e.g. Dixons, Currys, Comet). On a day-to-day basis these are serviced by sales people but are managed by the national accounts department at JVC House.

Business impact of IT

Since 1982 the company has managed its main merchandise stock control in the on-site warehouse originally via an off-the-shelf computer package. An IBM mainframe system was introduced in 1985.

In its use of computers for its business, the considerable change experienced by the company has been matched by developments in the skills and attitudes of staff working in end-user departments. From 1985 when the company first installed the system, data processing was the sole preserve of Computer Room staff. Employees in other departments were not fully aware of the benefits of using computers for their work. Gradually, as the computer facility has developed, individual departments have assumed responsibility for their own data entry. Employees in every department now use computers in their work.

Developing a pan-European system

Pan-European IT projects involve EDP managers from European subsidiaries together with the personnel from JVC Information Centre in Tokyo, which manages IT projects for the whole JVC group. In April 1992, following discussions with EDP managers representing all JVC European subsidiaries, head office in Japan developed a computer package to manage inventory, sales ledger and customer orders. This package was to be used by all JVC subsidiaries throughout Europe, including JVC (UK).

As local requirements differ from country to country within Europe, subsidiaries are allowed to develop their own domestic applications within the common pan-European system. Corporate policy prevents subsidiaries from changing any master computer programs supplied by head office. However, subsidiaries are free to adapt parts of the common system to their local requirements.

Predictably, subsidiaries make a number of changes to the common system to reflect local market conditions. They do so in collaboration with other national sales divisions. JVC (UK) and JVC Deutschland GmbH are currently working together to make changes to the pan-European system for mutual benefit.

Where several subsidiaries have similar local requirements, EDP managers request the systems development department in Japan to make changes in the master system. Head office evaluates such requests and decides what changes should be made. For example, JVC (UK) has a requirement for a bonded warehouse facility. As JVC (UK) is the only European subsidiary to make this request, head office systems development department will not make changes to the pan-European system. Consequently, JVC (UK) has initiated its own project and has engaged an outsourced software company to refine the pan-European system.

Product planning and procurement

JVC (UK)'s trading periods are twice-yearly from October to March and April to September. These periods correspond to the company's financial year which runs from April to March and are also planning cycles.

Sales divisions order stock by product line. JVC (UK) places stock-requisition orders on particular factories for part of their output. Close liaison between overseas sales divisions and head office product procurement department ensures efficient management of global manufacturing output and distribution.

In the marketing department product managers are responsible for different product categories (e.g. audio and video tapes, audio products, video products). Product department managers forecast product needs month by month over the six-month trading period.[2]

In July and February of each year, product department managers prepare product requisitions and discuss their proposals with JVC (UK)'s managing director and finance director. The managing director, finance director and sales director visit Japan for global planning discussions with their counterparts at head office. Global product planning negotiations take place in Japan between the managing director, finance director and sales director from JVC (UK) and their counterparts at head office.

Monthly IPS analysis

JVC (UK) conducts a monthly IPS analysis to examine its current Inventory, Purchase and Sales data. This audit reconciles purchases from Japan, sales to UK customers and inventory, and provides current trading information for forecasting purposes. The results of the IPS analysis inform the product marketing departments, sales departments, the managing director and the finance director of their discussions and are used to prepare documents for negotiations in Japan.

The Computer Room is responsible for producing monthly trading data at the end of every month. Product managers extract relevant data for their own physical records. At the end of the six-month trading period these records are passed back to the Computer Room who enter them on the computer database.

Spare parts ordering

In 1990 the company bought a Viewtrax system, including hardware and software, for its spare-parts ordering facility. Dealers use a monitor and modem to dial into JVC's system. An on-screen menu guides the dealer through various services. After validation,[3] dealers enter the common core system to order spare parts and enquire about part availability. Before Viewtrax was installed, JVC's dealers commented that competitors offered a better service for spare parts ordering systems.

When the system was installed, feedback from dealers suggested that a few changes should be made. These were duly carried out and dealers now find the system useful and easy to use. Spare parts transactions are quick with no waiting time and communications costs are lower than using a telephone to place a similar order.

In 1991 the company began to develop a common European spare parts ordering system. This was gradually introduced to European subsidiaries one by one. The system is intended to be in use from October 1993 by the larger JVC companies in the UK, France and Germany.

Electronic Data Interchange (EDI)

Where possible, the Computer Room manager responds favourably to requests from dealers for IT developments. A recent example is EDI. As dealers are aware that they have power in the supplier–buyer relationship, such requests are difficult to ignore.

JVC (UK) has had little alternative but to establish EDI links with dealers and in 1991 introduced EDI into the larger High Street retail outlets. Having decided to introduce EDI links, agreement was quickly reached on the most appropriate EDI standard package. Failure to introduce EDI facilities would undoubtedly have encouraged retailers to intensify their relationships with JVC's competitors.

Retailers' acknowledged strength in the supplier–dealer relationship compels JVC (UK) to make changes to its own computer system when retailers alter their own systems.

Managing IT

Computer facilities

JVC (UK)'s computer facilities are managed by the three members of staff in the Computer Room based in JVC House. The department is responsible for maintaining communications between local facilities on-site, and between JVC (UK) and its offices and warehouses in Leeds and Dublin. As a manufacturing site, the East Kilbride factory is not part of JVC (UK) and its computer and global communications links are with head office in Japan.

The Computer Room also is responsible for changes to JVC (UK)'s hardware and software, maintenance of software, arranging maintenance for computer hardware, and training end users. The computer manager reports to the finance director who is responsible for local IT budgets up to a certain amount. Larger IT investment decisions (over Y5 million) are referred to head office in Japan. Although he has no direct IT background, the finance manager keeps in regular contact with Computer Room staff and their work.

Head office in Tokyo develops standard software systems which are used in JVC offices throughout Europe. Managers from JVC's various European subsidiary companies meet to decide a common system. Local offices are allowed to develop their own domestic applications within the common standard system.

Planning IT

As all company departments are end users of the services and systems provided by the Computer Room, new initiatives and decisions to upgrade systems are discussed with all departments. From these discussions, the Computer Room determines user department's business concerns, which are invaluable when the Computer Room plans IT development.

The procedure in detail is that end-user departments outline their requirements on a request form, which is evaluated by the Computer Room. Requirements common to a number of departments, or which are beneficial to other users and the company, receive particular consideration. After further discussion with user departments, the Computer Room decides whether to accept or reject the request.

IT plans are submitted to the financial director and the managing director for approval. Once approval is given, the Computer Room can start development. The financial director and the managing director approve those projects that solely affect JVC (UK) Ltd. Projects which affect the JVC group are referred to head office. Two recent examples are: local directors approved bonded warehouse software which only affected JVC (UK); recommended changes to software for the system used by the JVC group were sent to head office for consideration.

Large IT projects are reported to head office to allow the appropriate department to make suggestions. When a system affects all subsidiaries, discussion takes place with departments in Tokyo. JVC (UK) is responsible for solely local systems used in the UK. The Computer Room contacts Japan on a daily basis using international close frame telephone link and fax.

When the request from the end user has been approved, new software can be introduced. The user is informed of the estimated time to write and install the software. Once the software is ready, the Computer Room and the end-user department conduct tests. The new software becomes operational when the end user is satisfied.

The department also analyses the effects of the new system on working practices. All department heads are informed by memo of the Computer Room's current ideas. Feedback replies are evaluated and included in future planning. Details are explained and agreed in meetings between the Computer Room manager, department heads and other members of staff affected by the new system. Computer Room staff and department heads welcome opportunities to discuss changes in existing computer systems.

New IT systems

IT budgets and IT investment spending are timed to fit into the company's two six-monthly trading periods. As a profit centre, JVC (UK) generates funding from sales activities. The computer manager makes proposals for expenditure on computer hardware and software and discusses these with the finance director who has board-level responsibility for the Computer Room.

As far as possible, the Computer Room staff try to be informed about the latest IT technological developments and to note products that could be useful to the company. For example, the Computer Room staff decided that laptop computers would be a valuable asset for the company's sales team. The Computer Room staff has recently recommended that JVC (UK) has replaced its existing computer system with a more recent model.

Head office is developing a new sales and accounting database that will preclude making hard copies as part of its initiative to produce a 'paperless' working environment. In the opinion of Computer Room staff, current working procedures generate an unnecessarily excessive number of hard copies of reports. Computer Room staff encourage end users to use information on their computer screens wherever possible. They and end users decide together whether it is essential to produce a hard copy of a report.

IT for management information

The Computer Room provides a number of services to other departments. Daily computer printouts are printed overnight and are distributed first thing the following morning to various departments (e.g. credit control, sales ledger, salesforce, personnel, management accounts, marketing, national accounts). Some departments occasionally request a special print run.

As part of its printing service for monthly reports, the Computer Room sends reports to senior managers for planning purposes. Most information contained in reports is an accumulation of the previous monthly and annual sales data, sub-divided by product line, retail outlet and sales targets. Data are updated in real time. The marketing department and the product managers use the accumulated data from the previous month or year to make strategic business decisions and plans for the following six months.

The Computer Room has created a new database for management planning purposes. Sales department managers and product managers ask the Computer Room to provide information in different formats. In this case the relevant department managers and Computer Room staff discuss possible ways of using available information more effectively by interpreting it in a different way.

Introducing laptop computers

In 1991 each member of the JVC (UK) twenty-three-person sales team was issued with a laptop computer. Prior to this, each salesperson received a daily sales report, printed manually. This procedure had three disadvantages: it was costly; posted sales reports took time and became dated; reports were sometimes lost.

The sales reports on the laptops contain a lot of information. For example, they show: sales up to the current day; current sales compared with the same day during the previous six-month period. The record of sales to a dealer is useful, particularly at the end of the month when dealers need to know their orders in order to reach their target. Salespeople use their laptops to keep track of their own targets. The sales reports show dealers' outstanding orders with JVC, including order details and forecasted shipping information. Messages can be transmitted to and from the laptops and JVC's offices in London and Leeds.

Sales data are now prepared every evening between 5.00 p.m. and 9.00 p.m. From 9.00 p.m. information is ready to be downloaded from the mainframe computer onto the laptop computers. After 9.00 p.m. sales staff make a telephone call via the PSS network. It takes approximately 15–20 minutes to download the same day's sales information from the mainframe computer to their laptop computers.

Additionally, sales staff can obtain up-to-the-minute sales information by connecting into the mainframe computer at any time of the day or night. In this way, the salesperson can, for example, verify current stock positions. However, for the most part the downloaded daily information on the laptop computers is adequate for everyday business purposes.

The salesforce is delighted with their laptop computers. Not only are these quicker and more convenient, but using them has a positive financial effect. Sales staff earn bonuses in addition to basic salaries and it is important for them to possess details of JVC's current stock position and dealers' latest orders. This information is available on the laptop computers and enables sales staff to see more readily their territorial sales position.

The laptop network has brought business benefits to JVC, for example by stimulating more orders for JVC. Dealers or salespeople can see when they are approaching targets and order more products to ensure that targets are met. Sales information on the laptop can be accessed very quickly and sales people do not need to telephone JVC to ask for the latest sales data. This frees head office telephone lines and computer screens.

Using laptops to help dealers

JVC dealers are aware of several key factors which affect their businesses. They are primarily interested in offers on current products and the prices of new JVC product lines. The JVC sales person advises a recommended retail price from which the JVC dealer calculates profit margins. Also on the dealer's mind are product availability and any order backlog to replace stock that has been sold.

Dealers place orders for several reasons. They may have a customer wishing to buy a particular JVC product. They may have sold a product for which replacement stock is needed. They may wish to take a new product line into stock.

Sales staff use their laptop computers to give JVC dealers more accurate information; particularly at the end of each month when dealers assess order requirements. Dealers qualify for discounts by reaching monthly sales targets. Sales personnel can stimulate dealers to place 'top-up' orders where information displayed on the computer screen indicates that by so doing the dealer qualifies for a discount.

Training

Prior to introducing new software, the Computer Room examines the effects on end users. A major issue is the time required for training.

The Computer Room manages training courses. At the initial stage, a series of meetings take place between Computer Room staff, department managers and key staff.[4] The purpose of this meeting is to analyse the new system. Especially important is the need to ensure that user-department staff are satisfied that the system has been developed to specification and meets the department's needs.

Approximately two weeks before a new system goes live, the Computer Room conducts user training. Training is conducted through systems manuals and computer screens with non-live data. In the interests of time saving and efficiency, key staff are responsible for training other members of the department.

Once the system goes live, members of the Computer Room make a post-implementation follow-up exercise. Computer Room staff visit each user department to check the effective working of the system, to answer questions from users and to offer help where needed. End-users contact the Computer Room informally as normal working practice. The three members of the Computer Room routinely circulate through the building as part of their effort to help end users.

Notes

1 The company originally established itself in the UK in 1973 and traded from premises in Caledonian Road, north London, until relocating to the JVC Business Park, formerly Eldonwall Trading Estate, in 1978.
2 Product managers are responsible for planning and purchase negotiation, liaison with sales departments and managing sales strategy to dealers.
3 Validation refers to the system of security checking by the computer to ensure that the user is still an active JVC dealer. This is done through the use of passwords. Checks are also made to ensure that incoming data comply with system criteria (e.g. format).
4 Key staff in a department are chosen from senior staff who show computer aptitude.

9
Kobe Steel Europe Ltd

Case profile

Kobe Steel Europe (KSE) provides procurement services for Kobe Steel's head office in Kobe, Japan. Head office in Japan asks its overseas subsidiaries to provide a variety of data in a readily accessible format.

Information is bi-directional: Kobe Steel in Japan sends KSE information about current projects, including project location, date of commencement, types of equipment required; KSE sends Kobe Steel in Japan the details of current procurement orders in Europe including names of vendors, order status and intended delivery dates.

KSE identifies vendors from business databases and other information services and correlates data from these sources to compile reports for head office. IT developments at KSE have replaced manual with automatic routines which have given increases in efficiency.

Information between KSE and head office is transmitted by telephone and fax. Personal contact between relevant departments (mainly Engineering, R&D, Finance, G&A) prevents undue costly delays at either end. An on-line facility would help to reduce communication costs and give longer lead times for procurement orders. In terms of IT, KSE recognizes the need to maintain a balance between serving the procurement needs of head office and maintaining its own local integrity.

Company background

Kobe Steel Ltd is based in Kobe, a city of some 1.3 million inhabitants situated on Honshu (the largest of the four main Japanese islands) 200 miles (320 km) south-west of Tokyo. It is one of Japan's top five steel producers and a major supplier of non-ferrous metal products, especially aluminium and copper. In Japan it also has strong competitive positions in the industrial and construction machinery markets. Kobe Steel Ltd has more than fifty overseas subsidiaries and affiliates in Asia, the Americas and Europe.

For a number of years the company has sought to diversify its business activities.[1] These now include the manufacture of industrial intermediate products from a number of metals (e.g. copper, aluminum). Kobe Steel's welding products division is Japan's leading supplier of welding materials and equipment. In the manufacture of industrial machinery and other engineering products, Kobe Steel undertakes turnkey projects which often involve the design, engineering, supply and construction of plant.

Kobe Steel has established a division to investigate new business opportunities as part of a longer-term strategy to diversify from its traditional base of heavy machinery manufacture. The company aspires to become an innovator of industrial materials and processes (e.g. metals, ceramics, plastics, information technology, electronics and robotics). In Japan, Kobe Steel is gaining a reputation for the development of urban infrastructure projects.

Business strategies

One of Kobe Steel's business strategies is the reduction of lead times for manufactured plant and equipment. In this business sector, companies achieve a competitive edge when tendering for a contract by being able to quote a shorter delivery time than competitors (i.e. giving a shorter delivery time *when quoting* provides a competitive advantage). For clients, reduced lead times for manufactured plant and equipment give shorter project times and consequent cost savings. As reduced project times also win business orders and reduce project costs, the successful company gains substantial competitive advantage through its ability to quote shorter delivery times. A reduced cost base would allow Kobe Steel to be more competitive.

Kobe Steel Europe

Kobe Steel Europe (KSE), based in London, is the UK subsidiary of Kobe Steel Ltd. It has no independent trading function, but provides European-based liaison, coordination and support services for the parent company. The London office contains departments responsible for Marketing and Business Development, Mergers and Acquisitions, Investor Relations (which deals with financial matters), and Procurement.[2] A liaison office in Düsseldorf deals mainly with the iron and steel welding divisions.

KSE identifies and generates new business in Europe and supports existing business relationships on behalf of Kobe Steel. KSE gathers business intelligence and commercial information which is forwarded to relevant divisions in Kobe Steel. It is a point of contact for UK and European customers, particularly in the field of engineering and machinery.

One of KSE's main activities is procurement services for the Engineering and Machinery Division in head office. This involves purchasing from UK and European suppliers equipment and materials which may be shipped to Japan or directly to various global sites. KSE is responsible for locating vendors, managing commercial transactions and coordinating these to ensure that contracts are completed on time, efficiently inspected and shipped in good order. Engineering and technical aspects are handled from Japan.

KSE has a Research and Development laboratory in Guildford, Surrey, whose current main research investigations focus on polymers, composite materials and diamond coatings. This research establishment reports to corporate R&D facilities in Japan.

KSE makes no input to corporate strategy and makes a limited input to IT strategy. The latter is limited because Kobe Steel operates no manufacturing plants within Europe, the area of KSE's operational responsibility.

Business impact of IT

One of the stated corporate IT aims for Kobe Steel is the pursuit of the 'paperless office'; to reduce the amount of documentation; and to transmit, as much as possible, business and commercial data electronically. Currently, Kobe Steel does not maintain a centralized IT strategy; at least, not at departmental level where decisions are made about PCs and related software. At this level KSE has freedom to choose its own IT systems. This can be illustrated by the corporate accounts facility, where IBM mainframes are centralized. Head office has sole responsibility and KSE has no need to link directly into the system. Consequently, it has the freedom to select and operate its own systems independently of the main accounting system.

As an overseas subsidiary of a multinational company, KSE is concerned that it maintains communications access to head office. However, at the same time, there is a need to retain local integrity over its own internal communications network. The General Manager for procurement at KSE, says: '...Our philosophy is put in a system that enables us to link in with whatever system Kobe Steel Japan wants in terms of its external communication and at the same time to avoid having a complete hardware and software solution imposed on us from Japan.'

Head office requires a variety of data from its overseas subsidiaries and these data must be in a readily accessible format. The General Manager continues:

> ...We provide data in a format that head Office requires. In terms of data we have to do whatever they require us to do in whatever format is required. That shouldn't necessarily mean that they tell us exactly what equipment to put on our desks. We have our own needs which we meet internally. When head office says this is wanted, we decide how we're going to provide it.

In practice, KSE has a certain degree of freedom because the amount of data demanded by head office is limited and there are as yet no direct IT links between KSE and its head office.

Two-way communication

When the communication system in Japan becomes fully operational the attendant benefits will be a more immediate exchange of information and the possibility of gaining 'real time' information. Information from head office to KSE relates mainly to the current status of projects; what items of equipment are required by various sites; and when. Information from KSE to head office reports the current status of procurement orders in Europe. This information is 'batched' and transmitted weekly or monthly depending on the nature of the information. Figure 9.1 shows the flow of procurement-related information.

> Kobe Steel Europe → Kobe Steel, Japan
> Status of procurement orders in Europe
> (vendors, delivery dates)
>
> Kobe Steel, Japan → Kobe Steel Europe
> Status of current projects
> (what items are required, where, when)

Figure 9.1 Procurement information exchanged between KSE and Kobe Steel in Japan

An on-line communications facility would potentially provide longer lead times for procurement orders and allow salient information to be gathered sooner so that closing deadlines could more readily be met. KSE could then undertake a more proactive procurement function.

Being linked more directly to head office in Japan has several benefits:

- KSE could get information earlier.
- Suitable procurement vendors could be more easily identified.
- KSE could receive a complete list of future requirements for a whole project.
- The procurement department could browse the list and suggest suitable vendors.

Current practice creates a time lag between the preparation of project specifications in Japan and the transmission of specifications to the procurement department in KSE. Personal contact between staff of KSE's procurement department and their colleagues in appropriate departments in Kobe Steel helps to prevent potentially costly delays. An on-line facility would bring potential savings by reducing current communication costs, particularly fax and telephone charges.

Managing IT

In 1984 KSE had one computer which was used for accounting purposes and which displayed Japanese characters. Not until early 1988 did the company purchase a PC for word processing purposes.

From 1985 KSE used a purely Japanese accounting system, using proprietary PC hardware purchased and imported from Japan. The software was a Japanese accounting system in the Japanese language. This proprietary accounting package was very slow and inflexible and was difficult to support locally. KSE's expanding business needs demanded a more sophisticated system and in 1990 the company decided to adopt a bilingual (Japanese–English) Sun Accounts system.

An internal proposal to expand this facility by adding more stand-alone machines and a laser printer prompted the local managing director at KSE to recommend that plans be more ambitious. KSE subsequently sent a more detailed proposal to head office which included a requisition for equipment to build an office-wide IT platform. Head office accepted the proposal which led to the establishment of a Local Area Network (LAN). The main applications of the new system were office support services (word processing, spreadsheets); a business contacts database; and on-line business and communications services.

Business databases and services

Business growth and the expanded number of locally employed staff have increased the level of English-language correspondence. KSE now has wider contact with a greater range of companies. The speed of information gathering has improved enormously and now takes minutes rather than hours. The presentation of work to head office and customers is of a more professional quality.

As a result of developments in its IT facility KSE is not only working more efficiently but is also able to work in areas previously unattainable. Automatic routines have replaced manual ones, particularly in the area of procurement report writing.

KSE uses a number of business databases and services to help identify suitable plant and equipment vendors. KSE combines elements of these databases for reports outlining potential vendors' capabilities. On-line databases include: Profile (a database of newspaper reports operated by the *Financial Times*); Kompass (a directory of UK and European companies); Pergamon Information Services; and Dun and Bradstreet financial data services. Completed reports are transmitted by fax to head office in Kobe. Since November 1992 the company has used an E-mail system for internal office communications.

The Machine and Engineering Division in Japan is using Businesstalk 2000 on a pilot basis to handle international communication for one of its projects.[3] If this pilot project is successful, the scope will be broadened for general business communication. KSE expects to link into this system at a future date. Head office provides the main drive for such communications development.

IT independence

In Japan the various divisions of Kobe Steel maintain their independence. KSE's operations restrict communication links to a limited number of divisions; mainly the Engineering Division, R&D laboratories and certain head office departments: Finance, General and Administration.

KSE is not pressured by vendors to install EDI systems which support communications links for procurement activities. Neither does the company insist on vendors having EDI networks. This is mainly due to the nature of capital equipment procurements. Although of high unit value, these are required and ordered in small batches, mostly on a 'one-off' basis, and are frequently custom-made to specification. Orders for three units per annum from one vendor are high-volume business.

Identifying new IT systems

Where new IT developments affect its own working practices KSE makes proposals to head office. However, head office customarily initiates projects for international communications links. For example, plans to implement a global VAN (Value Added Network) designed to link all overseas offices through an E-mail system.

Head office is currently evaluating different systems for this purpose. Similar consideration is being given to an Integrated Services Digital Network (ISDN) which would allow an interface between communication systems and computer facilities. Unfavourable economic conditions are likely to dampen any enthusiasm for major IT investment unless financial savings can be clearly demonstrated.

KSE provided information on global E-mail systems that would be suitable for its own requirements based on its knowledge and experience of systems such as British Telecom's Tymenet, IBM's IIN, and Compuserve. KSE expressed its concern to head office that a prime consideration should be mutual compatibility and that it would be laborious to access a range of different systems. The head office response to such suggestions was to create an investigative working party, called the SWIFT project group. The group interviewed relevant managers at KSE as part of its fact-finding mission. IT aspects of the SWIFT project findings are still in abeyance. However, administrative matters, including the documentation needed for collating internal office information, were comprehensively investigated and acted upon. One of the results of the SWIFT group's report is the establishment of a G4 fax network at key offices in Japan and overseas.

Video-conferencing

In Japan, Kobe Steel has an extensive video-conferencing facility. This consists of a private leased network for internal communications between corporate offices in Kobe and Tokyo where video-conferencing studios relay meetings of company executives. However, the insignificant amount of suitable 'traffic' between the UK and Japan does not warrant installing and operating this facility between the two countries at present. In a business climate where companies are trying to reduce communications charges, the capital and operating costs of such a system are greater than the benefits (at the moment). Video-conferencing facilities between Japan and the UK may be worth considering when the cost of videophones becomes comparable with conventional telephones.

KSE's business services for the parent company, where exchange of visual information is rare, do not urgently need face-to-face communication. Information relating to the current status of procurement purchase orders can be exchanged satisfactorily via a faxed spreadsheet message or via an E-mail link. Additionally, the time difference between the UK and Japan makes video-conferencing logistically awkward.[4] Managers at each end of the video-conference link would need to come to work early or remain late to converse with their colleagues on the other side of the world.

IT investment decisions

Each division of Kobe Steel has its own IT plans which are amalgamated into a division-wide budgetary framework. This is submitted to the data-processing department as part of the annual budgeting routine. IT strategy is not rigidly controlled by head office and IT departments of each division are allowed sufficient scope to make their own IT investment decisions. Within this framework some departments establish their own LANs which access company-wide MIS systems.

KSE has two half-yearly business plans. These are incorporated into Kobe Steel's capital and expenditure budgets for the following year. Applications made by KSE for budget funding are usually granted if they are supported by a sound explanation of expenditure intentions.

Notes

1 Kobe Steel is reducing its dependency on steel production. As a proportion of Kobe Steel's business activity this is now approximately 45 per cent; down from 70 per cent.
2 KSE has eighteen staff of whom the Managing Director, the Business Development Director, the Company Secretary, and the Treasurer are Japanese. Twenty-four staff are employed at the R&D laboratories in Guildford.
3 Supplied by General Electric Information Services Corporation (GEISCO), this is a business communication and information service. Businesstalk 2000 includes links to Quickcomm, GEISCO's E-mail service.
4 Japan time is GMT + 9 hours.

10
Nissan Motor (GB) Ltd

Case profile

Nissan Motor (GB) Ltd (NMGB) uses IT to manage its dealership network which is an essential aspect of business activities. In this respect, IT helps NMGB in three ways: to prepare information for new proposals; to provide dealers with business support; to provide and support Dealer Management Systems (DMS). Each of NMGB's six business management managers is equipped with a portable computer which they use to prepare viability studies for prospective dealers and sales targets for prospective and existing dealers.

A dealership uses a Dealer Management System (DMS) to manage its business (for example, inventory, sales ledgers, workshop scheduling and customer invoicing). Dealers and manufacturer communicate via a Dealer Communication System (DCS) (for example, concerning outstanding vehicle orders, financial matters, special promotions). To prevent undue duplication of data and effort, NMGB is seeking ways to transmit some business information automatically.

In addition to standard word processing and spreadsheet programs, NMGB is increasingly using E-mail facilities and diary management systems. Audio-conferencing equipment has been installed on a trial basis, and the potential benefits of video-conferencing are being studied. An end-user reporting (EUR) system enables desktop computers to receive information downloaded from the mainframe computer.

NMGB is a relative newcomer to the British car industry, and started trading almost from scratch. The Information Systems Department (ISD) mostly spent the first trading year developing systems infrastructure. ISD is now able to devote more time assisting with business development concerns. Information systems are now developed almost simultaneously with business issues.

NMGB believes that IT belongs to the business arena and should contribute to it as much as possible. Consequently, NMGB is keen to introduce new technologies and regards IT as an opportunity to improve, or remove, existing business processes and replace manual routines with ones that are automated. NMGB prefers to let business needs drive IT, rather than promote technology for its own sake.

NMGB would like to reduce the distinction between the business departments and ISD; ideally to a point where, for certain functions, they are no longer separate and each business department sees ISD as part of their own team dedicated to their particular business interests.

Company background

Nissan Motor (GB) Ltd (NMGB) is a wholly owned subsidiary of Nissan Motor Corporation (NMC), through its European headquarters and holding company Nissan Europe NV (NENV) in Amsterdam. Nissan's European parts centre, Nissan Motor Parts Company (NMPC), is also in Amsterdam. NMGB's parts warehouse is in Lutterworth, Leicestershire.

NMGB is responsible for the UK distribution of Nissan products through its network of 300 accredited dealerships. NMGB was established in April 1991 and began trading on 1 January 1992, selling 56 000 units in the first year of trading. Prior to 1983, Nissan did not have a single office or employee in the UK.[1]

Nissan Motor Manufacturing (UK) (NMUK), in Sunderland, Tyne & Wear, manufactures the Primera and Micro models and some car components. NMUK's output is a high-value product which does not attract quota restrictions from the European Union.[2] Consequently, NMGB is able to compete with the best European manufacturers on equal terms, thus making Nissan an attractive proposition for a car dealership.

Nissan occupies a trading position below the 'giants' of the motor industry (Ford and General Motors in international markets; Rover in the UK domestic market) and competes directly with European mid-range manufacturers such as Peugeot and Volkswagen. There is a very keen competitive relationship with other Japanese motor manufacturers, particularly Honda and Toyota.

NMGB's dealership network

NMGB's dealership network is growing rapidly. The network is planned to expand to 330 dealers by the end of 1993 and by the end of 1995 is expected to consist of approximately 360 dealers. The majority of dealers solely deal in Nissan cars.

NMGB is pursuing a partnership approach with dealers, with manifest benefits for both partners. NMGB deliberately rejects 'traditional' manufacturer–dealer relationships. Such relationships, in which both sides compete for superiority, NMGB regards as detrimental to both parties.

Although NMGB inherited some dealerships from the former Nissan distribution company, it is beginning with a 'clean slate'. However, nurturing an atmosphere of trust is not easy and elements of traditional relationships can upset trading negotiations and arrangements. That said, NMGB's continual efforts are bearing fruit.

The car-distribution industry is being forced into change by an evolving marketplace. Pressures from increased competition, consumers who are better informed, and the large amounts of start-up and working capital needed are making 'family-type' businesses obsolete. These are being replaced by car dealerships managed by qualified and experienced professionals.

Beginning a dealer relationship

Dealers are appointed by NMGB's Dealer Development Department based on an extensive analysis of a dealer's business background, business objectives and potential profitability. A dealer development plan in particular business areas plots potential profitability as related to volume per capita. NMGB looks for a dealership which is professionally managed with a professional business outlook. Included in this category are people who have had long experience in the car-distribution trade but who have not managed their own franchise. In common with other car-distribution franchises, NMGB is considering the introduction of dealer development sites where the manufacturer holds the freehold of the dealership property and the franchise operator is the tenant of the business.[3]

Teams of NMGB's business specialists visit the dealer's site and help a dealer to investigate every business aspect from initial profit planning to final implementation. Discussions with the dealer establish business needs and the optimum systems solutions for these needs. NMGB's business teams help to identify dealership objectives and priorities. NMGB's Business Managers educate dealers in NMGB's business policy and help dealers to produce a profit plan.

The Dealer Development Department makes recommendations to the Dealer Management Appointments Committee (DMAC), which consists of senior directors and line managers with relevant expertise. The committee meets once a month to review dealership projects and, where satisfactory, approve the appointment of new dealers. In some areas of the country there are sufficient numbers of dealership applicants, while in others suitable dealers are difficult to find.

NMGB's Business Management Departments encourage sound management practice within the dealership. They are also responsible for dealer profitability through profit planning and budgetary forecasting. An increasing number of NMGB departments become more involved with a dealer with the approach of the launch date for the new dealership. NMGB's sales forces become more involved as a dealer becomes fully operational. Day-to-day dealer management support is through one of the eighteen national sales zones.

NMGB's Dealer Council is responsible for developing and maintaining partner relationships with dealers. Business development issues are explored jointly with dealers almost from the initial concept. Business development plans include plans for IS systems. When drawing up business development plans NMGB takes into consideration feedback from dealers.

Business impact of IT

When it began trading, NMGB's first priority was to prepare IT systems which would allow it to conduct its core business activities, one of which involves its dealership network. This meant ensuring that dealer support systems were in place and functioning efficiently. Three examples of the ways in which NMGB uses IT for business management purposes are:

1. To prepare background information in support of a new dealership proposal
2. To provide business support to dealers
3. To provide and support DMSs

1 IT to support a new dealership proposal

NMGB equips each of its six business management managers with a portable computer, which they use in up to 50 per cent of their visits to dealers in their region.[4] The computers serve two main purposes: to provide viability studies for prospective dealers; and to produce sales targets for prospective and existing dealers.

Viability studies
NMGB's dealer development department assesses the potential market for a new dealer by using data and government statistics from the past ten years. NMGB's own records give details of a dealer's investment in terms of workshop space, specialized equipment and available labour. Together with information from the dealer concerning operating costs, each of these pieces of information is fed into the computer to derive a breakdown of a dealer's potential sales for new vehicles, servicing (in terms of mechanic-hours) and spare parts. Prior to meetings to discuss a dealer's application to sell Nissan products, hard copies are presented to the dealer manager.

NMGB assesses the new dealer's likely profitability based on this prediction and compared with current dealers' trading performance. The accuracy of such predictions can be tested by contrasting them with historical data from previous Nissan dealers and local competitors. As the objective of the exercise is to convince both the dealer and NMGB's executive committee of the viability of the new dealership project, predicted estimates are deliberately conservative.

Potential sales targets
Historical data are used to produce sales targets for each area of a dealer's business: vehicle sales, hours through the workshop, and volume and value of parts sales (for example, the likely hours needed to check a new car (pre-delivery inspection); to prepare a used car to showroom standard; and to calculate the volume and value of potential parts sales). As a next step, potential sales are converted into the number of staff required at the dealership to realize the potential. This is based on figures for the number of hours needed by mechanics or counter staff.

NMGB's business managers help dealers to manage their trading expenses for optimum profitability by using a 'what if...' program. This information builds up a picture of profit contribution from the sales aspect of the dealer's business.

A new dealer needs to consider an abundance of information. The business management manager calls back after a week or two to check that dealers understand all those data. Some larger dealers prepare their own figures prior to the meeting with the NMGB business management manager.

NMGB's business management manager calls at the dealer every 3–4 months to monitor progress and offer further advice, if necessary. Should initial trading be below projections, business management managers have a range of business strategies to offer dealers. One such strategy is to measure actual performance against standard indices (e.g. gross profit per vehicle sold).

2 IT to provide business support to dealers

Dealer support systems are of two types: DCSs and DMSs. A DCS is the interface between the DMS and the car manufacturer's head office distributor system. DMSs are the computer systems which a dealership uses to run its business.

Dealer Communications System
A DCS is a communications system which is used for transferring information between dealers and the car manufacturer and vice versa. DCSs are used to process vehicle ordering and to inform dealers of progress with their orders. Some of the functions of a DCS are:

Nissan dealers use a DCS to communicate with NMGB to:
- Make order enquiries
- Query the status of outstanding orders
- Order new vehicles
- Order spare parts
- Submit warranty claims
- Arrange wholesale funding for new stock
- Make general report printouts (e.g. dispatches).

Dealers use a DCS to communicate with other dealers to:
- Locate vehicles stocked by other dealers
- Transfer vehicles from one site to another
- Transfer documentation from one dealer to another.

NMGB uses a DCS to communicate with dealers to:
- Publicize special promotions and discounts
- Respond to dealers' enquiries
- Transfer new vehicle documentation.

Within the partnership concept a DCS has to provide mutual benefits to both NMGB and the dealer. However, who benefits at a particular time depends on the application being used. For example, the transmission of a stock order serves NMGB's data entry needs as well as helping the dealer process orders for stock replenishment.

NMGB constantly reviews its DCS system in line with its commitment to *kaizen* (continuous improvement). The current DCS is the first step in developing an efficient DCS system and is a foundation for a continuing growth strategy. NMGB seeks possible improvements to communications in terms of increased speed and diversity of applications.

NMGB has current projects to make the transmission of some of this information more automatic. For example, at the moment, dealers use information from their stock control system to produce an order for parts. They need to key parts numbers and quantities into the DCS for onward transmission of the order to NMGB's parts distribution centre at Lutterworth. Information about new vehicles leads to a similar duplication of effort. When the vehicle is sold the same basic information is entered into the dealers' own system and NMGB's system:

1 To produce an invoice
2 To raise a direct debit payment from Nissan Motor Finance to the dealer
3 To transfer the customer's name and address into central NMGB records.

In view of the relatively short time since NMGB began trading, DCSs currently offer dealers a limited range of IS Functions.

All dealers produce a monthly performance summary. This information, which at the moment is sent on hard copy, is processed by a specialist data-processing company. After processing the information the company sends it to NMGB in a summary format with other collated information. A number of departments at NMGB use this information to formulate policy relating to marketing, sales, credit and financial control. NMGB business managers have direct access to this information on either NMGB's PS2 computers or via the data-processing company's computer.

NMGB provides monthly projected figures for comparison with the dealer's actual figures. At the moment such information is transferred manually from NMGB's system to the dealer's PC because computer software between NMGB and dealers is, for the most part, incompatible. NMGB estimates that 40–50 per cent of Nissan dealers use this method to monitor projected and actual performance.

3 To support the Dealer Management System

A DMS is a computer system used in-house by a dealer to help manage and control the various aspects of the business. Some of the purposes of a DMS are:

1 Parts inventory and point of sale ledgers (e.g. stock records and sales records)
2 Administration of vehicle sales (e.g. monitoring stocks, creating invoices)
3 Use of information to generate further sales (e.g. marketing and promotional activities)
4 Managing workshop scheduling (e.g. retrieving car service history monitoring effectiveness of mechanics)

5   Management accounting functions (e.g. collating the work of each department).

When NMGB began trading it inherited a diverse range of DMSs from existing dealer networks. Some twenty separate systems are in current use. DMSs are another direction for development and an integrated part of NMGB's plan for its overall DCS.

Currently, some twenty-nine different suppliers produce DMSs for the motor industry, with some suppliers producing several different systems. This situation greatly inhibits NMGB's efforts to introduce common systems. NMGB is investigating ways to reduce this number, possibly through endorsing and recommending certain DMSs. This problem is exacerbated by the range of dealers' computer expertise as some DMSs are only suitable for dealers with a high level of computer literacy.

DMS systems tend to be expensive. A single-site model with several workstations has a starting price in the region of £40 000. NMGB has identified a need for a DMS for the smaller dealer who has limited computer expertise, and is encouraging certain DMS suppliers to produce a user-friendly DMS at a cheaper price.

Managing IT

Information Systems Department

When the ISD manager joined NMGB in May 1992 his main responsibility was to turn an IS concept 'on paper' into the reality where NMGB could start trading. That completed, his current concern is to provide strategy and direction for future growth. He provides the vision for the way in which IT should be developing in parallel with the business in response to the way in which the company is evolving.

ISD has thirty-one permanent staff. These are supplemented by up to twenty contractors, who are employed for the duration of a particular project. However, due to the nature of NMGB and its relatively recent entry into the industry, some projects run consecutively. A number of outside contractors are therefore employed for extensive periods and move from one project to another.

ISD avoids demarcation along the lines of development and maintenance; each business area has its own ISD team which is responsible for both of these areas. Projects are seen as evolving rather than having a beginning and an end.

ISD has regular departmental meetings which usually include a report-back on business activity and an 'open forum' for discussing improvements to work practices. Similar meetings are held in other business units in the company. Department members generate creative responses for IT strategies for business requirements e.g. databases, client server, networking.

Strategy workshops also take place on a regular basis. Due to its position as one of the larger units in the organization, the ISD needs to break the total number of staff into two groups. Each group meets under the leadership of a facilitator from a different business responsibility to ensure cross-fertilization of ideas. Open-plan office layouts stimulate informal feedback on an *ad-hoc* basis by encouraging impromptu meetings between colleagues.

In-house IT systems

In-house automated systems in general use include WordPerfect for word processing and Lotus 123 for spreadsheet work. Word processing and spreadsheet programs are standard, although some users have specialized systems. E-mail facilities and diary management systems are becoming widespread throughout the company. As the company expands, so these systems are 'rolled out' to encompass more users.

Audio-conferencing equipment has been installed on a trial basis. The company is presently studying the potential benefits of video-conferencing with an imminent trialling of a video-conferencing system. NMGB has isolated several 'communities of interest' and identified possible relationships within NMGB that would fully exploit a video-conferencing system and lead to cost savings.

Management Information Systems

As a newcomer to the industry, NMGB is trying to establish a share of a rapidly changing market which is shrinking.[5] Competition is fierce as rival manufacturers are attempting to maintain or increase their own market share. As a young organization with new information systems, all aspects of NMGB's business are under pressure. This, in turn, puts pressure on the ISD to react to business developments and provide the necessary information. For example, business departments need to know the location of vehicles in order to make decisions about offering a bonus scheme on a particular car, or beginning a product promotion.

Instigating an MIS system to provide such information can mean postponing a current project to concentrate resources on the latest business development request. ISD tries to absorb new requests into existing budget frameworks to prevent an increase in expenditure. Where this is not possible, ISD may request extra funding. The last option is to discard or postpone a project with a lower priority.

End-user reporting

The hub of NMGB's information system is its mainframe computer which serves several LANs. NMGB is a very young organization with one PC per desk. LAN-based software is used very extensively throughout the office.

NMGB has introduced an end-user reporting (EUR) system which provides the facility to download information from the mainframe computer onto desktop computers. This allows end-user departments to access information from four different sources quickly and efficiently using existing client server architecture and user-friendly desktop systems. The facility to gain access to any information on any part of the data base in the computer domain provides a very powerful business tool. Spreadsheet and word-processing packages on desktop computers enable information to be more effectively manipulated at a lower cost than in the mainframe computer.

The benefits of EUR are that the company can be very selective about information that is downloaded onto the LAN, thus optimizing performance. Business users can produce professional-looking reports, either for their own purposes or for submission to other management teams. Business report formats can alter as the market changes. EUR helps to ease development backlogs for standard, routine reports which change in the light of changed market needs.

An analyst with particular expertise in this area works in ISD. His task is to assist end users to exploit fully the technology available from their desktop PCs by accessing and interpreting the necessary information.

Identifying business needs

The ISD tries to harmonize its way of working with business departments' needs. As a support department ISD reacts swiftly to urgent business requests from end users. This often means suspending work on an existing project.

ISD and end-user departments discuss the appropriate solution for business problems. This helps to identify the type of information needed for both current and future needs in a changing business climate and the type of system that can best deliver this information.

An IS steering committee consisting of senior managers from all company departments meets regularly once a month to decide on priorities for information systems. The ISD reports to the IS steering committee on work in progress, available resources and business requests in hand. The ISD and the IS steering committee work together to schedule resources according to the business priorities.

Strategy and tactics

The IS steering committee decides business priorities and overall company objectives. The committee also decides on tactical development work. However, a decision by the IS steering committee to pursue a tactical development initiative would not necessarily mean that a major strategic programme is cancelled.

Long-term tactical projects which promote 'customer care' include an on-going development programme for the reconciliation of warranty claims. An example of a strategic project is customer-orientated price protection. This allows NMGB to protect the price of an outstanding order by 'freezing' the price of a particular vehicle, even if general prices are increased.

Wherever possible, the IS steering committee tries to develop tactically and strategically. Projects which are considered to be of strategic importance are 'ring fenced', to ensure that valuable time is not spent solely on tactical stratagems.

The ISD tries to keep in close touch with all parts of the business. For their part, business departments try to keep each other informed of developments in their particular area so that, for example, the parts department is aware of the situation in the vehicle-delivery department and the finance department is informed of other departments' circumstances. Various committees facilitate the exchange of information between departments.

Developing business strategies

Management's vision of business objectives sets the agenda for business strategy development, which is a continually evolving process. Business strategies and IT strategies are intertwined and are facets of the same business outlook. NMGB's development method involves examining business issues in terms of the opportunities afforded by IT.

Part of NMGB's business strategy is to use its IT capability for competitive advantage, wherever possible. Within dealership systems which relate to supply chain management, IT is used with the aim of optimizing the mutual benefits of the relationship. NMGB is concerned to change its business development methodology to encourage closer relationships with dealers.

When NMGB was in its early stages the company did much 'firefighting'. New recruits, who had been brought together in a relatively short time from diverse organizations with differing cultures, needed to adapt to colleagues and working practices. From an IT viewpoint, the first year was very reactive. Time was spent in infrastructure development. However, this meant that the department was less able to devote time and effort to business-related tasks, such as short-term tactical campaigns. Over time, the ISD has been able to align itself more closely with the concerns of the business development departments, each of which is responsible for developing its own area of the business. Systems can now be built almost simultaneously with the development of the business.

Business departments and ISD are trying to reduce the gap between their functions to the point where they are no longer separate departments in certain respects. Eventually, each business department will regard ISD as dedicated to their particular business interests and part of their own team. Once achieved, this will reduce the significance attached to conventional lines of reporting.

There is less likelihood of a clash of ideologies where ISD and business departments work closely and thoroughly understand each other. Discussions between members of different departments examine alternative viewpoints and prevent major differences of opinion. Individuals who are sufficiently well informed about colleagues' professional concerns are better able to comprehend diverse business perspectives.

NMGB's common culture encourages mutual understanding which is sustained by individualized awareness training. This nurtures a teamwork atmosphere which pervades the whole NMGB organization.[6] Cultural partnerships between individual departments reduce potential conflict.

Decision making at NMGB

NMGB has autonomy to make business decisions within the framework of the annually agreed business plan. As a matter of routine, NMGB reports to its parent company, Nissan Europe NV (NENV), in Amsterdam. Strong communication and commercial links are maintained between NMGB and its parent company to ensure mutual on-going reporting and cooperation. NMGB reports to Tokyo headquarters via NENV.

Both NMGB and NENV welcome opportunities to 'pool' resources, or share expertise and development costs. 'Dotted line' rather than formal reporting links ensure mutual cooperation on an equal basis.

Discussions between NENV and Nissan headquarters in Tokyo relate to IT strategy. Projects which have a pan-European or a global scope (e.g. E-mail, development technologies) are discussed at one of the regional or global meetings which take place at six-monthly intervals. Global meetings include such IT discussion topics as hardware platforms, database engines and consolidation of data centres on a regional basis. At a regional level such topics are discussed from the viewpoint of implementation. Other regionally relevant issues (for example, new ways of vehicle distribution) complete the agenda. As a result, IT tends to be involved very early in business strategy discussions. NMGB believes in taking innovation back to the business in terms of being able to say 'using this technology can remove the need for a certain process or can streamline a process'.

Nemawashi
An important part of the decision-making process within Nissan is the Japanese concept of *nemawashi*. Discussions among managers and directors take place outside the formalities of committee meetings. A manager circulates a presentation paper to committee members prior to a formal Executive Committee meeting. The manager can ask a director for help and advice prior to his formal presentation. This allows the manager an opportunity to answer a director's questions and clarify points arising from his proposals before presenting the paper to a larger collective audience. In this way managers receive guidance into the ways in which proposals will be more 'acceptable' to the committee and hence more likely to receive a successful hearing.

128 *The Japanese Advantage?*

Networking

When NMGB was first established a system of encouraging networking was set up. This involved most managers having a managerial grade adviser attached to them. Directors had a senior adviser, who was director grade, attached to them. When a business problem arose, the Japanese adviser assisted his newly recruited colleague to identify the appropriate person in the company who could help. Through this practice new managers were educated into Japanese business and cultural habits and also into the Nissan approach to working relationships, business practices and working routines.

Kan-doh

Kan-doh is a Japanese phrase meaning 'a feeling or emotion which touches the heart' and is the basis of NMGB's service ethos. Cards bearing the philosophy of NMGB are distributed to NMGB's employees and dealerships. Each division examines the corporate philosophy and decides its relationship with the philosophy for its own business issues. A *kan-doh* card is shown in Figure 10.1.

Senior management has a positive attitude towards technology as a means of securing business advantage. NMGB approaches technology from a business-driven perspective and does not believe in 'technology for technology's sake'.

At NMGB, IT is not a distress purchase that is seen as a panacea to business problems. NMGB is proactive in its introduction of new technologies and regards IT as an opportunity to improve, or remove, existing business processes. Technology can replace manual procedures with more efficient automatic processes.

NMGB's philosophy is that IT belongs to the business and contributes as much as possible to that business. Where IT strategic thinking is in advance of business strategy thinking, the business department is asked to consider the possible options for future business development.

Technical solutions may be available which the business is not yet ready to utilize. The use of peer-to-peer communication systems in the dealer systems arena is one example where the technology is in advance of the business. Development of this technology is already in progress but business departments need to be educated in the advantages.

In considering how IT can serve its business needs most appropriately, NMGB has to react to its changing marketplace. NMGB is very committed to technology, especially information technology. These include the use of the client server for end-user reporting, office productivity tools including electronic diaries and computer-assisted systems engineering (CASE). A youthful company culture means that there is little resistance to innovation or ISD responses to business needs.

NISSAN MOTOR (GB) MISSION
Our Vision
The natural choice will be NISSAN
Our Philosophy
Customer: *We continually strive to exceed customers expectations.*
People: *Employees are the heart of the company. Having chosen personnel with commitment to the highest standards, through teamwork we aim to create flexibility, corporate understanding and loyalty to one another.*
Partners: *We will work in long term partnership with our suppliers and dealers encouraging pride in NISSAN and being receptive to all suggestions and improvements.*
Communications: *We will foster an open environment where information and knowledge flow freely between all.*
We recognise our wider role as responsible members of society.

Figure 10.1 NMGB's *kan-doh* card

Matrix management and team building

NMGB builds project teams around particular elements of business, and tries to ensure that teams contain all areas of expertise. The aim is to build and maintain expertise in business and in the systems which support it; so interaction between team members is important. At any one time particular projects are being undertaken in areas of finance, dealer funding, parts distribution, corporate systems, vehicle management and sale or return. Two specialist teams, technical and personal systems, are involved in on-going projects which encompass all other business departments.

Employees are given opportunities to work closely with colleagues in other departments. In this way, individuals develop their professional skills and gain insights into the work of other departments. This encourages mutual cooperation and enlarges the skills base of each department. Each department gains a closer understanding of other departments' concerns so that, for example, business department team members grasp IT issues and ISD staff gain insights into business issues.

Business projects follow a matrix management style. Business teams and technology specialists form project teams. As projects develop, technology specialists are drafted into particular business teams. Individual expertise and contributions to the team's concerns are valued, and the team gains strength from the interaction between members from different disciplines.

At different stages in a project teams are supplemented by other members, according to when a particular expertise is required. Over the life of a project, team membership changes, although a team retains a nucleus of people who become expert in a particular project.

A nucleus of experts, which will not necessarily comprise the same people from one project to another, remains as a team over the longer term. The nucleus typically consists of people with certain individual expertise, which includes project leadership skills, business analysis skills and systems design skills. A skilled computer programmer may also be included, although this depends on the size of the business team. Computer programmers and systems analysts have key skills which require them to move around between various teams.

At NMGB people who constitute team nuclei now have up to two years' experience in particular elements of the business. A current priority is to rotate such skilled and experienced people around other teams in order to widen individuals' experience and allow their talents to permeate through the whole organization. This also has the effect of giving NMGB greater security in that a broader skills base exists throughout NMGB.

NMGB does not generally have job titles, preferring to retain an element of flexibility so that people can move from project to project to undertake different tasks. In this way, career progression does not depend on 'moving up the ladder' to the next available job position. At NMUK a similar flexibility applies and people can move between job tasks unencumbered by the constraints of job title.[7] Such flexibility of work tasks helps NMGB to optimize output per employee and also helps develop employees' own potential.

NMGB's philosophy is to recruit people who are thought to be the 'right' people and then develop them within the framework of the company. The development of employee's personal skills also helps the organization.

Due to the need to start up its new operation NMGB recruited high-calibre expertise in a short period of time. The company now has a youthful team with a diverse range of experience in the car industry, including manufacturing. In these circumstances, generating ideas is by no means a simple process but is more inhibited by logistics of meetings and the recording of ideas than by a lack of ideas.

Planning IT

IT planning falls within NMGB's five-year plan. Given the rate at which technology develops, IT planning for a period in excess of five years is pointless.

In the ISD, planning is a team effort. The department builds teams around projects. People with business expertise constitute the nucleus of business-related projects. Technicians and consultants are brought into the project team as their expertise is required.

NMGB has devoted much effort to planning IT strategy and building infrastructures. The ISD has possibly been more able to plan than have other business departments because it has had no systems history. Conversely, it has found itself in the unenviable position of supporting a mature business as an immature department. As a department in its infancy, IT has been compressed into a short time span and in many ways the company has had to adapt because of rapid development. At times it felt like twenty years of IT development had been achieved in twenty months.

A first priority was to set up and run systems which would enable the business to function. Now that has been achieved, it is critical to ensure that systems are built which will be able to support future business requirements.

IT investment decisions

NMGB prefers to integrate information systems into the business rather than operate such systems autonomously. IT investment decisions are dealt with at the level of the Executive Committee which comprises seven directors and five senior advisers.[8] Executive Committee approval is needed to countenance significant expenditures.

The Executive Committee works in a fairly formal style. In respect of IT investment, the ISD Manager makes the final recommendations concerning IT matters by presenting a working paper at an Executive Committee meeting. After discussing the issues raised, the committee usually makes an immediate decision.

The Executive Committee formulates the overall business plan and matches IT recommendations to business needs. The ISD's annual budget is decided in the same manner. IT investments are implemented according to the phasing of the annual budget allocation, which forms part of the business planning process. Smaller IT decisions are incorporated into the business plan prepared every October by the ISD Manager.

The level of budget is related to the outcome of negotiations (budget hearings) based on the overall business budget (e.g. sales volume, profit margin). These negotiations are part of the business planning process. NENV sets objectives for NMGB, e.g. to sell the vehicles in sufficient quantity.

NENV allocates NMUK's output from the manufacturing facility in Sunderland between UK and other European requirements. Production quotas, decided at a corporate level, for various countries can be rescheduled according to local market conditions. Sales volume forecasts are amended by the quantity that Nissan dealers think they can sell.

The budget for each department, including ISD, is itemized according to capital investment expenditure. When IT investments are to be made, the ISD Manager makes detailed proposals to the executive committee.

Occasionally, the business needs rapidly to change direction as a result of new legislation. A major investment may be required which does not appear in the business plan. In this eventuality, one project may be adopted at the cost of another, previously planned project. Alternatively, NENV may be asked to provide further funding. In this case, each request for funding is based on individual merits and in the light of other investment priorities within Europe.

Post-installation review

Between a week to a month after project installation the IT department conducts a formal post-installation review. At this stage, in line with the notion of *kaizen*, NMGB asks how the system could be improved for the next time. By re-examining the system some pointers can be discerned for improvement from the viewpoint of cost savings or systems effectiveness.

The nature of the project determines the ideal time for the review, as this affects the optimum point for judging effectiveness. Part of the systems development process involves acceptance testing which identifies any major defects in the system.

Business development teams meet on a weekly basis to report progress. Details are given to the development group when a system is performing inadequately or where business needs have changed and when consequent amendments need to be made to the system.

IT development teams are based around a business activity. Each system is continually judged in terms of its performance within the business. This ensures that ISD can constantly monitor the effectiveness of its own contribution in support of the business. For the ISD, systems are an evolving product and projects are considered to be on-going. The second stage of the two-stage process relates to the concept of *kaizen*.

Kaizen

Kaizen means constant improvement. NMGB extends this philosophy to all its business procedures. The principles of *kaizen* are applied with as much intensity as *kan-doh*.

At NMGB, *kaizen* is embodied in the ethos of the organization and pervades all aspects of business conduct: product launch, customer care, personnel planning issues. The principles of *kaizen* are passed from employee to employee by demonstration in daily work. Employees are encouraged to review constantly their own performance; *kaizen* sustains this self-awareness.

Supplier relationships

NMGB encourages partnerships and builds relationships with all key suppliers including technical software, communications systems and computers. A limited number of key suppliers benefit from a closer relationship with NMGB. These suppliers are fewer, but relationships with them are stronger.

Suppliers occupy business partnership status which includes mutual confidentiality agreements and a dedicated account manager (who may join the project development team). Such suppliers gain a greater insight into NMGB's business and are consequently more proactive in their dealings with the company.

Key suppliers are able to give business suggestions to NMGB and, for example, join with NMGB colleagues to present a case for business development. In one recent case a key supplier conducted research on behalf of NMGB, aware that as the supplier it had a vested interest in the outcome of the research. Some suppliers constantly review the service they give to NMGB with a view to improving the service and giving a higher standard of services.

The element of mutual confidentiality (according to circumstances) means that NMGB managers can reveal their business plans in greater detail than would otherwise be prudent. Suppliers can be party to short-term objectives (e.g. current market share) and longer-term company aspirations. They can plan business ideas ahead of time and not waste anyone's time (their own or that of the NMGB manager) seeking non-existent business opportunities.

Control and monitoring

On-going good communication with the business community, both inside and outside the company, facilitates control and monitoring of IT systems. In line with *kaizen*, the company is constantly seeking to improve its quantitative assessment of projects in terms of user satisfaction.

A method for improving quantitative assessment of projects is still being refined. Some of the parameters involve the reaction times of the IT department, the closeness of 'fit' of the systems for the purposes required by the business departments, the amount of post-installation work that is necessary and the costs of responding accurately to business needs.

A similar assessment is carried out, wherever possible, with vendors. Improvement programmes are often instigated by vendors, who assess the effectiveness of NMGB. For example, there was a joint project with BT to carry out a quality programme, where BT and NMGB each signed an action plan for improvements. NMGB aims to get the best value from available resources; its own and those of suppliers.

Notes

1 Nissan Motor Manufacturing UK (NMUK) opened in Sunderland in 1986. *The Road to Nissan*, Macmillan (1987) written by Peter Wickens, Director of Personnel and Information Systems at NMUK, describes Nissan's early years in the UK.

2. NMGB has an obligation to the British government to produce products which have 80 per cent local content. The British government then gives a certificate of origin which allows NMGB to sell these products within the EU. See, for example, ' "Foreign" cars are best of British' *The Sunday Times* 25 July 1993.
3. In a dealer development site project the tenant funds the working capital and the manufacturer provides the premises and facilities on a leasehold basis. NMGB have recently begun such an arrangement with their dealership in Romford, Essex.
4. Sixty per cent of the NMGB's dealership network is single-unit dealers who have one outlet. The remaining 40 per cent range from small chains with several outlets to national dealerships whose operation consists of up to 350 outlets.
5. NMGB plans to increase its share of the UK car market from its current 4 per cent to 10 per cent by the year 2000.
6. For further discussion of the Nissan ethos see Wickens, *op. cit.*, particularly Chapter 6, 'Teamworking and Commitment – Philosophy and Practice'.
7. See Wickens, *ibid.*, particularly pp. 7–21, 81–82, 88–89, 108, 120.
8. Senior Advisors are board-level positions occupied by senior executives from Nissan headquarters in Japan. Of the twelve committee members, four are European.

11
Nissan Motor Manufacturing (UK) Ltd

Case profile

At the Nissan Motor Manufacturing (UK) Ltd (NMUK) plant in Sunderland, IT helps managers to manage procurement, production and finished product shipment.

Systems project development falls into one of several groups, each relating to one of five areas of business: for example, commercial systems; systems related to vehicle orders; shopfloor systems related to manufacturing. Although a specialist team develops systems for the shopfloor, ISD staff are competent to work on any type of project. During a project a project group may increase or decrease in size, depending on whether extra staff are brought in at critical stages. Rotation of staff between different types of project exposes staff to different business areas and stimulates individuals' interest.

Company background

Nissan's project to build a car plant in the UK began in February 1984 with an agreement signed by representatives of Nissan and the UK government.[1] The factory site location was chosen in March and NMUK was established in April. To date, investment in the plant exceeds £900 million. At the current time Nissan has a 4 per cent share of the UK new saloon-car market.

NMUK is situated on an 800-acre site in Sunderland that was formerly the RAF Usworth airfield. Apart from the various manufacturing plants, the site contains three test tracks. Also on-site is the Sunderland branch of the Nissan European Technology Centre. This department, which tests prototypes, is sited away from 'public' areas.

There are 198 suppliers who make component deliveries to the plant on a JIT basis. Although there is no obligation for them to do so, a number of component suppliers have located themselves within the factory perimeter fence. The factory produces Nissan Micra and Primera models for Nissan Europe NV, Nissan's European head office. The majority of the factory's production is scheduled for export to all countries, including Japan. Various-sized freight ships take between 9000 and 15 000 vehicles from Teesside (for distribution via Amsterdam to other parts of Europe) or Southampton (for markets in the Far East). NMUK also makes spare parts for Nissan companies in Europe.

While the presence of Japanese senior managers has influenced the company to a certain extent, there has been no edict from corporate headquarters that NMUK should manage its business in a Japanese manner. In fact, when NMUK was established in 1984 the Japanese managing director emphasized his policy of 'anglicizing' the company.[2]

The current managing director is British, as are most other directors. The deputy managing director and the finance director are the only Japanese managers at NMUK. The engineering department has a number of Japanese advisors who are involved in transferring technology knowledge. Their presence at NMUK provides the company with a window on current Japanese engineering practices.

Corporate principles

Nissan works to three stated corporate principles:

- **Quality** We aim to manufacture the highest quality vehicles sold in Europe. It is the quality of our people that determines the quality of our product.
- **Flexibility** The motor industry is a highly competitive environment and the scene of rapid technological developments. To stay ahead of our competitors we need people who are imaginative and resourceful, people who take the initiative and are not restricted by traditional ways of doing things.
- **Teamwork** It is our aim to achieve mutual trust and cooperation between all people within the company. It is only by all of us pulling in the same direction that we will be able to achieve the tough objectives we have set ourselves. We believe that by operating this philosophy and by hard work and commitment we will achieve our goal of a product, and a company, that is continuously improving.

The workforce

NMUK has some 4600 employees, categorized as direct, semi-direct or indirect staff. Direct staff work directly in car manufacture. Semi-direct staff are involved in manufacturing support services such as maintenance or materials handling. Six hundred indirect staff provide administrative and office support.

All employees are salaried and work a 39-hour week. All work to 'common terms and conditions of employment'.[3] There are no productivity bonuses and no time clocks. The Company Council negotiates an annual pay award which everyone receives.

Recruitment for manufacturing staff takes up to 4 months and includes six interviews and aptitude tests. Employees recruited under the graduate recruitment programme are given two weeks' production line experience. Competition for jobs is fierce. In September 1991 the company advertised 1600 vacancies on the new Micra production line and received 38 000 applicants.[4]

Production teams

Four thousand manufacturing staff, of whom thirty to thirty-five are female, work in teams of up to twenty people. Each team includes a supervisor who has total responsibility for the team including safety and training. Supervisors also control a capital expenditure budget for the purchase of tools and equipment.

Each team has two team leaders, who can do any job in their area of the production line. Guided by a team leader, teams evolve working routines. Teams are trained to work at high levels of productivity. For example, an engine is fitted in 45–50 seconds; a windscreen in 37 seconds.[5] Each team has a specialist, called the check and repair man, whose job is to check the team's work and repair any faults before the vehicle moves onto the next team area. Faults are noted and brought to the attention of the work team during the next work discussion group.

Teams adapt their work environment to their own convenience, keeping tools and parts handy but unobtrusive. Nuts, bolts and other fasteners are ready to hand in open boxes. Team members learn to select by weight the exact number needed for a particular job. These practices allow each team member to maintain work speed and complement the team's routine.

Each individual team member's job capability is shown through a series of different symbols on an ILU board. Progress through the various jobs required by the team is shown by symbols. As a person achieves proficiency in a work task the appropriate symbol is shown next to his or her name. ILU boards are displayed prominently in each team's work area. This record of each team member's capabilities facilitates job flexibility within a team during a shift. An example of an ILU board is shown in Figure 11.1.

Teams are responsible for their particular work area of the factory floor, and are expected to keep it clean and tidy. The company is responsible for other areas of the factory floor. In team areas notice boards contain individuals' photographs and biographical details, safety notices (e.g. SAFETY IS NO ACCIDENT), work concerns, productivity charts and information about suppliers.

Areas of responsibility are defined by different coloured lines painted on the floor. Red indicates the company area, grey the work team area; blue designates pedestrian pathways. Yellow boundaries indicate robot work areas, which are protected by wire fences and infrared beams. If the beam is broken the entire production line comes to a stop, at a cost of £3000 per minute.

138 The Japanese Advantage?

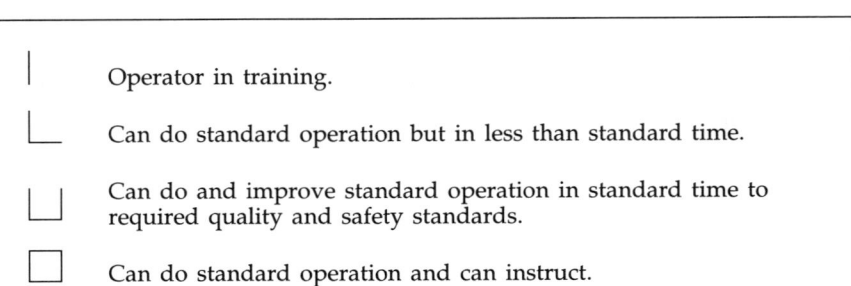

Figure 11.1 An ILU board. (*Source*: NMUK body shop)

There are 256 maintenance engineers responsible for maintenance in the whole manufacturing plant. Each shop has its own maintenance crew. In the body shop where the robots work, video cameras above the production line aid maintenance. A maintenance crew approaching close to the robots would break the infrared beams.

Business impact of IT

IT on the production line

In the body shop, at the beginning of the production line, pressed metal takes on a recognizable car body shape. At this stage an information tag is bolted onto the front of each vehicle. This tag contains a microchip which gives the identity of the vehicle, including its specifications and the source of each part. Information on the tag originates from Nissan Europe NV and identifies the options required for each vehicle. There are 350 variations, including body colour, left- or right-hand drive, four or five doors, sun roof, delivery place and date.

As the car body progresses through the body and paint shops, strategically placed sensors read the tag and pass information to other points on the production line. This advises the various work teams of the components required for a particular vehicle. Information is also passed to the Central Control Room (CCR) so that its staff can monitor the progress of the vehicle on the production line.

The tag also notifies JIT suppliers of progress of the vehicle on the line so that parts can be made ready (for example, seats from a supplier adjacent to the Nissan site). In the final assembly the tag is used to generate a computer printout of the vehicle specification. This information is pasted onto the car windscreen to identify the vehicle and its delivery destination. When the completed vehicle is finished the tag is re-used. Above the production line is an electronic monitoring board which shows the day's target and the actual number of vehicles produced.

The work of the manufacturing staff in the body shop is supplemented by 225 robots. Like their human colleagues, robots work on the vehicles as the line moves along. They do work that is repetitive, dangerous or boring, but are unable to carry ont intricate tasks (e.g. some aspects of painting).

Three phases of growth

The phases of growth for the ISD are slightly earlier than those for the company as a whole because ISD has the task of preparing systems to facilitate later company developments. Phase one from 1985 to 1986 related to the company launch and establishing a basic manufacturing infrastructure.[6] The company's first product, the Nissan Bluebird, was assembled mainly from Japanese kit components. Annual production rose to 24 000 units; this was a relatively small volume considering NMUK's current manufacturing output. Phase two from 1987 to 1988 saw annual factory output increase to 100 000 with a development from kit assembly techniques to real manufacturing methods. The range of cars in production increased many times as NMUK moved from the single UK market for its products to exporting left-hand drive vehicles to continental Europe.[7]

The move from phase one to phase two made obsolete almost all of the company's existing computer systems. From 1988, ISD prepared appropriate computer systems in readiness for phase two: the launch in 1990 of the Primera model.

Phase three began with the launch of the Micra model in 1992. Total output of both the Primera and Micra models increased from 100 000 to 275 000, primarily for export markets. This prompted expansion in business support areas. New warehouses were built and business partnerships were created with transport companies. For the ISD, phase three meant preparation and development of computer systems to cope with the rise in output and variety of manufactured cars and related distribution logistics. Comparatively speaking, these phases of development are very short, especially as the number of ISD staff is relatively small.

NMUK's manufacturing activities have always been supported by business systems. At each stage of growth, as it has expanded its manufacturing capacity these business systems have become more sophisticated to sustain increased output and diversity of product range. Examples of such systems are product specification systems; stock management systems, which enable the company to carry low stock levels; and logistics systems which manage the movement of larger volumes.

In 1985 the company decided to keep its computer systems as simple and as common as possible. This means that since 1985 NMUK has had a common user interface. From the start of the company ISD has developed on-line systems, wherever possible. User departments are responsible for writing their own procedures for their systems and for controlling and monitoring systems in use.

Throughout the period from 1985 to 1992 the company's computer systems have coped admirably with the pressures of rapid business growth. Other technologies, such as open systems, have not been considered as an option for NMUK. Since 1988, the company has used UNIX for its shopfloor computer system. This has grown in line with increased needs of volumes and manufacturing capacity.

At the current time NMUK has an integrated system. Almost all of the company's business systems are on mainframe computer, using Adabas and Natural. These systems are all home-developed. Since 1986 the company has developed all its computer needs internally.

Managing IT

The Information Systems department

The Information Systems Department (ISD) began in April 1985 with a staff of eight. The ISD manager joined the company at that time together with his two senior managers. The ISD has grown to its current strength of seventy-five staff in parallel with NMUK's three distinct growth periods. The ISD general manager reports to a local British director. ISD is not required to refer to headquarters in Japan for advice or approval.

The company uses IBM mainframe computer equipment and Hitachi and DEC process computer equipment. Since 1985 NMUK has had fourth-generation technology using as its computer languages Software AG's Adabas and Natural.

NMUK's ISD hires people who are more interested in developing systems to satisfy the business requirements than in IT itself. This recruitment policy reflects two insights: that it is relatively straightforward to train newly hired staff to use the company's computer languages; and that it is unlikely that newly hired staff would be able to offer both technological expertise and motor manufacturing business experience.

ISD staff show the high degree of loyalty evident in other departments of the company. First-line management in particular is very stable. Staff recruited in the first two years following the start of the ISD are still in the department. All ISD staff have worked for NMUK for an average of four years, giving the department a total of 300+person/years experience. A low employee turnover rate helps in building trust between members of the various departments.

In addition to financial rewards and company stability, the low rate of staff turnover is attributable to three factors. These are: staff are exposed to all types of business challenges, they are rotated between different types of project, and people enjoy working with the modern technology used by the company.

ISD planning

As much as any of the manufacturing departments, ISD plans its systems development workload on a production-line basis. Project managers assure themselves of the ability of the ISD and the user department to meet timetable deadlines for supporting and implementing the project. Throughout NMUK, at the beginning of each shift, each work team holds a review meeting. These meetings are informal and discuss the status of work from the previous shift and work tasks for the forthcoming one. Meetings provide an opportunity for team members to inform colleagues of any work difficulties. Every morning, each project manager holds a similar meeting so that each person in the project team can notify colleagues of the status of their work.

Workload is distributed among the department's fifty-five staff to achieve smooth working routines. In the event of a mismatch between staff and overall workload ISD negotiates with user departments to postpone non-critical work. This may happen when head office in Japan or NMUK raises new projects at mid-year after annual plans have been agreed.

The pace of change within the company has determined that plans are for one year, with a slight overlap. Longer-term plans would become meaningless very quickly. The company is now approaching relative stability and two-year plans may be feasible, supplemented by a document outlining a five-year vision. Financial planning is made on the basis of one- and five-year periods. ISD makes an input to the company's capital budget for each of the five years. This is based on ISD's projections of the growth of the processor and its database requirements.

Up to 1986 the intense demands of the initial launching of the company had created pressure on systems development methodology. Three (out of eight) staff reported to the systems development manager and this team of four worked to their own previous practices. In 1986 ISD decided to identify and consolidate a methodology for ISD systems development. This became an objective for 1987. Discussions between the ISD manager and the systems development manager followed and, in late 1987, a systems development methodology was initiated.

Data analysis was included in the methodology. Since 1987 ISD has been using a stable model on which to base all the company's subsequent applications. These factors also explain the ISD's relatively few staff. Any changes in ISD's data model relate to changes in the company, which were made in 1988, 1990 and 1991.

IT investment

ISD does not begin the process of helping its customers to solve IT problems with a contract in 'black and white'. Instead, user-department requests for project funding tend to be limited to two sides of A4 paper detailing personnel needs, expenditure and the benefits for the company.

The proposal allows scope for further changes to be accepted during later discussions, up to the point when the project is instigated.

ISD's philosophy is intended to give user departments what is right for the business – although this may not necessarily be what the departments themselves originally wanted. ISD works with user departments through planning and initiation phases to agree mutually acceptable business requirements.

ISD vets project requests when they are discussed with the manager of the user department. From its overall perception ISD advises how the request should be amended or whether it is better to withdraw it in favour of another. There is also the situation where insufficient resources are available to support all of a number of viable projects – in which case more stringent selection criteria are applied. In the situation where the investment request is refused or reduced, the ISD manager discusses alternative possibilities on a project-by-project basis with the user department.

Funding corporate objectives

Occasionally, head office systems department (called A60) has a corporate objective; for example, to create a network which requires ISD expenditure. In these instances the ISD manager approaches the finance and engineering departments for additional budgets for overheads or capital. The majority of ISD's expenditure relates to domestic concerns.

The ISD manager presents his case for capital investment by discussing his requirements with the engineering director, in common with other heads of departments. Meetings between the two managers consider the investment needed for a given time, and justification in terms of needs and cost savings. If investment for a project is approved by the engineering director, the ISD manager and the development manager meet the managing director informally to outline ISD's current focuses and the specific projects which address these.

The ISD is involved at an early stage when the company has a major project, for example when a major vehicle model is being replaced or when the company wishes to enter a new market. Discussions between the ISD manager, the development manager and the operations manager identify the direction in which the company is moving and the necessary computer requirements. The ISD manager and the development manager agree project time frames.

The development manager and the ISD manager work with managers and directors to ascertain the vision for the company's future growth. This has perhaps been less easy than in established companies. In 1990 NMUK discontinued the formal steering committee created in 1985 in favour of one-on-one meetings between the ISD manager and the managing director. User departments who are affected by proposed developments receive regular status reports. A report of ISD highlights is submitted monthly to executive meetings.

IT project management

From June to October project managers investigate potential new projects and familiarize themselves with related aspects of the business, including isolated projects and those interacting with other projects, either existing or requested. Project managers work closely with their contacts in related user departments to decide department needs in terms of future computer systems.

From discussions with representatives from the user department the project manager writes a project initiation document. The project manager discusses this document with other project managers and the development manager. The document is then passed onto the system analysis team who prepare a logical data structure for the project.

After several weeks' work the systems analysis team presents its project for comment by the project managers and the development manager. Project managers are thus made aware of all projects and any implications for their own areas of business. This procedure helps project managers to increase their knowledge of systems in other business areas so that they can be rotated between the various business teams. Such interaction between group members increases their business awareness and adds value to other projects.

This project procedure was successfully used to prepare systems for Nissan Motor GB (NMGB). NMGB now replicates this method of managing projects to develop the expertise of its own project managers. Nissan Motor Company in Japan has also evaluated project procedures developed at NMUK and is adopting these for global standardization.

Project development

Development falls into one of several groups, each relating to one of five areas of business. These are: commercial systems; systems related to orders for vehicles (e.g. order processing and tracking); systems for parts ordering and stocking; systems for product definition (e.g. bill of materials and engineering-related systems); and systems for the shopfloor (i.e. related to vehicle production). As expected in a manufacturing company, major users are those departments with a product-related function. ISD works very closely with the business areas and consequently has a strong relationship with these.

ISD staff do not specialize in particular areas of the business, with the exception of the team which develops systems for the shopfloor. The development department of fifty-five staff are competent to work on any type of project that the business needs.

All ISD development staff use the same computer languages and, should the need arise, the whole department can work on the same project. Using Natural a person can write a program in a few hours. On occasions, the whole department has worked over a weekend to produce programs for an urgently needed project.

Project teams can work on any project and individual members can be moved from one project to another depending on urgency of need. This flexibility is encouraged by the fact that everyone is trained in the use of Adabas and Natural computer languages and is an invaluable asset to ISD. User departments say that development teams add value to a project over and above expected outcomes.

Project groups increase or decrease in size during the life of a project. This is partly to provide extra staff at critical stages and also to expose staff to different business areas. Rotation between projects stimulates individuals' interest in the various aspects of NMUK's business.

In the absence of a formal structure for IT project management, project managers 'drive' their own projects towards deadline dates. It is important to complete one project on time because another will be waiting 'in the wings' and because a completed project relates to other parts of an overall business plan.

Control and monitoring

Although NMUK does not formally control and monitor its IT systems, or maintain an internal audit function, ISD monitors the performance of the mainframe computer and the service provided to business departments. ISD's procedure is to plan and monitor transaction volumes and plot trends. In this way, increasing or contracting user demands can be observed. ISD collates and investigates all transaction failures. Systems under operation are monitored by a problem-management system. Regular management review ensures that problems are investigated and rectified.

ISD carries out post-implementation audits to discover whether a system has produced the intended business benefits for a department. It sends a questionnaire to the user department, followed by discussions between users, project managers and leading analysts. These discussions verify that projects meet the user department's intended specifications or whether it is necessary to make amendments to the system. A follow-up report recommends any further work that is necessary.

Notes

1 In recognition of his contribution to the British motor industry, Nissan's chairman, Takashi Ishihara, was awarded an honorary knighthood, one of only three Japanese businessmen to receive such an honour.
2 See Emmott, W., *Japan's Global Reach*, Century Business Books (1991), pp. 46–50, for a discussion of the subtle differences between being a Japanese or a local car manufacturer.
3 For a full discussion of this system of employment see Wickens P., *The Road to Nissan*, Macmillan (1987), especially Chapter 1, 'Them and Us...to Just Us'.

4 This seems to be a common experience for Japanese car manufacturers. When Mazda set up its plant in Flat Rock, Michigan, near Detroit, almost 100 000 people applied for 3500 jobs.
5 Panel storage at the back of the press shop contains steel for only 1.6 days' work. For the Primera model, the actual work time taken for a steel sheet to become a finished product is $13\frac{1}{2}$ hours, although this time is lengthened by waiting time at various stages of the manufacturing process (e.g. in the paint shop).
6 Investment in the basic infrastructure for phase one was of the order of £60 million.
7 The introduction of left-hand drive vehicles into the manufacturing system changed NMUK's range of products dramatically, from tens to hundreds of possibilities.

12
Sony (UK) Ltd

Case profile

As the division of Sony Corporation responsible for sales and distribution of Sony products in the UK, Sony (United Kingdom) Ltd (SUK) uses IT systems for three main purposes: communicating with head office and manufacturing sites in Japan; communicating with Sony sites in the UK; and giving an efficient service to UK dealers. The STREAM system, designed to reduce product lead times and delivery times and reduce product inventories, provides information from manufacturing sites in Japan. STREAM enables SUK to predict stock deliveries with increased accuracy and gives greater efficiency in manufacturing procurement.

SUK's Information Systems Division (ISD) manages the company's UK computer network. All major Sony locations in the UK are linked to the computer centre in Sony's UK head office at Sony House, Staines, southwest of London. Additionally, ISD provides information systems services (e.g. technical support and computer service) to all divisions of SUK. Under the leadership of its General Manager, ISD has some forty staff who work in one of three sections: Development Services (which includes Database Administration); Computer Services; and Technical Support. ISD provides computer systems throughout the whole product life cycle, including systems which manage order processing and order entry, product component procurement, warehousing, spares and servicing; financial management; and control.

The mainframe computer at Sony House acts as a gateway for links between Sony's UK dealer network and Sony's UK spares depot in Thatcham, Berkshire. Sony's central computer offers various on-line computer services such as the sales order processing system, accounting systems and E-mail.

SUK has established EDI links with its larger retail customers. Using EDI, SUK can accept incoming orders and send out invoices. SUK intends to expand the system to transmit goods returns and credit notes. Through EDI, Sony receives distribution information from the major High Street retailers, which is used to supplement other commercial data. From the retailers' viewpoint, the introduction into EDI of multiple sales divisions will allow retailers to order products from Sony's different sales divisions. Retailers will be able to place one order and the EDI system will allocate the order between the different divisions according to product.

The warehouse and distribution point for all Sony products in Europe is the European Spares Centre (SEC) in Antwerp. Sony dealers in Europe order spares and make order enquiries by accessing SEC's mainframe computer. SUK users and SUK service dealers use the Sony international network to gain access to the SEC.

Company background

The company now known as Sony was founded in 1946 as a two-man partnership called *Tokyo Tsushin Kogyo* (Tokyo Telecommunications Engineering Company). The two partners were Masura Ibuka, an electronics engineer, and Akio Morita, a former university researcher in physics recently demobbed from the Japanese navy. Their company began operations in the bombed-out shell of a department store in war-devastated Tokyo. The company's first successful product, after an unsuccessful attempt to manufacture an electric rice cooker, was a suitcase-sized tape recorder for language learning in schools.[1]

In 1955, believing that a company with global ambitions should have a name that could be easily recognized and pronounced, the company changed its name to Sony. The name Sony, an amalgam of the Latin word *sonus* (sound) and the slang word 'sonny', was chosen for three reasons. It had no meaning in any language, it was short and easy to remember, and it carried optimistic connotations associated with 'sunny'. This name also became the company's logo.

After a series of ambitious experiments and unfortunate setbacks, including making Cellophane-based audio recording tape which distorted the sound it recorded, the company produced its first product: a weighty, expensive tape recorder. Needless to say, the product remained unsold – until it was demonstrated to the Japan Supreme Court, which bought twenty machines to alleviate a shortage of typists. Realizing its breakthrough, Sony developed a smaller machine for use in schools for teaching English.

From these modest beginnings Sony has established a reputation as an innovator with products such as transistor radios and solid-state personal television sets. This reputation continues today with products like the Walkman, the Discman, the Marvica filmless camera, the Trinitron television system, the $3\frac{1}{2}$-inch floppy computer disk, and Pyxis, a 24-hour global positioning system (GPS) used in aircraft navigation.

Sony's European operations began in 1960 with the establishment in Baar, Switzerland, of Sony Overseas SA, a financial services company. In the following years headquarters and support companies were opened in the Netherlands, Belgium, Cologne, Basingstoke and Fellbach, Germany.

In 1974 Sony established its first manufacturing facility in Europe at Bridgend, South Wales, which manufactures colour televisions and CRTs (cathode ray tubes). A later addition to the factory was officially opened by the Princess of Wales on 7 April 1982. The Bridgend factory was followed by manufacturing facilities in Fellbach, Germany, in 1975 (colour televisions and robots); Bayonne, France, in 1980 (audio cassettes); Barcelona, Spain, in 1982 (colour televisions, video tape recorders, audio products); Dax-Pontonx, France, in 1984 (video cassettes and coating); Ribeauville, France, in 1986 (compact disc players, car audio, video camcorders and tape recorders); Anif, Austria, in 1987 (compact discs and laser discs); Roverto, Italy, in 1989 (audio cassettes); and Bayonne, France, in 1990 (key components). The European Operations Office (EOO) situated in Cologne, Germany, is Sony's corporate headquarters in Europe. Sony is aiming for a single European zone of operations, managed and controlled from EOO.[2]

Sony sales organizations are usually of three types: Consumer Products (e.g. televisions, video and audio equipment); Professional Products (cameras, recording equipment); and Magnetic Products (magnetic and optical media). Sales and service companies were established in the UK (1968), Germany (1970), France (1973), Spain (1973), Italy (1973), Denmark (1974), Belgium (1977), the Netherlands (1979), Switzerland (1979), Austria (1979) and Portugal (1986). Also in 1986, Sony International Sales Division Europe (ISDE) was set up in Frankfurt, Germany, to develop sales in the former East European bloc and the former USSR.

In the UK, Germany and the Netherlands the company has established business groups which have responsibility for planning, engineering, production, quality control and strategic marketing of the respective product lines. The Software Engineering Company of Sony (SECS) is situated in Düsseldorf. Founded in 1991, SECS was established to write software for use by Sony companies in Europe. The software that SECS produces is for internal sale to Sony sales companies.[3]

Strategy and management

Sony works on the principle of 'global localization' defined by Akio Morita,[4] Chairman of Sony Corporation, as 'building a global corporation through commitment to local operations'. The philosophy 'think global, act local' enables Sony to 'explore and develop the unique features of each country while at the same time benefiting from the strengths of a global enterprise'.[5]

As a result of this corporate philosophy Sony is not a strongly centralized corporation. Tokyo headquarters avoids giving over-rigid guidance or control and subsidiaries are responsible for managing their own businesses and for maintaining corporate standards. Sony manages its operations in zones and has established these in Japan, the Far East (headquarters in Singapore), the United States (headquarters in New York) and Europe. Each zone receives corporate guidance from headquarters. Corporate plans and budgets are approved at zone level.

The policy of 'global localization' resulted in the current management structure in Europe. Tokyo delegates responsibilities to a European executive group led by EOO's chairman, who is also a member of the corporate board in Tokyo. Senior managers from Sony Europe make up the European management board which is responsible for deciding and disseminating European strategy. Approval is also required at this level for major decisions.

Mid-range plans, i.e. those of 3 years' duration, are prepared annually by each company. These are reviewed with EOO and adjusted where necessary. The consolidated results are reported to Tokyo. Sony United Kingdom Ltd makes a mixture of proactive and reactive responses to European strategy directives.

Sony United Kingdom Ltd (formerly Sony (UK) Ltd) (SUK)

In 1968 SUK was established in central London and is now based in Staines, Middlesex, some 20 miles south-west of London. SUK is an autonomous organization intended to manufacture, sell and distribute Sony-branded products in the UK. In addition, SUK provides communication services to Sony-approved service centres for repairs to Sony products. Specialized Electronic Services (SES)[6] companies are located in Cumbernauld, Dulwich, Leeds, Oldbury and Staines. SES companies order parts through the European Parts Ordering System (EPOS) run by SEC in Antwerp, Belgium.

SUK originally consisted of a single division for marketing and selling consumer products, later expanding into broadcast and communications products. A division was created to supply recording media for the various products. SUK has reorganized into divisions for consumer and non-consumer products.

Since 1990, SUK has operated three semi-autonomous sales divisions and a support division. A new sales division, Sony Components and Computer Peripherals Company (CCPC), was added in 1992. Figure 12.1 shows SUK's divisional structure.

Divisions are relatively free to make their own operating decisions within company-wide budgets and medium-range plans. Sales budgets are set for 6-month 'terms' (April-September; October-March) and for financial years (April-March). Each sales division prepares a sales budget report which describes their planned performance in terms of sales volume and value for each product. Sales budgets and related expense budgets for all divisions are reviewed by the European zone management at EOO in Cologne.

As a sales company, SUK is considered as an autonomous unit within Sony Europe and provides its own services from development through to operations. In 1993 Sony consolidated its UK hardware companies into one organization, Sony United Kingdom Ltd. The two main companies brought together were Sony (UK) Ltd which handles the manufacturing facilities at Bridgend and Pencoed, and Sony Broadcast and Communications Ltd.

Sales divisions are organized according to type of product and market:
- **Consumer Products** consumer electronics; televisions, video and audio equipment. These are sold by High Street multiples, such as Dixons or Currys, by Sony Centres and by independent retailers.

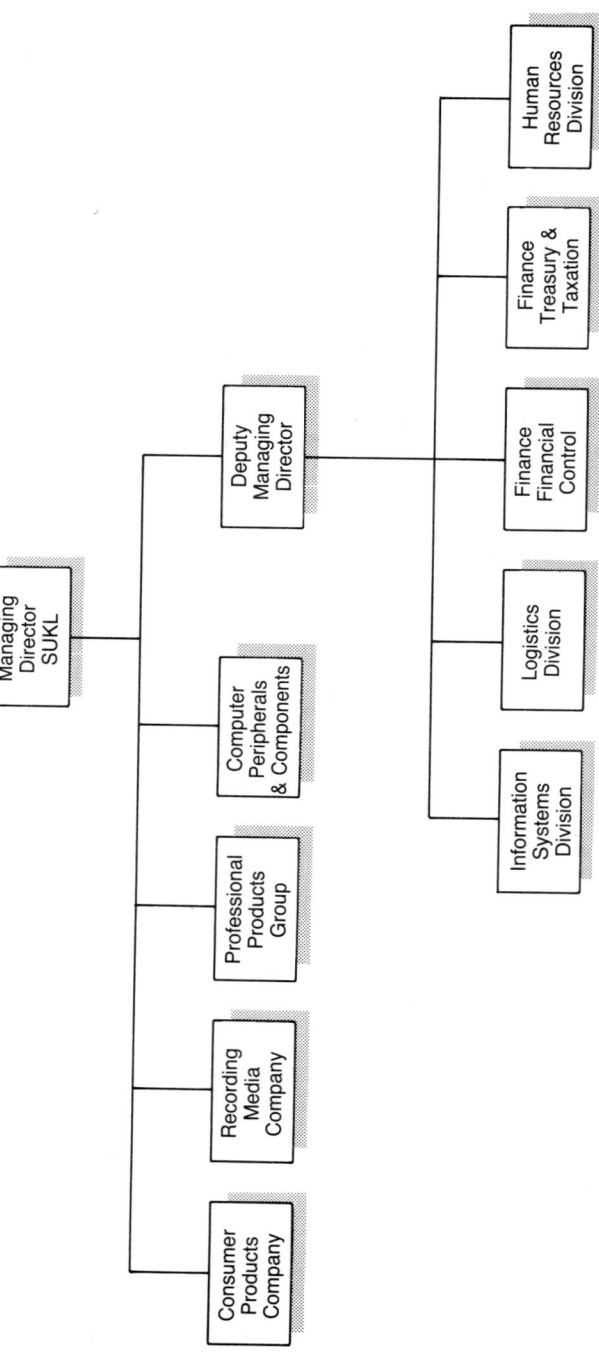

Figure 12.1 Divisional structure of Sony (UK) Ltd. (*Source*: Sony (UK) Ltd)

- **Professional Products** professional products for the broadcasting and industrial market, either direct or via distributors to large customers such as broadcasting companies.
- **Recording Media** all types of magnetic and optical media used by Sony products.
- **Computer Peripherals and Components** equipment and components, including semiconductors, to the OEM (Original Equipment Manufacturer) computer market.

SUK has four departments within the support division: Information Systems; Logistics (warehousing and delivery of finished products); Personnel and Administration; and Finance Group (which consists of two sub-divisions: Financial Control and Treasury and Taxation).

SUK distributes its products through three types of retailer. These range from Sony-branded dealerships to national multiple dealers. Sony Centres are independent dealers which sell only Sony products.

National Accounts include the well-known High Street retail outlets, e.g. Comet, Currys, Dixons. Independent dealers have a twice-weekly agreed call-off arrangement and can call up to 3.00 p.m. on a working day for delivery the next day.

Business impact of IT

Communications

Two networks serve national and international data communications for SUK. UK operations are the main priority for SUK. The main function of the international system is to support and inform. The UK network is managed by SUK's Information Systems Division (ISD) and links all SUK locations to the computer centre in Sony House, Staines. The major UK locations are the national distribution centre in Thatcham, Berkshire, which distributes consumer products and media products; the Broadcast and Communications warehouse in Staines which serves the London media distribution point; and the sales offices in Thatcham, Basingstoke, Leeds, Cumbernauld and Dublin.

The primary use of the UK network is to connect remote users of display terminals to the central computer so that they can use the various on-line computer services, such as the sales order processing system, accounting systems and E-mail. For example, a sales office would create and maintain orders, update customer details and manage similar information about its transactions with customers.

Increasingly, local area networks are being established in SUK offices and PCs are replacing 'dumb' terminals to provide additional services, such as word processing and spreadsheets. These PCs run terminal emulation software so that they continue to appear to the central computer as a terminal to allow the user to use existing on-line services. Figure 12.2 shows SUK's data communications network.

152 *The Japanese Advantage?*

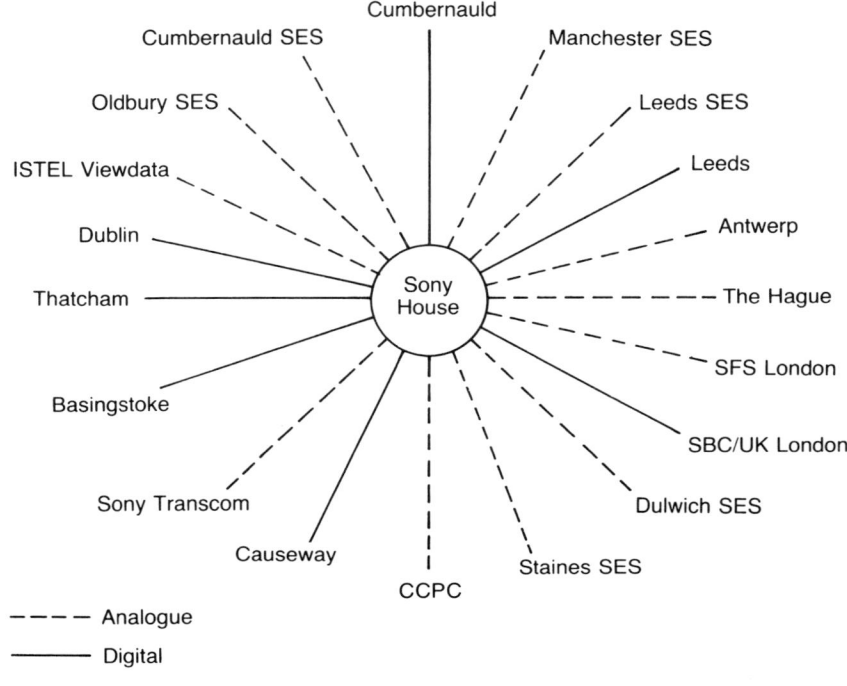

– – – – Analogue

———— Digital

Key

Cumbernauld, Leeds, Basingstoke, Thatcham – sales offices; SES – Specialized Electronic Services (independent service companies); Antwerp – European Parts Centre; The Hague – European Network Centre; SFS London – Sony Financial Services; PPG London – Professional Products Group; CCPC – Components and Computer Peripheral Company; Causeway – warehouse (Staines); Sony Transcom – service company for airline in-flight entertainment; Basingstoke – Sony Broadcasting; Thatcham – National Distribution Centre; Dublin – Sony Ireland.

Figure 12.2 Sony (UK) Ltd's data communications network. (*Source*: Sony (UK) Ltd)

Sony's European Network Centre (ENC) in The Hague forms one corner of Sony's international digital communications triangle linking Tokyo, the United States and Europe. The ENC is the conduit for communications from headquarters to Sony's European subsidiaries and from the European subsidiaries back to Sony headquarters. The components of this system are illustrated in Figure 12.3.

One layer is an IBM SNA (System Network Architecture) network which provides SUK with access to other computers in the Sony network. It is also used extensively for the exchange of data files between SUK, Sony Corporation, business groups and factories worldwide.

The majority of traffic over the Sony international network is the exchange of batch files of STREAM-related information. The sales company sends a rolling forecast of future requirements and firm purchase orders

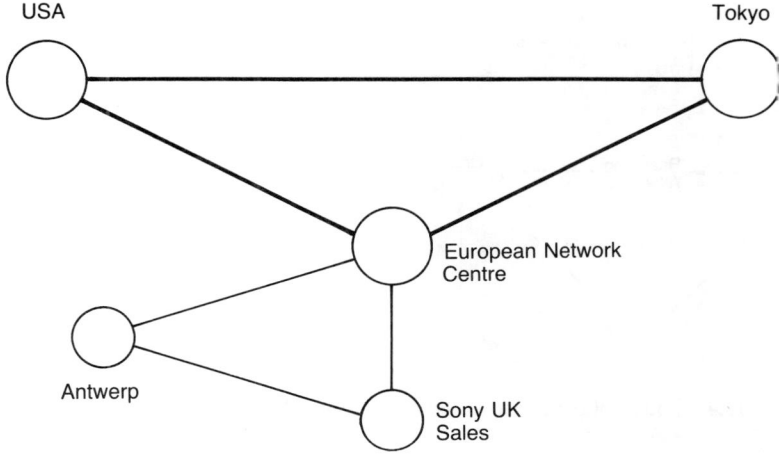

Figure 12.3 Sony's international digital network. (*Source*: Sony (UK) Ltd)

for each product on a weekly or monthly cycle. The Corporation returns status information on each order, such as confirmed quantity, production data and shipment details. The network is also used to allow SUK users and SUK service dealers (via Viewdata) to access spares ordering systems at the European spare parts centre (SEC) in Antwerp.

Major application systems

A similar system was initially developed in the United States and was copied for use in Sony's UK operations in 1986. Since then the business needs of Sony UK's sales companies have become increasingly diverse (reflecting their differently changing markets). Further development by SUK has produced different applications which have been incorporated into the original system, e.g. a telesales system for Recording Media Division and a Broadcast Sales Administration System (BSA). These are both 'front-end' systems for the respective divisions.

Figure 12.4 shows the components of the Sony Total Network (STN). While STN is capable of meeting current business needs, it has become clear that it is unsuitable for development to meet changing business requirements. Since STN was developed and introduced, business requirements have moved on. For example, EDI is now extensively used to handle the exchange of orders and invoices between SUK and its major customers. A multiple currency support system will be required if and when SUK moves into selling in other European countries.

Management have therefore decided to replace the system. Commercially available packages were considered but were rejected in favour of cooperation with Sony Europe.

154 *The Japanese Advantage?*

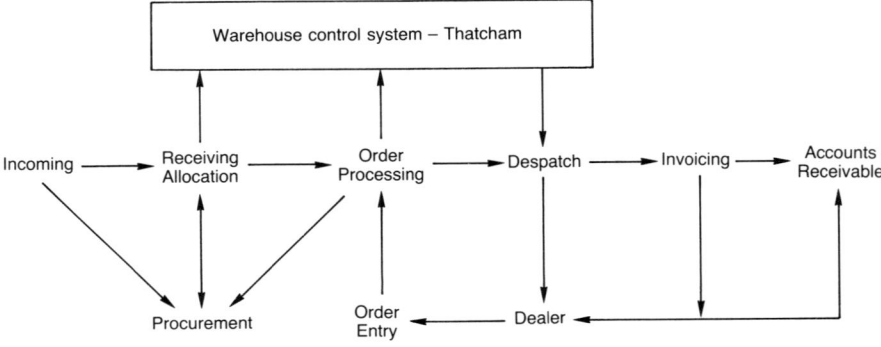

Figure 12.4 Sony total network. (*Source*: Sony (UK) Ltd)

STREAM

Corporate projects initiated by Sony headquarters in Japan span the entire Sony Corporation. One of these projects is a system called STREAM. This system was driven by a corporate need to improve communication between Sony's manufacturing and sales divisions, with the aim of reducing product lead times and delivery times. Before STREAM, sales divisions relayed sales forecasts (usually by fax) to the manufacturing plants on a weekly, fortnightly, or monthly basis, depending on the type of product. STREAM aids forecasting requirements and related purchasing decisions. Improved communication between the manufacturing and sales functions improves efficiency in procurement for manufacturing by facilitating up-to-date forecasting.

The primary aim of STREAM is to reduce product lead times and overall inventories of products held within the corporation. It is also improving information on status of orders, providing more accurate information on the arrival date of specific shipments. SUK uses this information to improve the service offered to dealers.

In the late 1980s a European STREAM project was developed. The project was designed to specifications defined by the corporation. Systems were then developed by each sales company. STREAM is the first corporate project to be handed on to sales companies for subsequent development. There are STREAM projects in other parts of the world where Sony has established itself.

Personal computers in the UK

Recent years have seen an increase in the use of PCs in SUK. This has been most noticeably evident in the setting up of local area networks. The company has 150 dumb terminals and 450 staff (out of a total workforce of 850) have a PC on their desk or portable PCs for use at home. The vast majority of staff use their PC to gain access to the mainframe computer for major corporate account details, as well as word processing, graphics and spreadsheet functions.

In an effort to improve internal communications, SUK has introduced an E-mail system as well as a system for on-line viewing of reports to make information more readily available. Reports can be 'bundled up' to allow users to select particular pages and these can be printed as hard copy if required. All daily and weekly reports are now processed through this software package.

A valuable by-product of E-mail has been saving paper as hard copies of reports are made in duplex (back-to-back), or reduced in size to fit more pages on an A4 sheet of paper. Printing costs have also been reduced by eliminating all pre-printed continuous stationery, excluding cheques, and replacing it with computer-generated laser-printed forms as an integral part of report printing operations. Single-sided continuous paper has been replaced by double-sided cut sheet A4, which is cheaper and easier to handle (and fits normal filing systems).

Such procedures are gaining popular support as people realize the implications for drastically reducing workload. However, in spite of the reliability of this service, there is still a psychological hurdle. This is the 'belt and braces' notion that a hard copy of every page of every report is essential 'in case the computer breaks down'.

EDI in the UK

EDI[7] is being introduced between SUK and its larger retail customers. SUK now accepts orders in and sends invoices out via EDI for a limited number of customers. The system is being expanded to include goods returns and credit notes.

The next stage of development, due shortly, is the introduction of multiple sales divisions. This will allow retailers to order products from Sony's different sales divisions (e.g. cassette tapes, consumer products). Retailers will be able to place one order with Sony's EDI system which will direct the components of the order to different divisions according to product.

Sales divisions exert pressure on ISD to keep abreast of EDI developments made by customers. Some competitors offer advanced notification of shipments which alerts dealers of the proposed delivery schedule for their outstanding orders.

Sony gains considerable advantage from receiving distribution information from the major High Street retailers. STN allows Sony to know how much stock is shipped to the retailers' warehouses but is not aware of the quantities sold by particular High Street stores. Once an extended EDI link reveals this information, Sony will be able to improve its delivery facility to retailers in towns and cities that warrant it.

A problem to be resolved is the tendency of some large retailers to attribute their own reference numbers to Sony products rather than the industry-standard barcode number. These differ from the Sony internal reference number.[8] Retailers use these for their own internal records purposes to enable them to cope with the almost identical products from various suppliers. Retailers who use such methods have undoubtedly evolved systems which translate one reference number to another. However, retailers prefer to use their own reference number when placing orders with Sony. This slows down the ordering procedure as Sony needs to check with the retailer precisely what product is required.

The major High Street retailers deal with a large number of suppliers (one major supermarket chain has more than 400). Such large organizations wish to increase staff efficiency by reducing order-processing time, thus increasing employees' work output. In such circumstances, EDI becomes a necessity rather than a luxury. Retailers are reluctant to establish separate manual procedures to manage suppliers unable to offer EDI.

The current market for audio and video tape is highly competitive and price is important to the consumer. A consumer is willing to take what is in a dealer's stock at the lowest price, even when this amounts to a few pence difference between recognizable brands. Consequently, a dealer is unlikely to tolerate a back-order system from suppliers for recording tape; if stocks are unavailable the dealer orders from the supplier's competitor. To survive in this market, suppliers must acknowledge an immediacy and respond to it.

The EDI power relationship between supplier and retailer influences decisions of EDI standardization. Once an EDI system is installed, a retailer is unlikely to agree to change the system at the request of a supplier who wishes to standardize to a different system.[9] Companies intending to globalize their electronic networks need to consider carefully the implications of EDI power relationships.

European Spares Centre

The European Spares Centre (SEC) situated at Antwerp holds spare parts for all Sony products. Other Sony dealers in Europe access Antwerp's mainframe computer for ordering and for their spares enquiries. The spares ordering system is a real-time order processing system. Dealers can enter the system (either via direct dial or AT&T's Istel network)[10] through the IBM 3090 mainframe computer, using Viewdata (the standard Sony videotext system). After entering their user's password, dealers are routed via the mainframe computer to the spares ordering system on Antwerp's machines. Any parts ordered are logged against the dealer's account number. For security purposes, the screen does not reveal a dealer's active account number and this prevents a dealer ordering parts against another account number.

The mainframe computer at Sony House in Staines acts as a gateway for Sony's UK dealer network and for Sony's UK spares depot in Thatcham, Berkshire, which holds stock of some peripherals: headphones, earpieces and manuals. Orders placed with Thatcham for non-stock items are ordered from the main storage depot in Antwerp. Antwerp aims for a 95 per cent 'first pick' rate,[11] and despatches orders for overnight delivery wherever possible, otherwise orders are despatched with a maximum of 48 hours after receipt of order.

Sony's main competitors offer similar parts-ordering services to their own dealership network. Some competitors offer additional services, for example fault-finding guides. This technology has been in existence for some years and Sony, their dealers and their competitors have come to rely on it. Six hundred Sony dealers (out of some 800 registered dealers in total for the Viewdata network)[12] use the computerized parts-ordering facility. Sony's spare parts department is actively encouraging other dealers to do the same.

Managing IT

International coordination

Guidelines from Tokyo define the framework of corporate IS issues. The most rigid controls relate to the communications network, which is very tightly defined and controlled for reasons of compatibility and access. The IS department in Tokyo determines naming conventions and allocates these to subsidiaries. Subsidiaries who did not comply would not be able to communicate with the rest of Sony.

Tokyo also provides guidelines on the type of operating system to be used by subsidiaries. Database management used to be controlled in a similarly tight manner but guidelines have recently been relaxed.

European Computer Services (ECS) was set up in 1991 and is developing a 'European harmonized data model' which, it is hoped, will form the basis of future application development within the European zone.

Within Europe, IT guidelines have been agreed informally among the major sales companies (for example, to use the natural programming language and the Adabas database). Common application systems have not been agreed between sales companies. Each sales company is responsible for its own information systems services. Sales companies have their own computers and their own IS departments.

Sony Corporation gives overall guidelines on IT expenditure. However, within agreed staffing levels the local divisional management has the responsibility to assign staff to each job function. The headcount level assigned to its ISD is determined by local management.

The ISD budget is decided by SUK directors as part of the overall company budget. As a separate exercise by Sony Corporation to gather information about the IT function, details of the ISD budget are reported to EOO.

An example of the liaison between Tokyo and Europe is the European STREAM project. A corporate project team in the IS Department in Tokyo provided the initial impetus for the project, which was subsequently publicized to overseas sales companies. The IS Department invited an informal grouping of sales companies within Europe to discuss the project and to make development proposals.

In essence, Tokyo headquarters outlined the information required from rolling sales and purchase forecasts. The sales companies were encouraged to develop the system to their own specifications. Individual sales companies redeveloped their own individual procurement systems and purchasing systems to produce the data required by Tokyo. Local development teams in each country wrote applications for the system.

STREAM is now managed by Sony's European headquarters in Cologne and is used by SUK's sales divisions to procure product. User responsibility rests with the Procurement Manager of the sales companies where STREAM is used.

On occasions, systems that are 'inherited' from Tokyo headquarters, such as the STREAM project, are difficult to manage. Decisions made by the IS Department in Tokyo, perhaps in collaboration with other departments, may stray from informal specifications as originally agreed. If this happens, SUK makes a constructive analysis in an attempt to clarify the situation and suggests how it can be rectified. Usually this is conducted in the form of lobbying, through personal contact, between managers in departments in SUK and their counterparts in Tokyo.

Information Systems Division

Information Systems Division (ISD) is responsible for providing information systems services to all divisions of SUK. These services include technical support and computer service facilities. ISD also provides communications services to other Sony companies located in the UK. ISD's annual objectives describe services that the department will provide, projects that are expected to be undertaken and agreements on service levels for end users.

ISD is headed by a general manager who reports to the financial director (also the deputy managing director) of SUK. The department has a total of forty staff and is organized into three sections: Development Services; Computer Services; and Technical Support. A fourth section, called the Database Administration (DBA) Group, has recently been established and currently operates within Development Services. In time, this section may become a separate unit. Figure 12.5 shows the organizational components of ISD (numbers indicate staff).

SUK makes its own IT decisions, as long as these conform to general corporate guidelines. Where decisions are thought to be contentious, or where corporate policy is unclear, ISD seeks guidance from EOO or from Tokyo.

ISD provides computer systems throughout the whole life cycle of the product. These include systems which manage order processing and order entry, product component procurement, warehousing, spares and servicing. Systems for financial management and control are proprietary packages which operate on Millennium software. These packages include systems for accounts receivable, accounts payable, general ledger, and financial reporting systems.

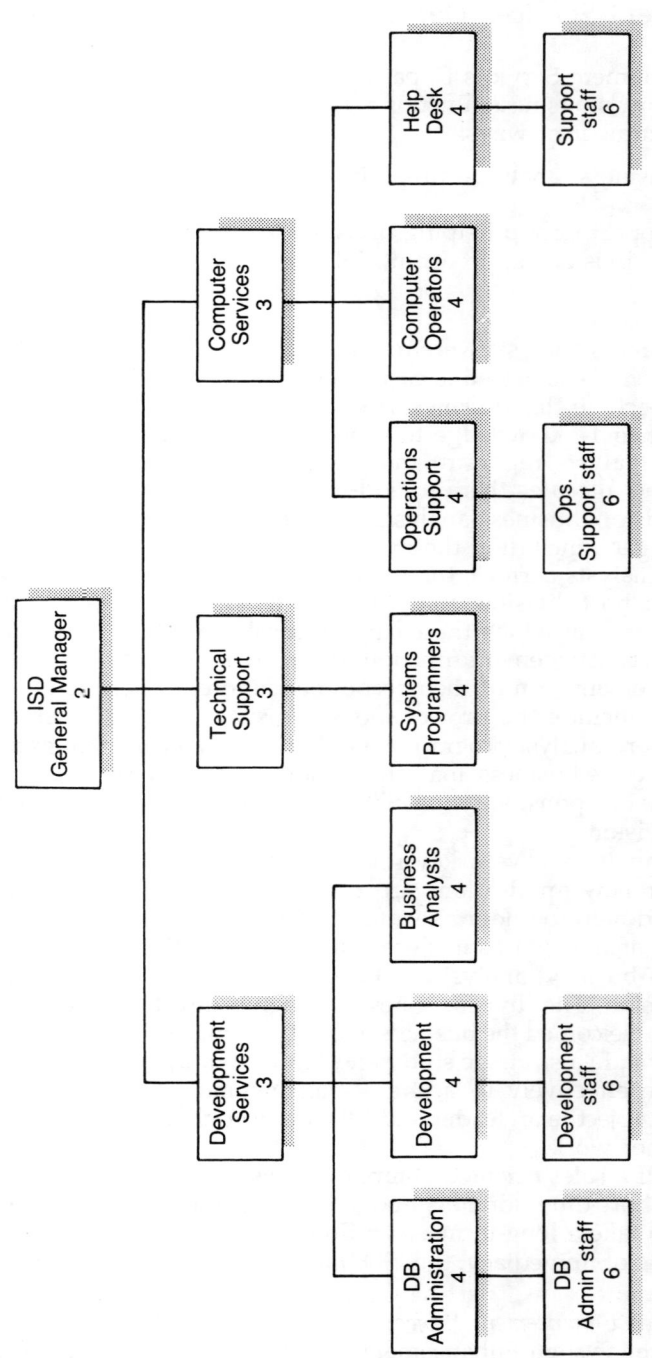

Figure 12.5 The organization of ISD. (*Source*: Sony (UK) Ltd)

Development Services Department

ISD's Development Services Department provides new computer applications to Sony's business functions. The department identifies business needs in a number of ways:

1 ISD's business analysts preparing strategic studies for end-user divisions
2 ISD's Support Group helping divisions with smaller IT projects
3 End-user divisions approaching ISD directly with new ideas.

1 Strategic studies
The first business analysts were recruited in mid-1991. Ideally, one business analyst will be allocated to each sales or support division, but present resources preclude this. Business analysts function as hybrid managers and apply their IT knowledge to solve business problems.

Business analysts report to the Development Services Department Manager who allocates them to end-user divisions. In their work with the host division, business analysts are expected to foster contacts with senior managers, including the managing director.

Business analysts perform three roles. First, they investigate a business area for their host division, analysing the division's business needs and identifying ways in which these can be translated into IT. Second, they have a project management function. In this role business analysts manage the implementation of their recommendations. Other members of a project team include the project sponsor (usually the end-user department manager), analyst programmers (APs), analysts and programmers. In a third role the business analyst functions as an account manager and takes financial responsibility for ISD services from the perspective of the end-user division.

Business analysts have a key role to play in clarifying users' needs. When major new applications are concerned, they draw up terms of reference and help to undertake a feasibility study. In subsequent stages the business analyst works in close collaboration with a systems analyst.

To date, a business analyst has been most successful in Sony Broadcasting Division. The division's new managing director, who has an IT background, welcomed the business analyst into his division. The business analyst has made a strategic study and has drawn up a five-year plan to use IT more effectively to address management needs. The business analyst is a project team leader and ISD has brought in outside resources to support her work.

As parts of a sales-oriented company, divisions are used to operating with quite short time horizons and it is a struggle for ISD to persuade end users to take a long-term view. Conversely, in the area of logistics, with its sense of immediacy, the ISD business analyst is quite successful.

2 The System Enhancement Project
The role of the System Enhancement Project (SEP) is to manage small IT projects and to be the first line of support for production. User divisions

approach this group directly even when a business analyst is working in their division. Every six or eight weeks, ISD has a meeting with each of the divisions. In these meetings divisional management raise ideas for business changes and request the assistance of ISD. The Planning and Control managers of two of the divisions are very alert to personal computers and are keen to introduce new ways of using them. This procedure enables ISD 'to win friends and influence people'.

3   External demands

ISD is involved in a number of the systems which have a broader usage than SUK. One example is the STREAM project. In such cases the initial impetus for the system originates from outside SUK, possibly from EOO or Tokyo. ISD prefers to be involved in such externally directed IT projects at an early exploratory stage in order to provide a driving force.

Computer Services Department

The Computer Services Department is more technical and consists of three groups. The first group, Operations Department, comprises three senior operators. This group provides services for running and monitoring on-line systems, managing batch work and composing production reports. The second group, the Operations Support Group, comprises a supervisor and two operations analysts. Their main responsibilities are production scheduling of batch work, change management and quality assurance (QA), and implementation of new applications. In the event of any batch failure the Operations Support Group provides first-line support and is on call 24 hours a day. The third group is the Help Desk. This comprises a supervisor and three support analysts and supports both mainframe and PC equipment.

Support teams

The support teams are the Operations Support team, Technical Support team and the System Enhancement Project (SEP) team. The last is within the Development Group. The SEP team consists of three to five programmers whose function is to provide production programming support and to manage minor enhancements to existing systems. Programming problems are escalated to the SEP team. Systems software problems are passed to the Technical Support team, which has responsibility for both hardware and software.

Technical Support

The Technical Support team consists of four people who are responsible for day-to-day management of the network infrastructure and network definitions. The team is also responsible for installing operating system software over the major software packages that are used by SUK. Once installed, software packages are passed onto the Operations Department or the end-user sponsor of the software project.

Another function of the Technical Support team is to ensure that software (which may not be standard) is set up to support new hardware. The Technical Support group is consulted when new hardware is introduced or there are problems with the mainframe computer.

Project teams

As you would expect, project teams approach their work systematically. An initial feasibility study is undertaken by the project group. The study contains an analysis of a division's business needs and attempts to clarify the division's IT requirements. Agreeing project specifications with the commissioning division is becoming more formalized. The Development Service Department (DSD) has increasingly encouraged divisions to define closely what a project involves and to signify agreement by 'signing off' the agreed specifications. Part of this development has involved educating DSD staff to see which are important aspects in a project and to clarify matters with the host division.

From the initial feasibility study project work is passed on to a development group who will be responsible for designing and building the system. A subsequent group is responsible for installation and testing the new system.

The project process resembles a relay race. The ISD tries to analyse the various skills of its members with a view to encouraging staff to become specialists in their particular fields. Current priorities include educating DSD staff to be more aware that development on mainframe computers or PCs is equally important. In any case, it is vital to increase user access to available data.

ISD is attempting to inform colleagues in other divisions of the value of their resources. In a company such as Sony where technology development is the nature of the business, other divisions are well informed about computer software. Armed with this knowledge, it is tempting for their staff to pursue interesting developments which may be beyond the support capability of ISD. Concerted public relations strategies, complemented by personal contact, go some way to correcting existing misinformed impressions.

End-user departments are involved in making design specifications for the new system. Representatives from production divisions are involved in new project planning from the earliest stages. Final operations acceptance testing takes place at the same time as unit testing. It is important to distinguish between design problems and operations problems.

Planning IT

IT planning meetings for the European zone are held on a quarterly basis. These meetings are attended by managers from ISD and their

European counterparts and are primarily a forum for exchanging information and experiences. During September and October, annual planning meetings take place at SUK between ISD management and senior management of the sales and support divisions. During these meetings managers discuss projects and planned new computer applications to ensure that end-user needs and IT development are in lockstep. Decisions relating to appropriate computer needs and applications are thus a joint decision between relevant parties, with ample opportunities for mutual feedback and discussion. These meetings are in preparation for a review with the IS Steering Committee, which is made up of the SUK board directors and the ISD manager. The committee approves proposed IS strategy, project plans and budgets.

IT decisions made in these planning meetings are timely for budget planning meetings scheduled in January of each year. Heads of all divisions attend budget meetings. A series of pre-budget meetings helps to establish sales divisions' priorities. In late January the annual budget is finalized in time for the forthcoming financial year beginning in April. Once the ISD budget has been approved by company management as part of the overall company budget, it is reported to EOO for consideration. EOO reports to Tokyo on behalf of the European zone.

Evaluating ISD services

There is no formal process to evaluate and quantify the benefits for IT projects. If the IS Steering Committee considers a project to be of sufficient value or importance to the company and the cost is acceptable, then it will normally be carried out when resources are available.

Sales divisions are responsible for demonstrating and justifying business needs for IT development. They are also responsible for justifying the value to the business of new development projects, including possible cost savings.

The other side of the IT cost equation is the continuing costs of providing production computer services for the business. These costs are easier to define. ISD has accounting software to apportion service charges to end-user departments. Although end users are not charged for minutely itemized aspects of the service, the software can indicate appropriate usage charges and thus alert end-user departments of the cost of ISD services.[13]

Allocation of development costs are based on the cost of each project in terms of personnel, which includes overheads. The project cost is apportioned to the user divisions involved, i.e. those receiving benefit from the project. Computer services costs are analysed by production service. The cost of each service is then allocated to user divisions in proportion to service usage. Equipment costs for terminals, PCs and printers are charged to users at a flat monthly rate per unit.

Costs are allocated to other divisions who decide for themselves any additional expenditure on ISD services. Costs incurred by ISD to provide

IS services to SUK are allocated on a monthly basis to the sales companies, with a final reconciliation at the end of each 6-month period. Should a sales company decide it wishes to have additional IS services beyond those included in the ISD budget, then they would bear the costs directly out of their own budgets. If, for example, they want to buy additional PC software then they can buy it themselves. ISD does not run a billing system and charges users for each service used.

ISD costs allocated to support divisions are reallocated to the sales companies as part of their own costs, usually in proportion to annual net sales. Corporate targets state that the cost of ISD services of any sales company (or group of sales companies) should not exceed 1 per cent of net sales.

In practice, a company the size of SUK faces certain unavoidable cost levels to manage an order-processing system. Sales divisions have no viable alternative as they are not big enough to contract outside. There is no element of charging as this is not thought to be particularly helpful. If sales divisions feel that costs are too high, budget meetings provide a forum for expressing their concerns.

As a service function ISD must constantly seek ways of providing its services more cheaply while maintaining or improving their quality. ISD aims to show reducing unit costs over time. The main targets for cost control are quantifiable targets (for example, production services, development programmes). There are routine active measures to control costs including: constant monitoring of expenditure; inventory control measures; postponing planned upgrades to computer systems; renegotiating the terms and conditions of renewed contracts.

ISD maintains regular contact with management from each of the main user groups. Review meetings take place every one or two months. Key users advise ISD if services are provided too slowly. ISD tends to notice this fact first through use of monitoring software, which helps ISD to restore performance levels.

The role of ISD's general manager is to create optimum benefit for the company from the IT resource. This is achieved more easily if user divisions are able to state their business objectives. Objectives which are shared between the user division and the ISD are more likely to result in successfully completed projects. Prior planning on the part of user divisions enhances IT project work and helps conserve resources.

However, ISD's limited resources are further inhibited by requests for urgent work, including resolving 'bugs', supporting PCs, helping users to develop better ways of managing work on their PCs, taking on new projects and developing new systems.

Undoubtedly, ISD's biggest challenge is managing available resources for optimum effectiveness. As much as possible, ISD collaborates with end users in order to prioritize its resources. ISD prefers to be led by the business needs and ISD seeks users' business priorities as an input to planning. Although it is sometimes necessary for ISD management to make a value judgement, this is tempered by quarterly meetings at board level with the IS steering committee.

The future role of ISD

Historically, ISD has been a 'traditional' data-processing department and has controlled the functions where computers have proven effectiveness. ISD has been responsible for managing the operations systems, processing and shipping of orders, and the accounting system for sales.

However, the role of ISD is changing. The advent of an increased number of PCs brings additional responsibilities and opportunities for the ISD. These PCs are changing the way in which people work, not least the way in which ISD staff work. PCs have accelerated the rate of change and increased the number of business possibilities. The information held in the mainframe computers can be shared with people in other departments. Sales personnel, middle management and senior management are now able to work with PCs and ISD is involved in helping such staff to discover how best to use whatever computing power is available.

ISD regards itself as setting company standards in conjunction with the users. In this role it tries to maintain central control over a number of aspects of computing to prevent longer-term problems of communication or sharing data. ISD's general manager is responsible for deciding how to exploit the computer resource for the best advantage of the whole company.

Notes

1. For an interesting account of the life of Akio Morita, one of the founding partners of Sony Corporation, and a description of the company's growth into a multinational enterprise, see Morita, A., Reingold, E. and Shimomura, M., *Made in Japan*, Fontana Books (1988).
2. In 1990, European operations were approximately 25 per cent Sony's world turnover. (Source: *Sony; 30 years in Europe*, Sony Corporation (1990).)
3. Sony sales companies are located in each of the major European countries. SUK sales company is one of the biggest, by turnover.
4. Akio Morita was awarded an honorary knighthood by the Queen in 1992. 'Mr Walkman gets an honorary knighthood', *The Times*, 5 November 1992.
5. *Sony; 30 years in Europe*, Sony Corporation (1990).
6. Specialized Electronic Services companies are 49 per cent owned by SUK. SES companies were originally integral parts of SUK until they were sold, mainly to their own management, in the mid-1980s.
7. SUK uses a system called Supertras. This is being installed in Europe as a standard EDI system.
8. Model names designated by retailers are similar to Sony model reference numbers, but are sufficiently different to cause confusion.
9. The 'balance of power' with EDI trading links lies with retailers who provide the vital link between suppliers and consumers. A retailer's

implied threat of changing to a competitor, especially when the product concerned is a commodity (e.g. blank video tape cassettes), is a strong incentive for a supplier to trade electronically. The power structure changes in the relationship between components suppliers and Original Equipment Manufacturers (OEMs). Divisions of Sony who deal with suppliers of component parts (for example, Sony Manufacturing) wield power over EDI decisions.

10 Istel is a package-switching network. As national telephone calls are at local tariff rate, using Istel saves a dealer making a long-distance telephone call. On entering the Istel network the dealer will be confronted with a list of code reference numbers. Selecting the particular code which refers to Sony's spare parts ordering service will direct the dealer towards the machines in Antwerp.

11 This means that 95 per cent of orders received by 3.00 p.m. are picked that day and despatched immediately from available stock. Antwerp orders the remaining 5 per cent from elsewhere.

12 Sony are willing to register free of charge existing owners of Viewdata. Dealers without Viewdata equipment are frequently sold one at cost.

13 One of the major users is another support division which runs financial packages on Millenium (and uses 40–50 per cent of available processing power daily). Charging the support department for this amount for terminal use presents the company with a circuitous situation: the support division will need to recharge the sales division for whom it manages the financial services.

13
Toshiba Information Systems (UK) Ltd

Case profile

Toshiba Information Systems (TIU) uses IT for several purposes, including warehouse and distribution systems, management information systems (MIS) and an executive information system (EIS). A relocation to new premises enabled TIU to install a new warehousing management system. The system incorporates barcode reading facilities, radio data terminals and a spare parts retrieval system using computer-controlled racking carousels. TIU invites customers and potential customers on a guided inspection tour. In addition to expected business benefits, the warehousing and distribution system has had a positive effect on contracts with customers to whom business benefits are demonstrated and has enabled TIU to negotiate sole sales agreements with national and multinational companies.

A group of managers on an in-house management course suggested that the company install an Executive Information System (EIS). Although the project was developed in semi-artificial circumstances, users like the new system and are requesting changes to meet their specific needs.

Unlike EIS, a project to introduce E-mail has been driven by business needs. The ISD manager realized that E-mail would be relatively easy to install as TIU did not share their building with other occupants. An internal audit provided the justification for such a system as it revealed that employees were unhappy with the telephone system and internal mail service. Using previously prepared plans, ISD implemented the project in 1992, and completed it seven months ahead of schedule thanks to company-wide support.

Company background

Toshiba Corporation is one of the world's leading electrical and electronics manufacturers. Toshiba manufactures products in five main sectors:

- Information and communications systems
- Electronic components

168 *The Japanese Advantage?*

- Consumer products
- Heavy electrical apparatus
- Materials and other products

The roots of what is now Toshiba Corporation began in Tokyo in 1875 when Tanaka Seizo-sho founded Tanaka Engineering Works, Japan's first telegraphic equipment plant. This company grew to become one of Japan's largest producers of heavy electrical apparatus.

In 1890 a Tokyo-based company called Hakunetsusha established Japan's first electric incandescent-lamp plant. This company expanded into producing electrical appliances, manufacturing and marketing various innovative consumer products. In 1939 the two companies amalgamated to form Tokyo Shibaura Electric Co. Ltd, manufacturing integrated electrical equipment. In 1978, the company was officially renamed, adopting the previously established abbreviation Toshiba as its new name.

Business strategy

Toshiba Corporation's business strategy centres on the two business fields of Electronics and Energy (E&E). The company perceives enormous growth potential in these two business areas for the twenty-first century. Electronics helps to create, store, process and control vast amounts of information, and energy will provide the basic foundation necessary to power tomorrow's societies.

In Electronics, the company is making significant developments in semiconductors, computer telecommunications, office-automation systems and space development. In the field of Energy, the company has advanced into the development and marketing of nuclear power plants, new energy sources such as fuel cells and future applications of nuclear fusion.

In 1963 Toshiba Corporation established a representative office in Zurich. In 1969, Toshiba became the first Japanese company to open a European industrial electronics subsidiary with its subsidiary in Germany, which had seventeen staff. Toshiba group companies in Europe now directly employ over 5400 staff with five offices, thirty-four subsidiaries and seven factories.

European subsidiaries manufacture the whole range of Toshiba products. Each subsidiary engages in one of Toshiba's five core business sectors and in diverse business activities including marketing, manufacturing and engineering. Each subsidiary is supported by marketing and sales networks throughout Europe from Sweden to Greece and from Ireland to Poland.

Toshiba has a policy of locating manufacturing facilities for individual products in specific countries. Accordingly, colour televisions and air conditioners are manufactured in the UK; microwave ovens, facsimile (fax) and photocopying machines in France; personal computers, semiconductors and VCRs in Germany. Toshiba's factory in Regensburg, Germany, manufactures PCs for distribution in Europe and spare parts for the UK.

The Toshiba Europe Office (TEO) was established in London in 1989 with the task of overseeing the activities of the five business group headquarters companies: TEG (Information and Communication systems), TEE (electronic devices), TCPE (consumer products), TMSE (medical equipment) and TIL (industrial equipment). TEO represents Toshiba at corporate level to national governments and the European Union. TEO also oversees the sustained development of the Toshiba group network.

Toshiba Information Systems (UK) Ltd

Toshiba Information Systems (UK) Ltd (TIU) is a subsidiary of the Toshiba Corporation and was set up in the UK in 1986. TIU occupies modern premises in Weybridge Business Park and has approximately 200 employees.

TIU distributes products manufactured by companies in the Toshiba group for the UK market. These products include photocopiers, fax machines, personal and portable computers, and electronic key telephone systems.

In its PC business, TIU's portable computers are sold exclusively through a network of authorized resellers providing service and technical support (e.g. warranty service) to end users. TIU markets its photocopiers through its network of authorized dealers who provide service and technical support to end users. In addition, TIU sells these products to national account customers, service and support being provided by authorized dealers.

TIU has a stated policy of differentiating itself from competitors, by whatever possible and appropriate means. Recent initiatives include distribution, product quality and reducing the length of time needed to respond to customers' complaints. All letters of complaint must receive a reply within 24 hours. If a customer orders a product which is out of stock, Toshiba's policy is to give an honest delivery promise, even when this means a lost sale.

TIU aims to improve its own performance in competitive terms. Company culture encourages constant improvement to customer service and productivity through various internal initiatives and programmes. The Toshiba corporate handbook, *Standards of Conduct*, explains Toshiba's principles of management. Toshiba has two company mottos: 'In Touch with Tomorrow', and 'Committed to People, Committed to the Future'.

Business impact of IT

TIU enjoys a competitive edge in product distribution. As long as a product is in stock, customers' orders received before 2 p.m. will be delivered by midday the following day. This delivery promise is met 99 per cent of the time.

Warehousing

In just under two years after being established in the UK, TIU planned to move its warehouse from a single building in Sunbury, Middlesex, to a new site in nearby Weybridge and a larger building in Sunbury. Two strategic decisions were needed: how to design the infrastructure in the Weybridge building for future use and how to improve the efficiency of the warehouse system. Each of these areas became the focus of a significant project.

Prior to relocation, structured cabling systems were installed throughout the new Weybridge building. Much more cabling was installed than was then necessary to anticipate future needs. In the light of later applications this decision was justified.

In November 1989 the board of directors approved the move to the new warehouse. Lease contracts were exchanged shortly afterwards and the building given a major refurbishment.

TIU wanted to improve the efficiency of the distribution system in the new warehouse, which had high bays and narrow aisles. Once the location and size of the new building was known, the ISD manager and distribution manager began work on defining requirements for the distribution system and deciding an appropriate computer system. ISD provided information on suitable types of systems, project costings and budget estimates in cooperation with the operations director, the 'owner' of the project.

The system has brought a number of business benefits:

- Increased information about stock levels
- Stock location is known with greater accuracy
- Status and flow of stock can be seen more clearly
- Stock levels are more apparent.

Sales staff, who rely on stock information when dealing with customer enquiries and orders, now give stock information with more confidence.

Distribution system

The new warehousing management system was to be integrated into the main business system. After systems definition and tendering, a letter of intent was signed with a systems software supplier in March 1990. The project gained senior management approval on the basis of an operational need, without a detailed cost justification.

The system went live in July 1990. It incorporates barcode reading facilities, radio data terminals and a spare parts retrieval system using computer-controlled racking carousels. Software and hardware, including radio-based terminals, for the warehouse management project cost £160 000. The overall project was completed within its total budget of £1.5 million.

The system, which meets specification BS 5750 (ISO 9000), is a showpiece of distribution operations. TIU invites customers and potential customers on a guided inspection tour. Visitors see for themselves that not only will their delivery requirements be met, but in a shorter time than TIU's competitors.[1]

With hindsight, the initial investment proposal envisioned only a necessary business requirement, and was too modest in outlining the project's potential benefits. To be fair, the range of cost benefits could not easily have been predicted. The project was planned around observable benefits such as the number of locations and picks per hour for warehouse staff, staffing levels and the number of forklift trucks that would be needed.

Staff productivity levels have surpassed expectations. Warehouse staff can locate stock with increased accuracy and select it more quickly from the storage racks. A reduced staff (from three to one full-time and one part-time) now picks two to three times the previous stock volume per hour.

Since installing the system, stock accuracy is 99.998 per cent. It is no longer necessary to conduct bi-annual stock checks. The finance department now only makes stock checks on high-value items over £100.

TIU has made cost savings in two major areas. First, it is no longer necessary to pay overtime or to close down the business to take stock. Second, improved accuracy in housekeeping has had a positive effect on contracts with customers, who realize the intrinsic business benefits.

The project has more than recouped investment costs. The unexpected psychological gains are incalculable. On the strength of its warehousing and distribution system, TIU has negotiated sole sales agreements with national and multinational companies.

Executive Information System

At the request of a group of managers ISD considered a different type of project. This was an Executive Information System (EIS); a type of system notably difficult to install.

As part of an in-house management course, groups of senior managers were required to develop a project as a way of improving their team-building and cooperation skills. One group chose to investigate the installation of an EIS so that monthly review meetings (MRMs) could become Electronic MRMs (EMRMs). Four senior managers from different departments comprised the project group; the project owner was from a fifth department.

The exercise had benefits for management training and project administration. However, group members subsequently admitted that the project was prompted by a semi-artificial activity rather than a genuine business need. This made the project complex to manage as well as taking longer than planned.

The project team completed their work. The EIS was installed and became operational. The system produces useful, though basic, information. Users are now requesting changes to the information format to meet their specific needs. These requests will make the project more 'real' but will also stretch available resources.

The EIS was demonstrated at a recent MRM to an enthusiastic response. However, it is not without difficulties. The nature of the EIS project with various strands of information made it difficult to designate a single project owner. This, in turn, made training tasks more complex than otherwise need be.

EIS is currently managed by ISD. However, as the first EIS application was sales-oriented, ISD is ceding responsibility to each sales division. ISD is training other project team members who, in turn, will train colleagues in their department.

E-mail and networking

One project which has been driven by business needs is E-mail. The ISD manager was keen to install an E-mail and networking system which he thought would be beneficial for the company. Installation would be relatively simple as TIU occupied the whole building which was recabled prior to tenure.

The ISD manager did not have a sufficiently strong justification until an internal audit provided him with one. The audit questionnaire circulated to every employee revealed that people were unhappy with the telephone system and internal mail service. Responses to the questionnaire indicated that it was difficult to contact colleagues by telephone. This was understandable as the company was now on two sites and everyone was very busy.

This information gave the ISD manager the opportunity to meet a stated business need. ISD had already prepared background details and the project was implemented in 1992. The impetus provided by the company-wide request meant that the project was completed in five months instead of a scheduled twelve months. Every employee, whether in an administrative or operations function, now has access to E-mail. Both management and staff consider E-mail and networking a great success.

Training in the new system

Towards the end of a project ISD conducts system testing with users and trains them on the new system. If a large number of people is to be trained (as was the case with E-mail) training may be in collaboration with the TIU training department. This was set up to train TIU dealers but its facilities can be used for training TIU staff.

As part of end-user training ISD draws up procedure documents. However, users are responsible for producing user documentation to encourage ownership of the new system.

A current training project parallels upgrading to a five-year old computer system. As an induction to the new system, ISD is helping groups of users to work with the parts of the upgraded system which relate to their job.

Managing IT

Information Systems Department

The Information Systems Department (ISD) has a staff of ten. Five people work on IT development and five on operations support and end-user computing. Outside contractors provide additional expertise, when necessary. A number of ISD staff from Weybridge have been on secondment to the German subsidiary.

The ISD manager joined the company in June 1988. Computer systems and staffing levels had failed to keep pace with rapid company growth at an annual rate of 100 per cent for each of the previous three years. A newly installed AS/400 was in the process of 'bedding down' and was generating inaccurate and unreliable data. This caused employees to lack confidence in and distrust the systems. Initially, the ISD manager's main job was to ensure the efficient working of the new systems.

The first six months were devoted to consolidating the systems to the satisfaction of ISD and end users. For the ISD manager one of the major projects was to ensure that the systems were running as he wanted them to run and to improve the service for end users.

IT planning and decision making

TIU has no formal business strategy which includes IS/IT. Planning for IT relates in part to TIU's mid-term business plan, which has a fixed three-year time horizon. The mid-term plan outlines annual targets and is coordinated by the planning manager. ISD is one of several internal sources which has an input to the mid-term plan.

The ISD manager monitors the plan for any implications to his department (e.g. systems changes, increases or decreases in capacity). This allows ISD to react to imminent changes. Other factors in the mid-term plan may have indirect implications for the ISD. For example, renegotiated leasing arrangements, where the company may need to relocate, could affect company infrastructure.

IT planning tends to be a reaction to business decisions. The ISD manager stresses the importance of his involvement at an early stage of business planning as a prerequisite for timely implementation of systems for business purposes. TIU's business departments give feedback to the ISD manager on what TIU needs to do in comparison with competitors, although competitors' IT capabilities remain obscure.

Occasionally, senior managers from Tokyo request a short-term plan in which ISD outlines its intentions for one year ahead. Part of this plan contains projects outstanding and the status of projects from the ISPWG (Information Systems Planning Working Group).

Senior management is responsible for the accuracy of mid-term planning. The ISD manager outlines his plans to the financial director, to whom he reports. As a board member the financial director is involved with his fellow directors in agreeing the contents of the mid-term plan. This makes the ISD manager's task more straightforward, as the financial director is aware of the company's business direction.

TIU monitors the effectiveness of its IT systems through the work of two distinct groups: the Information Systems Planning Committee (ISPC) and the Information Systems Planning Working Group (ISPWG).

Information Systems Planning Committee

The ISPC is fundamentally a steering committee which makes and implements IT-related decisions. Membership comprises the four general managers and the three local directors (two of whom are Japanese managers on UK assignment).

The ISPC determines major strategic issues pertaining to IT and makes decisions on IT projects, particularly those which are resource-intensive and thus likely to be large and expensive. The ISPC does not originate projects (this is the function of the European Steering Committee).[2]

However, the ISPC has several important duties. It approves company-wide IT projects: prioritizes IT proposals; monitors IT-related activities; and arbitrates in IT-related disputes between business groups. The ISPC also resolves issues arising from the ISPWG.

Information Systems Planning Working Group

The ISPWG functions at a lower managerial level. Membership of the ISPWG comprises senior managers including department heads and senior managers responsible for marketing, finance and distribution. The ISPWG is responsible for:

- Determining IS priorities
- Determining resource allocation
- Raising IT projects
- Making recommendations to ISPC.

The ISPWG meets every two months. Interim meetings are held every month to review current projects.

ISPWG meetings are chaired by the ISD manager who is also responsible for preparing working papers for the group's consideration. The working group considers recently completed projects, work in progress and planned projects. Projects which are not contentious and within agreed budget limits originate from the ISPWG. Those that encounter opposition are passed up to the ISPC for review and a decision.

Budgeting for IT projects

Budgets and objectives are set in 6-monthly periods: from April to September and from October to March. ISD needs to consider a 12 months' time frame to take into account the 6 months' budgetary period and include a forecast for the following 6 months. The ISD manager and the commissioning department manager negotiate budget overspending when departments submit their IT requirements late, and these have not been included in the current budget.

The ISD manager next creates a budget, based on his awareness of future projects, to cover the requested project. The finance director gives budget clearance as the ISD manager has a relatively low 'sign-off' budget ceiling.

In order to gain budget clearance the ISD manager first briefs the finance director on aspects of the proposed project still being discussed, including potential benefits and financial implications. Briefings usually take place on several occasions over a period of time and include the different options available and cost implications over different pay-back periods.

The ISD budget covers all IT expenditure throughout the company. Exceptions are individual PCs and standard, non-networked PC packages for which individual departments are responsible. The ISD manager budgets for projects, including pilots, for all other departments. Capital equipment is depreciated at differing rates. Computer hardware is depreciated over four years (25 per cent per annum); software for the mainframe computer and networked computers over five years (20 per cent per annum); personal computers over two years (50 per cent per annum).

Project objectives determine which major projects are raised and carried forward, unless projects are the result of an urgent mandatory requirement. Objectives usually relate to improvements to services or projects.

Implementing IT projects

Individual managers generate most IT projects, which begin with a formal written request. This pro-forma request document is signed off by the requesting head of department, as the cost centre manager. TIU follows this conventional procedure whether the work is for one day or one year.

The ISPWG gives approval for the project, which will be allocated a level of priority. ISD discusses proposed projects with each requesting division and helps the division to prioritize its projects according to the benefits to the company. Urgent requests, for example responding to government or EU legislation, receive highest priority and total ISD effort.

ISD presents the ISPWG with a 'top five' priority list from each division. Only the top five requests are discussed, thus saving time. Projects which are one of the top five priorities for more than one division gain an overall priority rating. When a large project is proposed ISD allocates a percentage of its own total resource to the project. ISD normally works on two or three projects concurrently.[3]

Projects are planned task by task and resources are allocated on a task-by-task basis using the software Project for Windows. ISD has attempted to spread experience through company-wide projects.

Project teams are set up at this time. The ISD manager and the project originator nominate a project leader and decide other members of the project team. An informal project team may consist solely of a small number of on-site staff. Larger projects may need external consultants.

The ISD monitors projects against a plan and discusses progress with the project originator. Written reports on status and progress are sent to the ISPWG every two months. To save time during urgent projects, decisions between project members are communicated by E-mail. Project team members have an opportunity to respond without attending formal project meetings.

Auditing IT

TIU has two sets of audits. An independent external IT or financial audit is conducted by an international firm of management consultants. Audit teams from Toshiba Corporation conduct an internal business audit, which includes IT.

In preparation for their annual statutory audit of the company, external auditors carry out an IT risk audit to assess the degree to which systems are tamper-proof. Auditors investigate logical or physical access to the computer system software and data. The investigation includes the use of profiles and passwords; how regularly passwords are changed; how back-up files are made and where these are stored. If TIU demonstrates secure procedures to protect its computer systems, these need be audited less frequently.

Internal audit

Approximately every five years audit teams from Toshiba Corporation carry out extremely rigorous internal audits in Toshiba subsidiaries worldwide. A four-man audit team spends approximately ten days with the company and audits all aspects of the business. The team spends between 1 and 2 days in each department and uses an IT specialist on a part-time basis to help audit ISD.

Prior to the internal audit exercise, the audit department in Tokyo sends the subsidiary company a 30-page questionnaire. Each department head completes the questionnaire and returns it, together with supporting documentation, retaining one copy for his department. The audit team uses these documents to prepare for their practical inspection 2–3 months later. The audit team brings copies of the questionnaire, annotated for reference. The team also reads the subsidiary's previous audit report.

The team has universal access to information and can, and does, ask anyone for any company document. The investigation is very thorough and precise. It includes how often door locks are changed, how business forecasts are made and how quickly staff submit travel claims. The team also checks that every item of equipment valued at more then £500 carries an asset identification sticker. Naturally, with this attention to detail, the team works a 12-hour day.

The audit activity completed, the team submits a written confidential report to the board of directors. Although this is not available to departments, managers generally receive a one-page list of objectives. The managing director informs staff of the result of the audit.

In the most recent internal audit, Tokyo awarded TIU an A1 rating. This signifies that it is one of the best-run Toshiba subsidiaries worldwide.

Notes

1 TIU delivers product in 10–12 hours. Commercial feedback suggests that this is faster than most competitors.
2 The European Steering Committee, of which the TIU Managing Director is a member, holds meetings in Germany and is charged with developing IT systems for Toshiba's European subsidiaries. Systems for the various business groups at TUI are developed by the European Steering Committee.
3 Day-to-day project support accounts for approximately 10 per cent of ISD's resources. Another 20 per cent is allocated to a major project, of which more than one may be running at any one time. A further 20 per cent is added to unplanned or small tasks for other departments.

Part Three
Weighing the Evidence

In Part One we provided the essential background against which to view our case studies. We reviewed the current state of the strategic battle between Western and Japanese companies and discussed various perspectives on the strengths and weaknesses of the participants. In particular, we looked ahead to the coming strategic battles between Japan and the West which are likely to be fought in Europe. Next, we moved to the strategic role of IT in this battle – a minor role in the past but increasingly significant in the future. Finally, we considered certain aspects of Japanese management style which seem to differ fundamentally from those in the West.

In Part Two we presented the ten case studies. In each case we concentrated on the business impact of IT, especially the strategic impact, and the way in which IT had been managed.

Now, in Part Three, we revisit the themes of Part One in the context of the case study material. In Chapter 14, **Japanese management of IT**, we examine how the IT resource has been perceived and managed in the companies. Chapter 15, **The business impact and strategic use of IT**, analyses the cases by means of the frameworks provided in Chapter 2. These frameworks allow us to assess the role of IT in the various companies with greater precision than purely descriptive methods would permit. A particular dimension of IT management, **Head office control**, is the subject of Chapter 16 and here we draw on information collected during visits to company headquarters in Japan and by means of interviews conducted there. In the final chapter, **Eclipsing the sun?** we draw our conclusions and make some predictions about the likely outcome of the strategic battle.

14
Japanese management of IT

'The Japanese manage by panic' a number of British managers replied when we asked them to describe how their Japanese colleagues manage IT. Several anecdotes usually followed describing painfully slow decision making; decisions made in Tokyo which were inappropriate for local operations; ill-advised decisions to purchase obsolete computer equipment; purpose-built software that was years out of date. Several managers described a mismatch between their own experiences and publicized Japanese success stories. 'Day-to-day reality,' they said, 'is vastly different'. One manager expressed the opinion that 'the Japanese don't know how to use the technology they've created'.

We were intrigued. Could these statements and anecdotes be referring to the same managers whose style and techniques have made corporate Japan the envy of the world? Whose manufacturing ingenuity has stretched the boundaries of what is technologically possible? Who have earned a deservedly celebrated reputation for using advanced technology to produce state-of-the-art products? Or could there be an obverse side to Japanese manufacturing and technological know-how? We considered the different implications of using technology for product and process technology and using information technology for business benefits and competitive advantage. What are the implications of managing IT and IT used for management benefit?

Product and process technology

Since the late 1960s and early 1970s when Japanese goods began to gain noticeably increasing market shares, consumers and competitors have grown used to high-tech products from the drawing boards and robot-populated assembly lines of Japanese manufacturing plants. Innovative companies have used technology to design new processes and gain competitive advantage over their Western counterparts.

Well-publicized success stories of Japanese ingenuity and expertise have described how companies use state-of-the-art technology to produce manufactured goods which consumers want. Some, like the Sony Walkman, were completely innovative products that consumers did not even know they wanted. Credit card-sized radios broadcast travel, tourism and topical news to Japanese tourists and retirees in Australia. Securities houses have software programs which match clients' repayment and debt preferences with worldwide investment choices. A major convenience store chain in Japan uses point of sale data to reorganize its product displays twice daily.

These examples merely describe the present. For the near future a world-class consumer goods manufacturer has announced plans to make cameras that operate without film; TV screens flat enough to hang like a picture on a wall; telephones able to translate multi-lingual conversations; and tape recorders as small as a matchbox.

Japanese companies are undoubtedly highly competent at using technology for product innovation and process technology, as these and similar well-publicized success stories testify. Our case studies show that Japanese companies have used IT extensively for basic business automation and that IT for this purpose is competently managed. However, as the following incidents exemplify, there are startling contradictions, even at this basic level of computer operations:

- One company installing a mainframe computer with a computer language that was superseded in the mid-1970s
- Financial traders who use outdated software
- A company which waited patiently for two years for head office to produce purpose-built software discovered maintenance instructions written in Japanese when attempting to rectify a fault
- A newly hired manager who found that his department's mainframe computer was so old that the manufacturer had long ceased to service it
- A computer network in which information sent from London to Paris is routed through Tokyo
- Company directors needing help from lower-level colleagues to access computer information.

We wondered what accounted for the mismatch between the management of product and process technology to design and produce state-of-the-art consumer products and the management of information technology for business benefit. In our opinion there could be a number of explanations.

Turning to the case studies for enlightenment, we reviewed how Japanese companies manage their IT resource. We considered a number of issues, including cultural aspects in a Japanese subsidiary company, Japanese management practices, management attitudes towards IT, identifying business benefits, IT development, organizing projects and learning from past experiences.

The culture of a Japanese subsidiary

In a Japanese subsidiary a number of influences affect the cultural aspects of the working environment and encourage or moderate Japanese management practices. These factors are both internal and external and include the length of time that a subsidiary company has been established, the percentage of Japanese managers in the total workforce; and the degree of intention on the part of senior Japanese managers to apply 'home-grown' management routines and conventions. In practice the management styles within a Japanese subsidiary company are the subtle combination of a range of such factors.

Arguably, senior Japanese management attitudes most determine the degree to which Japanese management styles are part of company culture. The dispositions of the senior Japanese director and his fellow directors sets the ground rules for management practices, if not throughout the company, certainly at the higher levels of seniority. The degree of 'Japaneseness' in the behaviour of a company's managers is likely to be diluted by directors who have had previous overseas assignments in a foreign environment. Japanese managers who are familiar with non-Japanese working environments are less likely to insist on Japanese work procedures. Such managers are also more likely to promote a more 'neutral' working atmosphere in the workplace and to work more successfully in its cultural landscape.

A number of our informants suggested that one distinguishing feature of a successful Japanese manager working overseas is an ability to switch appropriately between home and host cultures. Some Japanese managers are able to maintain Japanese protocols when dealing with head office colleagues while continuing to meet the cultural expectations of local managers. Conversely, a Japanese manager who has sole recourse to Japanese management styles risks nurturing ill will of local colleagues. Unfamiliar practices may make local managers feel uncomfortable.

One British manager explained the resentment felt by himself and his colleagues when their managing director bought an expensive leaving present for an employee and divided the total cost between the number of staff. This conflicted with the accepted local practice of circulating a memo or greetings card and allowing individuals to decide how much to contribute; the total collected being the amount that would be spent on a farewell gift.

According to our informants, local staff who feel uncomfortable with the management style of a senior Japanese colleague may distance themselves from the person concerned thus reducing their contribution to the team effort. Once noticed this could cause friction on both sides and encourage the Japanese manager to exclude local expertise from his team.

A subsidiary company's culture can be identified by a number of subtle clues. For example, subscriptions to Japanese newspapers and magazines which are placed on tables in reception areas next to copies of *The Times* and *Financial Times*. Some offices displayed glass cabinets containing Japanese artifacts, others proudly displayed framed head office commendations and award certificates. In some subsidiaries, particularly the dealing rooms of securities houses, some computer screens displayed information in Japanese.

In one subsidiary in the City of London a head office inspection team congregated in the reception area. The group of *salarimen* dressed in

184 *The Japanese Advantage?*

identical dark blue single-breasted suits, white shirts, and dark blue ties could have been transposed directly from a Tokyo subway station.

As Japanese subsidiary companies have established themselves in Europe, they have extended their supplier and client bases. Initially trading solely with other Japanese subsidiaries (overseas, Japanese companies noticeably congregate together for example in Dortmund, The Hague, South Wales), Japanese subsidiaries now use more local suppliers and serve the needs of local communities. Under these circumstances, Japanese middle managers are replaced by other nationals. Some financial services companies who deal in newly emerging markets now employ various European and Middle Eastern trading staff.

Japanese management practices

While not all companies in our study replicated all the practices found in a Japanese company on its home territory, most used one or more recognizably Japanese management techniques. The most common is the use of *nemawashi*: the system of consensus decision making.

As we explained in Chapter 3, *nemawashi* allows middle managers to inform superiors of their ideas and opinions and enables senior managers to keep in touch with 'grassroots' thinking. *Nemawashi* is said to be a more democratic form of management as subordinates feel that they are shaping corporate decisions. However, in the opinion of some British managers, *nemawashi* has two disadvantages: decision making tends to be slowed down when opinions are sought from all parties; and some managers lamented the 'difficulty of getting Japanese middle managers to make a decision'. Some Japanese managers we spoke to sympathized with these opinions.

At NMGB *nemawashi* lubricates decision making. Directors and managers meet informally outside formal committee meeting arrangements. When managers are scheduled to make a formal presentation to an Executive Committee their papers are circulated prior to the formal meeting. Executives can give managers help and advice prior to their formal presentation and presentations can be clarified before being made public. From their committee experience, executives can advise managers on how discussion papers should best be presented. NMGB's open-plan offices encourage spontaneous meetings between colleagues at lower levels of management.

Hitachi Europe Ltd (HEL) also practises *nemawashi*, which it has adopted to prevent lower-level management decisions from giving unexpected surprises to senior managers. The system gives all parties in a decision the opportunity (and obligation) to inform colleagues of their thoughts and opinions. The managing director receives a copy of the *ringisho* document listing people who approve a proposal. At Japan Travel Bureau Europe (JTBE) *nemawashi* allows senior managers to confer with colleagues in other departments and clarify proposals before approaching the managing director for a decision.

The two Nissan companies in our study stressed the importance of individual self-development for their workforce. NMGB's end-user reporting (EUR) systems enables employees to process on their desktop computers information that was formerly available only on the mainframe computer. An analyst helps users gain maximum benefit from the system. Users can now produce reports with a more professional appearance. An adjunct to self-development of the individual is *kaizen* (constant improvement). At NMGB the *kaizen* philosophy is a fundamental part of the organization. *Kaizen* guides all business practices, for example the launch of a new product, customer care, personnel development and planning. Employees use the principles of *kaizen* when reviewing their own performance.

NMGB's encouragement of networking by allocating a Japanese adviser to newly hired managers is another way of enriching individual expertise. This is supplemented by the company's practice of matrix management through team building. NMGB encourages team members to accumulate a broad base of expertise by asking them to work on a variety of business projects. This is integral to an individual's understanding of business issues from an IT standpoint or IT issues from a business point of view. Rotating expertise in this way strengthens individual employees and the company. In such an atmosphere, specific job titles are deemed to be an encumbrance to flexible attitudes and working methods.

Like its sister company, NMUK manages ISD projects so that individual project members are able to work on any project. NMUK believes that the individual employee and the company are both best served by flexible working routines. NMUK's ISD prefers to recruit people who are interested in working to resolve business problems, rather than in IT for its own sake. The company's restriction to two computer languages makes post-recruitment training relatively straightforward. Having only two computer languages gives ISD staff a flexibility to work on any project. When a deadline becomes urgent ISD staff can complement any existing project team.

Japanese management attitudes towards IT

Our research evidence suggests that, generally, senior Japanese management is not as well informed about IT as their less senior colleagues would like. However, there are exceptions. In some companies a senior manager is sympathetic to the work of the IT department and gives encouragement and backing to IT projects. However, few members of a senior management cadre have an IT background; those who do are regarded, according to one IT manager, as a 'prize catch'. Conversely, when the managing director and his fellow board members lack awareness of IT issues this is liable to adversely affect IT decision making. In such a situation IT decision making may be slowed down considerably as explanations are sought and given.

Aversion to conflict and risk

Respondents from a variety of Japanese companies describe Japanese management as exceedingly cautious in their business decision making. This feature is compounded in certain industries, e.g. banking and financial services, where prudence is a way of life. However, Japanese managers are said to be averse to conflict rather than to risk.

Some decisions, for example those which relate to IT, may foster a cautious approach. This may be amplified by unfamiliarity with the topic and an inclination to prevent loss of face by making an unsuitable, and potentially costly, decision. A high-profile decision would be readily apparent to end users and most other employees. Several managers told us that when faced with uncertainty, Japanese management would most likely take a 'wait and see' approach.

In Japanese companies in a variety of industries, including banking, financial services, consumer goods and industrial products manufacturing, both Japanese and British managers reported evidence of changes to this way of thinking. Some IT department managers have noticed increased responsibility for IT decision making since joining their organizations. In some companies regular briefing meetings take place in which the middle manager formally updates the senior-level manager on IT-related matters. This is particularly important when the senior person has little or no IT training or expertise.

Positive attitudes

One recent managing director at JTBE was an enthusiastic supporter of IT projects and constantly 'pushed' the IT department to explore new IT project areas. The current managing director has given his official support to plans to upgrade the JETS I booking system. At JVC (UK) the computer manager reports to the finance director who is responsible for local IT budgets up to a certain amount. Although he has no direct IT background, the finance manager keeps himself informed through regular contact with Computer Room staff and their concerns.

The managing director of Kobe Steel Europe (KSE) saw an IT opportunity when he recommended colleagues to be more ambitious in their plans to expand IT facilities. KSE subsequently included a requisition in an otherwise routine proposal to head office for equipment to build an office-wide IT platform. Head office created an investigative working party, which interviewed managers at KSE on a fact-finding mission in London. The investigation has led to improvements in some administrative procedures using IT. The new managing director at one of Sony's sales divisions with an IT background gave encouragement to the work of the business analyst from Sony (UK)'s Development Services Department when she came to his division to prepare a strategic study of IT possibilities.

In general, IT managers felt that it is useful for their work to report to a senior manager who is an 'IT champion' willing to 'wave a flag for IT'. Companies with such managers are more likely to use IT more creatively.

IT for administrative support

In a number of the companies researched, IT is regarded by senior management mainly as an administrative support function. IT systems remain a 'back-office' function intended to support the company's main area of business activity. In some companies IT is the responsibility of the administrative manager. Few companies reported plans to use IT as a strategic resource to gain competitive advantage. Although respondents may have used different phraseology, the gist of their feelings is described by one manager:

> As a division of a large corporation, we are not our own masters. We can't draw up our own business plans without being conscious of what is happening in Japan.

A manager in another company spoke of being 'at the end of the value chain from Tokyo' and outlined the decisions that his division inherits from head office in Tokyo. His division's function, he said, is

> ...to sell what the factory makes. We can, and do, make suggestions about what should be made, but our main role is to sell what the factory produces.

For some companies, relocation can provide the necessary stimulus for a fresh management viewpoint about the place of IT. HEL's relocation in 1990 from an urban site to rural surroundings on the River Thames at Maidenhead prompted management to bring IT nearer the mainstream of corporate activity. HEL, which sees itself as a flexible organization, regards IT as the means by which it can react swiftly to changing customer needs. HEL believes that the ability to make rapid responses to changing market conditions leads to competitive advantage.

At NMGB, business issues drive the use of technology and senior management sees technology as a means of securing business advantage. NMGB's philosophy is that IT belongs to the business and contributes as much as possible to that business. This view is also evident at Sony (UK), where the Development Services Department section of the ISD helps business departments to identify how IT can resolve business needs.

IT expenditure as a cost

Japanese management regards IT expenditure as a cost, partly because managers have difficulty in demonstrating that IT is a source of generated income. In some companies, sales divisions are responsible for showing the business benefits of IT development.

Managers in various companies stated that functions which generate income take precedence over those that do not; an important distinction where budget considerations are concerned. Unless expenditure patently enhances corporate development (e.g. by improving production or manufacturing), expenditure is curtailed. A composite of what several managers told us is :

> IT is not seen as the top job as it doesn't generate income. The functions which don't generate income tend to take second place to those that do create income...IT is seen as a cost rather than an investment and this has prevented expenditure of, for example, PCs due to cost reasons. Unless expenditure can be demonstrated to benefit corporate development, e.g. to augment a marketing strategy, expenditure does not go ahead.

Some managers we spoke to expressed their frustration that IT expenditure can sometimes be misdirected. For example, when expenditure is approved it is for the senior Japanese managers, and may sometimes be unjustified on work grounds. Newly purchased PCs may be sitting unused on a desk in one part of the building while in another a team of people are trying to work without a PC. However, things are changing and computer-literate staff are showing their Japanese colleagues how to attain the optimum use of their machines.

A number of companies have introduced cost-cutting initiatives. These are being used to identify operating costs with a view to instigating cost-reduction programmes. In the financial services industry, companies are trying to reduce technology costs per trading desk.

Some companies assess the worth of IT investment by evaluating IT expenditure with its potential to generate income. Japan Travel Bureau Europe (JTBE) is one company which is conscious of a balance between expenditure and income generated. New IT systems are assessed in terms of the income they are likely to create which is compared with development and implementation costs. The company seeks IT systems which allow an increased volume of work to be produced by the same, or reduced, number of staff.

Outsourcing IT

In common with their Western counterparts, Japanese managers are debating the advantages and disadvantages of outsourcing IT. A number of Japanese companies have chosen to outsource parts of their IT facility. For some this is seen as a way to gain cost benefits; for others it is regarded as common sense to leave IT to experts and 'stick to the knitting' of core business activity.

Along with a number of other companies in its business sector, DEL regards itself primarily as a financial services house not a communications engineering company. Company policy advocates that IT systems are to be outsourced to suppliers as much as possible. As DEL is now responsible for European-wide IT, the alternative to outsourcing would bring about vast increases, particularly in staffing levels. For some companies the maintenance and servicing of PCs may be all that is allowed to the outsourced agency. DEL, for example, augments its own expertise by using an external contractor for routine servicing and maintenance of its PC network.

Other companies engage an outsourced agency to manage their global communications network. Global communications companies maintain staffing 24 hours a day, 365 days per annum. Most companies would be perturbed by the expense of managing such services on this scale. Senior management at DEL believe that the quarterly network management fee paid to the outsourcing agency represents a small fraction of the cost that would be incurred if DEL decided to maintain its own communications systems.

Identifying business needs

It is interesting to compare how the companies in the case studies identify business needs. In some, the procedure involves regular personal contact between ISD staff and end-user departments in order to identify business concerns and match these to proposed IT systems. Other companies, perhaps because of their larger size, supplement personal contacts by a series of IT planning committees. In a third approach, companies nurture hybrid managers who have both IT and business knowledge and who can use skills and knowledge from both disciplines to help the company fully to use its IT potential. Some companies blend these approaches.

JVC is one company where business concerns are identified through personal contact between ISD staff and end-user departments. JVC's Computer Room serves all company departments so it is vital that regular contact between staff is maintained. Initial discussions help the Computer Room to gauge departments' concerns. The user department then completes a request form and sends it to the Computer Room for detailed evaluation. Highest priority is given to requests which overlap with a number of departments. The issues involved are clarified during further discussions between the Computer Room and the department, which also enable the Computer Room to decide whether the request should be approved.

Daiwa Europe's Systems Planning Department is responsible for managing IT communications and providing MIS for trading activities. As part of its working brief, the Systems Planning Department looks for ways in which existing systems can be upgraded. Accordingly, the department is the first point of contact for departments requiring IT solutions to their business problems.

Hitachi Europe's ISD manager maintains regular contact with other company departments to ensure that user departments are kept informed of IT projects. In its quest to use IT to provide a more proficient service for customers for its semiconductors, HEL organizes liaison meetings between a Marketing Systems Coordinator and the customer. These meetings aim to discover customers' concerns and needs. Consultations between HEL managers and customers drive the development of IT systems at HEL. At TIU, the various business departments inform ISD of systems that they would like to see implemented. The company's ISD manager emphasizes the importance of involving his department at an early stage of IT planning.

Committees play a part in IT planning at Sony (UK). ISD managers and senior representatives from sales and support divisions attend annual meetings to decide systems planning. Meetings are scheduled between September and October to prepare for a review by the IS steering committee. With membership comprising SUK directors and the ISD manager, this committee examines and approves IS strategy, proposed projects and related budgets. Decisions made by the IS steering committee are passed to budget planning meetings which take place every January. Budgets passed during this round of meetings are thus in place for projects to be implemented after the start of the next financial year in April.

At NMGB the IS steering committee decides business priorities and company objectives. The committee meets monthly to decide company-wide IS priorities. ISD reports on the current status of projects and resource allocation to the steering committee.

NMGB and NMUK nurture hybrid managers who have both IT and business knowledge in the firm belief that such managers are best placed to help their organizations to manage IT. In the opinion of NMGB's management, business strategies and IT strategies are facets of the same business perspective. Each business area has its own ISD team which helps to bridge any gap between IT and business interests. Over time, NMGB intends to narrow this gap until it is no longer perceptible. The narrower the gap, the greater the possibility of improved communication flow. This, in turn, will bring about a closer relationship between IT systems and business developments.

NMUK plans its systems development work on a production-line basis. Project managers make themselves aware of business priorities by working closely with user departments. Project managers are responsible for writing a project-initiation document and discussing implications with other project managers and the development manager. This document is passed to systems analysis teams for appropriate action. These teams present their work to project managers, a procedure which helps project managers to be better informed about systems in different business areas. In this way, project managers build up a company-wide expertise that is of practical benefit when they manage further projects.

The Development Services Department of Sony (UK) has a number of business analysts whose work involves investigating possible new computer applications for business departments. With a background in IT and business, business analysts are strongly placed to identify business needs which can be fulfilled with appropriate IT systems. Sony's business analysts are seconded to sales divisions where they analyse business needs and propose appropriate IT systems. Their dual background enables business analysts to manage projects, including the financial aspects.

In the case studies, companies identify business needs in a number of ways. Personal contact between ISD staff and user departments ensures that business needs originate from user departments, that the departments' needs are clarified and that decisions can be explained. However, other departments and the company at large may remain unaware of proposed IT projects unless some form of communication, e.g. a company newsletter, publicizes these.

When companies use committees to identify business needs, representatives from user departments can constitute committee membership. This helps to ensure that business needs are subject to cross-functional discussion, during which alternative viewpoints can be raised and IT proposals can be potentially shared between departments. Using specialists with business and IT knowledge who work directly with user departments means that these departments gain additional expertise from hybrid managers.

IT decision making

In Chapter 3 we identified some of the contributory factors which influence Japanese management decision making. So far in this chapter we have outlined some of the management styles found in the companies in the case studies. Needless to say, IT decision making, or indeed decisions made in any company department, are much more complex. IT decisions are influenced not only by the cultural factors which we have discussed but also by, among other things, relations between the subsidiary and its head office.

At Hitachi Europe Ltd (HEL) the relationship between HEL and head office in Japan is a predominant factor in IT decision making. Prior to 1989, the group was organized into divisions according to product function (Semiconductors, Computers, etc.), and each division was empowered to make its own overseas organizational decisions, including choice of computer systems. After reorganization, decision-making parameters had a geographical basis. HEL, one of the results of the reorganization, inherited diverse computer systems on different platforms e.g. IBM mainframes and operating systems, UNIX machines and systems. A major IT priority for the new company was to ensure that all systems could communicate with each other.

At Kobe Steel Europe (KSE) local IT plans are amalgamated into the divisional budget, which is submitted to the data-processing department in the annual budgeting exercise. Head office does not exert rigid control over IT strategy and divisional IT departments are allowed sufficient scope to make their own IT investment decisions. Some departments use this freedom of action to establish their own LANs which access company-wide MIS systems.

In a number of companies the ISD manager (or one of his team) is responsible for discussing possible IT projects with end-user departments. Frequently, the speed with which projects are implemented depends on the urgency of the business need or the number of departments that will benefit.

NMGB's ISD takes pains to harmonize its way of working with business departments' needs, and reacts swiftly to end-users' urgent requests, even when this means suspending existing project work. Discussions between end-user departments and ISD analyse the business problem in terms of information needed and attempt to identify the type of system that can best deliver it. An IS steering committee meets once a month to decide IS priorities for information systems. Senior managers from all company departments make up the committee to prevent bias. The ISD works closely with the IS steering committee (for example, reporting on work in progress, available resources, and business requests in hand) and scheduling available resources.

Due to the global nature of its CRS systems, the amount of decision-making freedom allowed to ANA's overseas subsidiaries is limited to the kind of PCs that are preferred for the office. Overseas offices decide their own back-office systems, which include databases for business intelligence. New systems are requested from head office.

JVC (UK) operates two six-monthly trading periods, and IT budgets and investment spending are timed to fit into these. As a profit centre, JVC (UK) generates funding from local sales activities. The computer manager makes proposals for expenditure on computer hardware and software and discusses these with the finance director who has board-level responsibility for the Computer Room.

At NMGB ISD avoids boundaries between development and maintenance as each business area has its own ISD team which is responsible for both areas. Regular departmental meetings usually include a report-back on business activity and an 'open forum' for discussing improvements to work practices. Other business units in the company hold similar meetings. With its large number of staff, ISD separates into two groups for such meetings. Leadership of each group by a facilitator from a different business responsibility ensures cross-fertilization of ideas.

HEL identifies requirements for IT systems in a variety of ways. At customer liaison meetings a Marketing Systems Coordinator and other members from the customers discuss various current problems. Consultations with MIS development staff attempt to develop appropriate systems to resolve perceived problems. Improvements in HEL's warehousing system and consignment documentation were prompted by customers' suggestions. Government and EU regulations also give impetus to IT systems development at HEL.

At JVC (UK) the Computer Room serves all company departments and discusses new initiatives and decisions to upgrade systems with all departments. Such discussions help the Computer Room to determine user department's business concerns, which in turn inform IT development plans. End-user departments send a request form to the Computer Room outlining their requirements. This is evaluated by the Computer Room which gives particular consideration to requirements common to a number of departments or which are likely to benefit several users as well as the company. The Computer Room decides whether to accept or reject the request after further discussion with user departments. End-user department managers (e.g. sales, marketing) who found themselves inheriting systems which they considered unsuitable for their department's requirements spent resources to 'customize' non-business systems for their own purposes.

At Sony (UK), identifying systems to meet business needs is the function of the Development Services Department, which tackles this situation in three ways. First, business analysts work with user divisions to assess business needs and to propose appropriate systems. As 'hybrid managers' business analysts bring their specialist knowledge of IT to business issues. Their expertise enables them to analyse business needs; manage projects to implement recommendations; and take financial responsibility for users' ISD requirements.

Second, the ISD's System Enhancement Project (SEP) concentrates on smaller IT projects which divisions may wish to undertake. This is a separate line of contact between users and ISD, and can be additional to work that a business analyst may be undertaking. Third, the relationship between the ISD and its client divisions means that the latter can approach ISD's specialist units with suggestions and ideas for projects.

IT systems development

Our research indicates that Japanese multinational companies generally choose from three alternatives for IT systems development:

1 Buy in IT expertise from a local software house
2 Develop IT systems locally in the company's own Systems Development Department
3 Develop IT systems in a Systems Development Department at head office.

As a company moves from 1 to 3 costs increase and flexibility decreases. Smaller companies take the first option. Larger companies may have progressed through each of these stages as their funding and IT commitment increases.

1 Buying in or developing in-house?

Buying in local software house expertise gives a company most flexibility at lowest cost. Smaller companies and those newly arrived in the UK market often choose this method. However, off-the-shelf products are not always available for some tasks (for example, sophisticated trading activities in the financial services industry).

Once established, a subsidiary can start its own IT development capability. This can ensure purpose-built software in line with the company's new market-entry strategies. However, recruiting software expertise on a direct-hire basis is expensive and some companies employ consultant software engineers full-time. The third alternative, IT systems development in a corporate Systems Development Department in Japan, ensures global compatibility but may necessitate local enhancement to meet particular market needs.

The choice of buying in or developing in-house depends on a number of factors, not least of which is the availability of a ready-made, off-the-shelf product. When a suitable product is available, buying in is less costly. An off-the-shelf product is unlikely in some industries. In the financial services industry, for example, purpose-built systems are a major source of competitive advantage. When spare capacity and resources allow, it is preferable to develop IT systems in-house to ensure a purpose-designed product and allow greater control over product development.

When appropriate technology is innovative (and costly) a company has little option but to commission development externally. One Japanese financial services company followed this option when the company realized that it would be prohibitively expensive to employ on a direct-hire basis the required number of engineers with the necessary software development skills. To conserve costs, the company employs several outside contractors to work exclusively on software development within the company. Japan Travel Bureau Europe employed a 'Special Projects Adviser' who worked at JTB for the duration of an IT project.

In the financial services industry many new financial software packages are originally developed by software houses in the United States; New York and Chicago have a particularly good reputation for such products. US software houses excel in designing futures trading software. London also has an active financial software development market. Not infrequently, software developed in the United States is further enhanced by software houses which service financial institutions in the City of London. Software houses frequently employ former financial traders as software development engineers.

Deregulation in the City's financial markets encouraged financial services companies to expand into new markets. With an increasing dependence on IT a number of companies established an internal software development capability. One Japanese bank undertook a joint project with a software house to develop purpose-built software to the bank's specifications when it wished to begin trading in financial markets for which no software was available.

2 Systems Development facility in Japan

Head office systems development facilities can be quite large: in some companies up to 250 full-time staff supplemented by as many as 1000 specialist engineers and systems designers join particular projects as outside contractors for the duration of development. Of these numbers as many as 50 per cent will have specialist industry expertise and the remaining 50 per cent will be specialists in systems development. Some companies, e.g. Nissan and Sony, realize the advantages of recruiting business specialists who can subsequently learn computer skills.

The existence of a Systems Development Department in Japan does not automatically mean that overseas branches use the latest technology. Several major Japanese banks devote the major part (as much as 90 per cent) of their Systems Development Department resources to developing

IT for domestic banking needs. Nor do innovations by a head office Systems Development Department necessarily imply immediate transfer to overseas subsidiaries. London-based officials of at least one Japanese subsidiary realize that it will be some time before they use the new technology demonstrated on an in-house video produced by its Systems Development Department.

3 Software from Tokyo

Head office Systems Development Departments often develop software programs for use by overseas subsidiaries. When this is the case head office will send a team of specialists to 'migrate' the program onto the local system. These specialists are also responsible for pre-operational training and post-migration monitoring of the system in use. Such a procedure can bring difficulties. A migration team insensitive to local self-esteem can adversely affect the morale of local staff. Instructions written in Japanese not only preclude local managers rectifying errors but can also promote a 'them and us' mentality.

During the run-up to the migration, as many data as possible are transferred manually, a procedure that helps to detect 'awkward' data. The migration itself is concerned mainly with the successful transfer of information which defied manual transfer. Checkpoints during the migration identify 'rogue' information which has evaded manual transfer. The specialist migration team returns to Tokyo shortly after the new system has been implemented.

ANA's head office in Tokyo has a team of programmers whose function is to enhance current systems. End users suggest additions to the existing system at annual CRS development meetings. HEL is obliged to follow the head office lead in terms of IT development in the interests of mutual compatibility of systems. However, each of Hitachi's trading zones has a level of internal autonomy, although they are obliged to maintain a dialogue with head office in Japan.

Head office in Tokyo develops standard software systems that are used in JVC offices throughout Europe. Managers from JVC's various European subsidiary companies meet to decide a common system. Local offices are allowed to develop their own domestic applications within the common standard system.

Migration from one system to another is very strictly controlled. Specialist migration teams from head office implement new systems and most companies have recognized routines for migrating systems developed in head office. Teams travel to a particular branch prior to the implementation, and remain on-site for the duration of the implementation period. Prior to the actual migration, training teams may conduct training sessions. A migration team is usually in constant touch with head office colleagues, who monitor the migration. Invariably, a collective decision is made to progress to the next phase. Regular reporting back to Tokyo during migration indicates any discrepancies which arise during the changeover.

Organizing IT projects

The companies in the case studies described their organization and management of IT projects. Procedures varied according to company size and the number of staff composing the IT department.

IT project management at JTBE involves a team from the company's IT Department with additional members from other relevant departments. Personnel from JTBE's European offices are included in some project teams, particularly where IT developments are intended for use throughout Europe. In addition to working with outside contractors and managing projects, the IT department has responsibility for in-house training. JVC (UK)'s Computer Room is responsible for IT systems which are used in the UK. Working closely with user departments, Computer Room staff write software programs according to UK business needs. The Computer Room is also responsible for managing training courses for users.

NMGB uses a matrix management style to manage business projects. Project teams consist of people with a range of expertise in business or technology. Project teams work to provide specific areas of the business with IT solutions. Team members are encouraged to work in a wide variety of projects (e.g. vehicle finance, dealer funding, parts distribution, corporate systems) so that they accumulate knowledge and expertise. This way of working builds up each department's skills base as well as developing the individual's competence in IT and business areas.

Over the life of a project, different people contribute their skills as needs arise. Certain individuals, for example those with a broad knowledge of business issues, form the project core. People with specific skills, e.g. computer programmers and systems analysts, move between different projects as their skills are needed. Needless to say, in such an environment friction-free interaction between members from different disciplines is vital. NMGB's corporate culture, where a minimum number of job titles gives individuals flexibility, encourages this.

NMUK manages projects in a similar way, indeed NMGB inherited some of its procedures from NMUK. NMUK's ISD recruits people who are interested in satisfying business requirements using IT, rather than those people who are solely interested in IT. Staff are rotated around different projects to develop their expertise. The department believes that this makes the work more interesting and contributes to the low turnover of staff (all ISD staff have four or more years' experience in the department).

Learning from past projects

Some companies frankly described IT projects that were not as successful as expected and which the company was able to use as a learning experience. Managers at JTBE outlined two instances where the company was able to learn from past experiences. The first related to the development of the JETS computerized booking system. The first model of the system, called JETS I, was developed for use in JTBE's European office by a project team consisting of staff from Europe. When the project was completed, the project team instigated training sessions on using the new system. At this stage, end users (operations staff from a sector generating a large volume of business) expressed their reluctance to become involved with the new system, and requested postponement of their involvement for several months.

One result of this situation is that publicity and training for the JETS II system have been brought forward to an earlier stage of development, so that end users have a greater involvement in the new system. A period of pre-training helps to explain the benefits of the system. This message is reiterated through articles in the JTBE newsletter. JTBE's managing director, an avid supporter of IT projects, has expressed his enthusiasm for the new system in written memos to all divisions of the organization.

The second example from JTBE relates to a project for a service for cost-conscious travellers on low budgets. After receiving recommendations for a number of available software packages from software houses, JTBE shelved the project. The project team noticed that the recommended systems involved a change in working routines which management could not endorse at the time.

The ISD at TIU faced a situation with an Executive Information System (EIS), which it introduced at the request of a group of senior managers participating in an in-house management course. The proposed benefit from the system was to convert monthly review meetings into electronic monthly review meetings. As part of a management training activity the project lacked an authentic business need, which gave it an unnecessary complexity, resulting in a longer than planned time frame. However, an enthusiastic response to the system from senior management and staff, coupled with genuine requests from users for changes to the system, means that the EIS has become a success.

Summary

Highly publicized reports in newspapers, journals and books have illustrated the remarkable successes of Japanese management in product and process technology. The plethora of Japanese-branded calculators and computers, televisions, radios and hi-fi equipment, cars and motorcycles bears witness to the uncanny ability of Japanese companies to design and manufacture products which satisfy consumer needs. For managers, the acknowledged advantages of Japanese production methods, including quality circles, TQM, *kaizen*, JIT and zero-defect manufacturing have made Japanese management techniques the envy of the world.

Our research suggests that Japanese management is also good at managing IT for automating business processes, although some of the examples we cite of mismanagement suggest that for some companies there is scope for improvement in this area. In some aspects of IT management, e.g. outsourcing, Japanese companies face decisions similar to their Western counterparts. In other aspects, e.g. management attitudes towards IT, culturally bound decision-making procedures and systems development in Tokyo, Japanese companies face challenges of a different nature.

Japanese management has a number of attributes which support judicious management of IT for strategic benefit. The process of consensus decision making (*nemawashi*) is suited to the exchange of IT ideas and proposals across departmental boundaries. This would be a useful forum for exploring IT possibilities on a pan-company scale. Similarly, there is the notion of rotating employees around a variety of projects to develop their business competence. This matrix style promotes individual learning and creates a learning atmosphere for the organization. Some companies were willing to share with us their experiences of earlier projects which enabled their organization to develop its facility for improvement.

However, as there are strengths, so there are weaknesses. In the opinion of some of the managers that we interviewed, commendable though *nemawashi* is for involving everyone in the decision-making process, it has at the same time the deficiency of slowing down corporate decisions. Other critics of *nemawashi* would also say that it encourages middle managers to rely on decisions from higher up in the hierarchy and to release middle managers from responsibility for creative thinking or from making decisions.

Positive attitudes by management contribute to an atmosphere which can induce IT creativity. We have cited some examples of senior management figures who realize this, but some of our research indicates that middle managers, especially those responsible for IT, are somewhat disappointed in the support they receive from their senior colleagues. Some managers, particularly IT and DP managers, said that professionally informed recommendations which they make about appropriate IT systems for their organizations seldom receive a reaction from management. Most likely, the recommendations disappear from the corporate landscape. However, not infrequently they tend to reappear at a later date as policy decisions under senior Japanese initiatives.

From our research evidence it seems that few Japanese companies have been, or are currently considering, using IT creatively for business *transformation*. If anything, some Japanese companies do not give IT the same high place on the management agenda as their more proactive Japanese and Western counterparts. We consider these issues in the following chapters.

15
The business impact and strategic use of IT

Chapter 2 presented and discussed the concept of information technology (IT) as a strategic resource with the potential to gain or lose competitive advantage and to be a key factor in deciding the outcome of international competitive battles. Strangely, although strategic IT has been regularly discussed in journals and magazines of all kinds and although the power of Japanese companies has been repeatedly analysed in much the same publications, the two themes have rarely been brought together. Even writers such as Emmott, Jackson and Ohmae[1] who have discussed extensively issues such as the competitive strengths and weaknesses of Japan and the West, the difficulties of managing across cultures and the blurring of international boundaries have barely mentioned the strategic role of IT.

It has to be reiterated that 'strategic' does not necessarily equate with success or the achievement of competitive advantage. Strategies can be defensive, and they may not work out as planned, sometimes resulting in disaster.

Until the last few years IT has not been a strategic factor. IT used to be applied exclusively to mechanize and automate support functions such as accounting systems. The purpose of the automation was usually to increase efficiency, reducing staffing and other, mainly clerical, costs. The major management concerns were whether the projects were completed on time and within budget, and responsibility for the projects rested with the IT manager. Of course, automation still goes on, and continues to bring business benefits to organizations.

Strategic IT, however, differs from automation. It is a senior management issue because it has a significant impact on competition, revenue, costs, human resources and survival. In fact IT is now a major influence in all the areas that fall within a senior manager's domain.

IT now does more than automate *support* processes. It is increasingly being applied to the *cores* of businesses and is transforming industries, organizations, business processes and management methods. When applied in this way IT gives benefits much wider than those of traditional efficiency. The new benefits sometimes amount to competitive advantage, usually occurring when IT is associated with business transformation, rather than automation.

If we accept this concept of IT's strategic potential then it follows that IT could be a decisive factor in any future competitive battles between

Japanese and Western companies. This is especially likely to be the case, since IT is having a major impact on the development of truly global companies. It is breaking down barriers, both organizational and geographical, between organizations, governments and nations.

Writers such as Kenichi Imai[2] reinforce this view. He sees IT as having a crucial role in the growth of Pacific Rim economies, Malaysia, the Philippines, Indonesia and Thailand, as well as Japan.

Japanese companies have clearly been highly successful in competing with their Western counterparts for the last two or three decades. Their expertise in marketing, new product development, flexible and cost-effective manufacturing and purchasing and supply has been the subject of numerous studies. Their success has been well documented and universally admired. IT, however, was not generally a factor in the battles of the past. IT, at least when deployed strategically, is new and the Japanese have no clear track record of success in this area.

In fact there are some tentative reasons for supposing, *a priori*, that they may not be good at it. For example, the populist view, which has also been discussed in the writings of management gurus, is that Japanese organizations, and indeed Japanese minds, are good at linear logic and incremental reasoning, and not at creativity, lateral thinking and quantum conceptual leaps. We might therefore expect Japanese organizations to have done well in using IT for automating and securing efficiency benefits but to struggle with the more imaginative qualities needed for using IT strategically. An hypothesis is therefore that if 'strategic IT' is a key factor in future business competition then Japanese organizations might be outperformed by their Western rivals.

On the other hand, the idea that Japanese management generally lacks the capability for creative thought may just be a myth, like so many others. The West has continually been lulled into a sense of false security by myths about the Japanese. At the time of Japan's entry into the Second World War received wisdom on the part of the Allied military was that Japanese fighter aircraft were sub-standard and that the Japanese people had bad eyesight which made them poor pilots. Subsequent air battles revealed the gap between myth and reality.

The purpose of this chapter is to investigate, using the case study data, whether there is evidence that Japanese organizations have used IT strategically to achieve wide-ranging business benefits. Unfortunately, it is difficult to assess and analyse the deployment of strategic IT: there are no precise measures or even established analytical methods. However, Chapter 2 described four 'dimensions' of strategic IT and in this chapter they will be used to provide a framework to guide our thinking. The four dimensions are:

- How strategic IT is for a particular organization (Strategic Grid)
- What the business benefits of strategic IT are (Index matrix)
- The extent to which IT is being used to induce transformation (Five-level graph)
- The view of IT held by the senior management of an organization (three views of IT graph)

The rest of this chapter is an analysis of the case studies along these dimensions.

How strategic is IT for a particular organization?

In general terms IT is strategic but its potential impact varies from one organization to another. If the strategic potential of IT within a particular organization or industry is low then a capability to exploit strategic IT is of little significance. McFarlan[3] of the Harvard Business School developed a Strategic Grid, shown in Figure 15.1, to help answer this question.

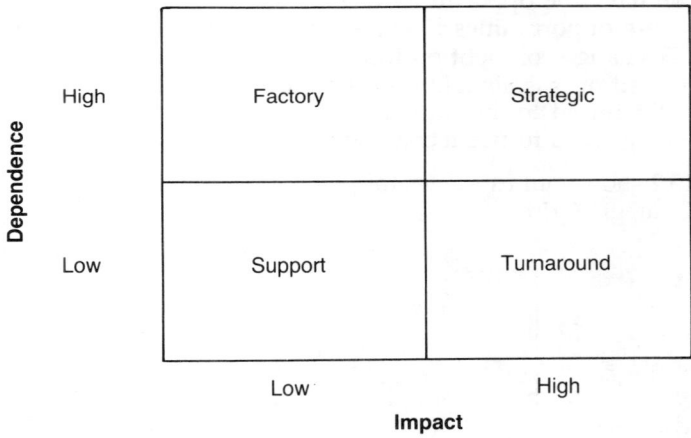

Figure 15.1 The Strategic Grid

The Strategic Grid was described fully in Chapter 2. A summary is given here to refresh the memory. The Grid has two dimensions:

- *Level of dependence* on existing operating systems. *High dependence* means that the reliability of the core systems is essential to the company's well-being. *Low dependence* means that unreliable functioning of systems is frustrating but of minor business importance.
- *Strategic impact* of planned IT developments. *High impact* means that IT is crucial to the organization's future prosperity. *Low impact* means that IT development may be useful, but is not critical.

McFarlan gives labels to the four boxes of the matrix shown in Figure 15.1.

1 *Strategic* The organization is critically dependent on IT now and in the future.
2 *Turnaround* Existing technology is not of critical importance but the organization is moving to a situation where IT will be a key determinant of success or failure.

202 The Japanese Advantage?

3 *Factory* Existing systems are the backbone of the business but new developments are not going to alter its competitive situation.
4 *Support* IT has not been, and will continue not to be, a major determinant of success or failure.

McFarlan suggests six questions that will help an organization to determine its position on the Strategic Grid. The questions ask whether IT can be used to achieve competitive advantage by one of the classical methods. All 'no' answers mean the organization is probably on the Factory–Support side; one or more 'yes' answers suggest a position on the Strategic–Turnaround side.

1 Are there ways to use technology to create defensible entry barriers?
2 Do we have the opportunity to induce switching costs?
3 Are there opportunities to change the ground rules of competition?
4 Can IT change competition from cost-based competition to competition based on sustainable product differentiation?
5 Can IT be used to link in suppliers?
6 Are there ways to use technology as a product?

Figure 15.2 shows our estimates for positioning the case study companies on the Strategic Grid.

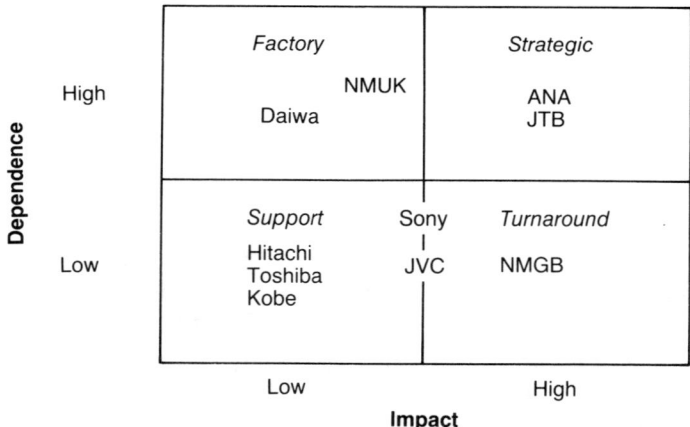

Key

ANA – All Nippon Airways; JTB – Japan Travel Bureau; NMGG – Nissan Motor GB Ltd (i.e. distribution); NMUK – Nissan Motor Manufacturing (UK) Ltd

Figure 15.2 Positioning on the Strategic Grid

As an international airline with ambitions to grow, *ANA* falls clearly into the 'strategic' quadrant. Its reservation systems are critical now, even though they are not as advanced as comparable western systems such as British Airlines' Galileo. The ability to use them to make 'seamless' worldwide bookings and tailor travel products means they will continue to be critical in the future. The entry barriers for would-be international airlines are formidable. Reservation systems have shifted the ground rules for competition between international airlines, away from service in the air towards service on the ground.

Daiwa's trading systems are essential to their present operations, as for any financial services company. However, there is no evidence from the case to suggest that future systems will be any more than operational, rather than strategic necessities. Our interviews showed they considered themselves 'at par' with the rest of the industry. Daiwa falls into the 'factory' quadrant.

Hitachi has some important information systems, especially those which provide customer service. The case study describes a system that was intended to build closer links with distributors but which had not worked out as well as hoped. Despite the element of disappointment, this can be seen as a strategic initiative. Even so, there are no signs that IT is viewed as a major strategic factor for the future. Hitachi is somewhere between 'support' and 'factory'. This view is confirmed by the MIS manager: 'IT is a support factor for the users of our products, rather than a component of strategy.'

Japan Travel Bureau (JTB) is not dissimilar from ANA and is placed in the 'strategic' quadrant. JTB presently relies on some essential information systems for integrating group and individual travel arrangements. These systems provide extensive coverage across a range of organizations and countries. They are a crucial part of strategy since they give a capability for tailoring holidays and travel to individual customer needs.

Although it does not have any information systems which could be said to be critical, *JVC* is nevertheless taking initiatives for establishing pan-European systems linking different countries, functions and processes. This could prove to be the basis for more strategic developments and, in any case, the systems are erecting substantial entry barriers for rivals who plan to become a global organization. Therefore JVC is positioned between 'support' and 'turnaround'.

Kobe uses IT in a 'support' role and the case study does not suggest that this will be different in the future. However, it should be noted that Kobe in Europe is much smaller than Kobe in Japan, where diversification plans may involve a different use of IT.

NMGB, the distribution division of Nissan, is in the 'turnaround' quadrant. The use of IT has been limited in the past but future plans for drawing together, using and controlling car dealerships depend heavily on IT for their success in meeting growth and quality objectives. Dealers will become 'locked in' to Nissan's systems, providing long-term opportunities for training and development.

NMUK, the manufacturing part of Nissan, is heavily reliant on information systems for its manufacturing processes and its process technology, like that of many Japanese companies, is highly sophisticated. IT supports JIT policies and many other aspects of manufacturing. This platform could form the basis for further initiatives but it is not clear from the case data exactly what future strategic intentions may be. NMUK is positioned between 'factory' and 'strategic'.

Sony falls near the middle of the Strategic Grid. There is evidence of both present reliance and future strategic intentions, but the company may not yet view IT in such a clear strategic light. But, like JVC, the entry barriers for smaller rivals are beginning to look daunting.

Toshiba Information Systems uses IT in a 'support' role. It has many systems but none can be thought of as absolutely essential for the present nor do future plans appear to carry major strategic significance. Even so, many of the systems are advanced technically (for example, the executive information system).

Overall, the case study organizations are spread over the quadrants, although we might have expected more of them to have been on the strategic/turnaround side. It is worth noting that the Strategic Grid looks at the strategic relevance of IT to an organization given its current situation and the way its plans are moving. The Grid is not suggesting how 'in a perfect world' companies *should* be applying IT.

The range of IS benefits

Strategic IT provides a wide range of substantial business benefits. The Index matrix, described in Chapter 2, is one method of classifying them.

	Individual	Function	Organization
Efficiency	Task mechanization	Process automation	Boundary extension
Effectiveness	Work improvement	Functional enhancement	Service enhancement
Transformation	Role expansion	Functional redefinition	Product innovation

Areas of impact (columns); Benefits (rows)

Figure 15.3 The Index matrix

Shown in Figure 15.3, it categorizes them according to their level of impact, individual, function or whole organization and according to type, efficiency, effectiveness and transformation – nine categories in all. The categories are:

- *Process automation* (function/efficiency cell). For example, automating stock control to reduce warehousing costs.

- *Functional enhancement* (function/effectiveness cell). For example, automating the sales/ordering process provides better information on the state of an order or invoice, resulting in better customer service.

These first two cells above represent *Era 1*, the earliest type of benefits sought and achieved.

- *Task mechanization* (individual/efficiency cell). For example, word processing mechanizes secretarial activities. The ability to make changes quickly and to store standard letters and documents should reduce staff costs.
- *Work improvement* (individual/effectiveness cell). For example, desktop publishing not only automates document production but also improves the quality of the end product. This should result in the document being accepted more easily by those to whom it is being sent and, therefore, perhaps stimulate faster decision making.

These above two benefits represent *Era 2*, the benefits that came about when computers were decentralized to the individual level.

- *Role expansion* (individual/transformation cell). For example, computer networks can transfer documents rapidly backwards and forwards between departments. As a result, they can be handled almost simultaneously by different functions instead of in strict order. This has led to the streamlining of management processes and created a need for the development of team-working and for managers to assume new coordinating roles.
- *Functional redefinition* (function/transformation cell). For example, clothing retailers have been able to transform their distribution systems because the availability of information from EPoS gives daily, accurate information on sales. Distribution schedules for each store are devised overnight in response to the previous day's sales. The traditional method was to forecast and guess, weeks in advance, resulting in unacceptable levels of overstocking and stockouts.
- *Boundary extension* (organization/efficiency cell). For example, white-goods manufacturers have computer links with many of their suppliers allowing the manufacturer to specify up-to-the-minute distribution and delivery requirements. The manufacturer has extended its boundary to include the supplier in its domain, at least electronically, leading to efficiency benefits.
- *Service enhancement* (organization/effectiveness cell). For example, insurance brokers are linked electronically to most major insurance companies. Brokers take only minutes to search through insurance companies' databases to find the policy best suited to a client's requirements.
- *Product innovation* (organization/transformation cell). For example, American Airlines sell the facilities of their reservation system to other airlines. This is a new product for the airline which has transformed the scope of its business.

The above five cells represent *Era 3*, the strategic IT era when a much wider range of benefits are being sought and achieved.

206 The Japanese Advantage?

The Index matrix is not a precise classification system, nor are the names given to the cells tight definitions. It is intended only to illustrate the range of potential benefits.

Eras 1 and 2 are the traditional areas for IT applications. Few present-day organizations do not continue to be active in these cells. On the other hand, few are firmly established in Era 3. Organizations active somewhere in these cells are the ones trying and perhaps succeeding in implementing strategic IT.

Organizations do not progress through the matrix one cell at a time. An organization is likely to be operating in several cells at once. In particular, organizations that are involved in Era 3 projects will almost certainly still be heavily involved in Era 1 projects seeking efficiency benefits.

What is of interest is whether an organization is making some attempt to use IT strategically, i.e. whether it is engaged in Era 3 activities. Figure 15.4 shows our assessment of the positioning of our case study companies in the Index matrix.

		Areas of impact		
		Individual	Function	Organization
Benefits	Efficiency	Era 1 Task mechanization All	Era 2 Process automation All	Era 3 Boundary extension ANA JTB NMUK SONY
	Effectiveness	Work improvement All	Functional enhancement All	Service enhancement SONY
	Transformation	Role expansion DAIWA JVC NMGB	Functional redefinition JVC SONY	Product innovation

Figure 15.4 Index matrix for the case studies

The case study evidence showed, as expected, that all the organizations were active in Eras 1 and 2; that is, they were involved in projects which gave efficiency and effectiveness benefits at the individual and functional levels. Few, however, appear to have ventured into Era 3. In placing organizations in Era 3 cells we have looked for *significant* developments and have not counted more marginal ones. There is plenty of room for debate about what to include and what to exclude:

- *Role expansion. Daiwa*, and indeed any major international securities house, must be located in this cell because of the way IT has changed and continues to change the way business is done by individual traders

and managers. *JVC* is here because of the impact of its spare parts system on dealer relationships and also because of the way it is developing its use of personal computers. Likewise, *NMGB* (Nissan sales and distribution) is transforming the way its dealers work.
- *Functional redefinition.* *JVC* can be clearly placed in this cell. Again its spare parts system and its use of laptops have altered the boundaries of functions. *Sony* is here because of its current plan to transform the sales ordering process for dealers so as to make it a 'one-stop' ordering process.
- *Boundary extension.* Developments in *ANA*'s reservation systems, although not radically different from those of other airlines, nevertheless put it in this cell since the effective boundary of the organization now includes many other travel companies. For similar reasons, *Japan Travel Bureau* (JTB) is in this cell. Like other international car manufacturers, *NMUK* (the manufacturing part of Nissan) have extensive and close supplier links which can be thought of as bringing the suppliers within the corporate boundaries of the company. *Sony*'s STREAM initiative seeks major efficiency benefits encompassing the entire organization.
- *Service enhancement.* Only *Sony* can clearly be placed in this cell, on account of the potential effectiveness benefits sought through the STREAM project.
- *Product innovation.* As far as we can discern from our investigations, no organization is making or moving towards new information products of a radical nature. Nothing approaching the American Airlines example could be detected.

The Index matrix suggests clearly that the case study organizations are conservative in their application of IT. Few far-reaching developments can be found. To say this is not, of course, pejorative. It may well be that pursuing excellence in terms of efficiency/effectiveness is entirely the right approach. Even so, these organizations might, on the other hand, wish to move up the learning curve in terms of radical IT initiatives.

The link between benefits and business transformation

Surveys suggest that transformation benefits are now the major goal of capital IT expenditures. This is a recent development and the resulting projects are proving difficult to manage. So what efforts and progress are the case study organizations making in this direction?

As described in Chapter 2, the MIT90s Research Programme proposed five levels of IT-induced business transformation, each corresponding to a range of potential benefits. The levels are illustrated in Figure 15.5:
- *Level 1: Localized exploitation*   Localized exploitation refers to the application of IT to different parts of an organization, in isolation one from another, with a view to achieving mainly efficiency benefits. It implies automating processes and tasks rather than transforming them.

208 The Japanese Advantage?

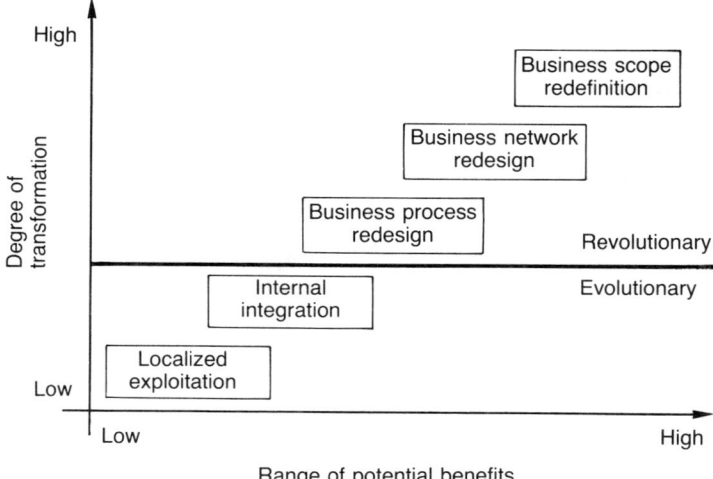

Figure 15.5 The five levels of transformation

- *Level 2. Internal integration*   Internal integration is the development of IT-based links between different parts of an organization. If accounts, customer records and stock control have been computerized separately, these are level 1 developments. Connecting the three systems together so that a customer can immediately know everything about the status of his or her order would be a level 2 transformation.
- *Level 3. Business process redesign*   Levels 1 and 2 are evolutionary, developing almost naturally over time from the first introduction of IT. Levels 3, 4 and 5 are revolutionary and do not follow in a smooth logical progression. They are radical jumps. Level 3 relates to the redesign of business processes. It implies a radical transformation rather than tinkering at the edges.
- *Level 4. Business network redesign*   Whereas level 3 concerned redesign within the organization, level 4 concerns inter-organizational redesign. The other organizations may be suppliers, customers, services or competitors. Level 4 refers to a radical change in the nature of the relationships between organizations. Electronic links which automate existing processes and relationships do *not* constitute a level 4 redesign.
- *Level 5: Business scope redefinition*   Level 5 refers to extending the scope of an organization's business, usually by means of a new information-based product. The emphasis is on using IT in some way as a new product in a new area of business rather than to enhance existing products or to speed up new product development.

The first important point to note about the transformation graph is the distinction between the evolutionary levels, 1 and 2, and the revolutionary levels, 3, 4 and 5. They are very different concepts: there is a gulf between levels 2 and 3 and different management approaches are needed. The second is that an organization does not move through the levels in the strict sequence 1–2–3–4–5. Organizations generally start at level 1 and move on to level 2 but after that there need be no definite pattern.

Where, then, are the case study companies in terms of transformation? Have they reached the revolutionary levels? Our assessments are shown in Figure 15.6.

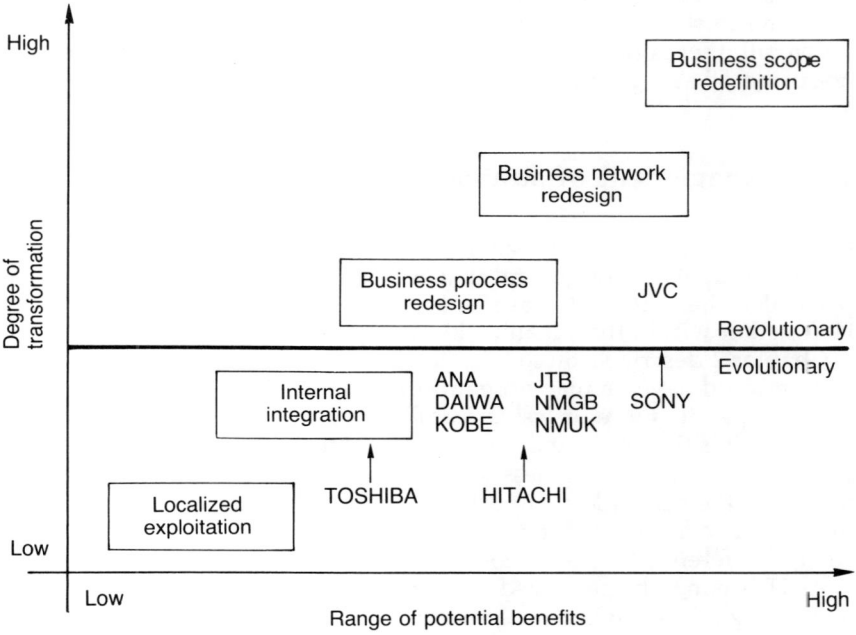

Figure 15.6 The transformation levels of the case study organizations

In our view the organizations are more or less uniform in their achievements. Only one, *JVC*, was, we thought, unquestionably at a revolutionary level. JVC have made substantial changes through their reassessment of spare parts ordering and through their application of laptop computers. It should be noted that it is not laptops in themselves that represent a transformation but the way they were applied to transform working practices and business processes.

Sony could also be placed at this level because of the STREAM project but the degree of transformation being brought about by STREAM is not clearly revolutionary. This is not to say that STREAM is not an important system with strategic implications for future global management. Likewise, *NMGB* could be placed at this level because of the way business managers use laptops to communicate with dealers but, again, the degree of transformation is not clearly revolutionary.

There is an argument for putting *Toshiba Information Systems* and *Hitachi* at level 1, but recent plans suggest that they are moving rapidly to level 2. All other organizations were placed at level 2.

As with the Index matrix, there is no intrinsic merit in being placed in one cell or at one level rather than another. The point is to be at the right level for that organization at that particular time. This depends upon the particular circumstances of the organization. Our only reservation in saying this is whether at this time every organization should be learning more about the role of IT as a truly strategic resource, and therefore engaging in some activity, however minor, at the higher levels.

Overall, then, our conclusion is that our case study organizations are not using IT as a factor in radical transformations of their businesses.

The management of strategic IT

Research has shown that the successful deployment of strategic IT depends upon the capability of general management to manage this resource. In particular, the *view* of IT that management holds and the position of the IT function within the organization is a prime indicator of success.

Chapter 2 described three 'views', or approaches to, IT that an organization could have. In many organizations IT functions have operated, or still do operate, more or less *independently* of the main business. Within this view it is the job of senior management to deal with strategic matters such as what area of business to be in and how to improve competitiveness; it is the (much less important) job of the IT manager to find tasks that could be automated. He or she would usually do this with, at most, cursory reference to the corporate strategy.

As IT began to be perceived as a strategic resource, there was evidence of organizations having a *dependent* view of IT. In this approach the corporate strategy comes first. When it has been finalized, the IT manager develops an IT strategy which spells out how IT can contribute to corporate objectives and plans.

The most recent developments, however, show organizations with an *interdependent* approach to IT. Here there is interaction between devising the corporate strategy and devising the IT strategy. The development of both is interwoven, with the result that the IT strategy is aligned with or even integral to and indistinguishable from, the corporate strategy.

These views of IT are summarized in Figure 15.7. The implication is that, in order to be in a position to use IT strategically or to reject the use of strategic IT, organizations should be at or moving towards an interdependent view of IT.

What, then, are the approaches to IT adopted by the case study organizations? The case study interviews produced clear evidence concerning the management of IT and our assessments are shown in Figure 15.8.

Surprisingly four of the organisations, *Daiwa*, *Hitachi*, *JVC* and *Kobe*, appear to have an 'independent' approach to the deployment of IT. The search for profitable IT opportunities makes little reference to the corporate

The business impact and strategic use of IT 211

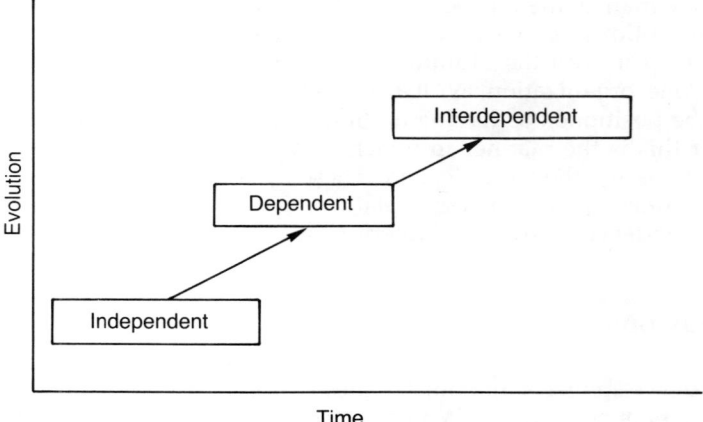

Figure 15.7 An organization's vision of IT

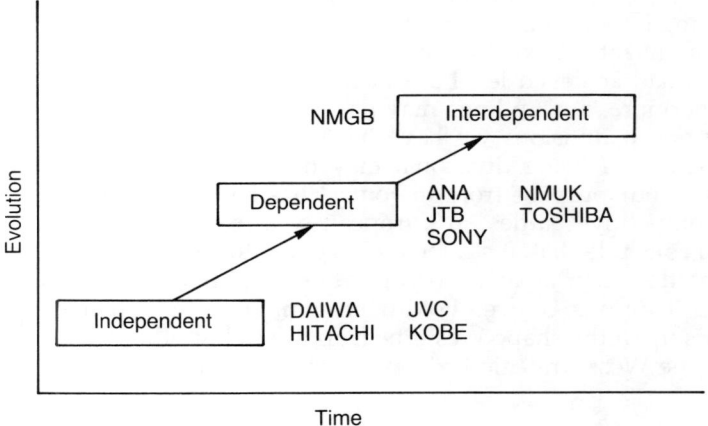

Figure 15.8 Views of IT from the case studies

strategy and there is no indication that corporate and IT strategies could be aligned. In these companies there are, of course, visits from board members from time to time but this is not the same as the implementation of management procedures to align strategy. The 'independent' approach may be accounted for in part by the fact that the case studies are based upon investigations into the European divisions of the organizations. The next chapter, however, describes our investigations at the head offices of some of the companies and picks up on this issue.

Most of the case study organizations have a 'dependent' approach.

They have management processes and procedures, clearly detailed in the case descriptions, which encourage IT management to work within the constraints (or with the illumination) of the corporate strategy.

Only one organization, *NMGB* (Nissan's distribution company), can clearly be positioned as having an 'interdependent' approach. The evidence for this is the manner in which they are developing new information systems for their car dealers. These systems are closely integrated with the development of new relationships with the dealers. There is definite evidence of two-way interaction.

Conclusions

The evidence suggests that our Japanese case study organizations are not major users of strategic IT. Whichever aspect of strategic IT and its management we have investigated we have found them to be efficient and thorough but conservative.

Of course, our analytical methods are limited and data are not easy to find. More investigation, particularly from other organizations and Japan (but see next chapter for our Tokyo data), would be valuable. It is also interesting to note some contradictions in our findings. For example, one of the organizations with a non-strategic 'dependent' view of IT was also one that had achieved level 3 transformations.

Furthermore, our findings may partly reflect the fact that it is mainly the European divisions we have been studying. Geography, language and the fact of being divisional may have constrained the role of IT. However, our purpose from the outset has been to consider the role of IT in competitive battles on European soil. Extrapolating our data, we have to conclude that, if strategic IT is going to be an important factor in these battles, then Japanese organizations will not be in good shape to emerge victorious, or even hold their own. Of course, such a conclusion depends upon the shape Western rivals are in but other studies[4] suggest that in the West strategic IT is more firmly on the agenda.

Notes

1. Emmott, W., *Japan's Global Reach*, Century Business (1992); Jackson, T., *Turning Japanese*, HarperCollins (1993); Ohmae, K., *Borderless World*, Fontana (1990). Some of the important issues raised by these authors are summarized in Chapter 1.
2. Imai, K. in Soesastro, H. and Pangestu, M., *Technological Challenge in the Asia Pacific Economy*, Allen and Unwin (Australia) (1990).
3. McFarlan, FW., 'IT changes the way you compete', *Harvard Business Review*, **62**(3) (1984).
4. See, for example, Wiseman, C., *Strategic Information Systems*, Irwin (1988). Also Brady *et al.*, 'Strategic IT issues: the views of some major IT investors', *Journal of Strategic Information Systems*, September (1992).

16
Head office control

After all he had read and heard about Japanese management, the newly appointed manager was greatly looking forward to working in a Japanese company. At first, his dealings with head office contacts were cordial. His counterparts in Japan sounded eager to hear his opinions and learn from his expertise. His recommendations that his department's existing computer hardware was obsolete and should be replaced as quickly as possible were graciously received. His projects to improve his department's computer facility were authorized almost immediately.

Increased subsidiary business justified his request for two new mainframe computers to cope with increased workloads. At a later date, head office in Tokyo recommended and shipped an additional mainframe built by another computer manufacturer. Although unexpected, the subsidiary found a use for this machine.

Head office insisted that the subsidiary install software developed by the company's extensive Systems Development Department in Japan. On delivery, it proved to be fifteen years behind the latest technology available in the UK. A later system was even more dated.

Naturally, as part of his everyday work, the manager makes recommendations to head office. Recently head office contacts seem to disregard reports from the subsidiary. Unanswered reports are compounded by reports of outstanding items and follow-up reminder memos. When head office replies, instructions are unlikely to be error-free, and at times head office and the subsidiary appear to be thinking on different planes. However, it would be a grave loss of face for senior management in head office if this were pointed out. Subsidiary staff now refer irreverently to head office as 'the black hole'.

Japanese technology lag?

We asked this manager and a number of his colleagues for their explanation for this situation. We also related the episode to other managers in Japanese companies. Expecting vehement disagreement that we must have misunderstood, they nodded sympathetically and said that the situation was all too familiar.

In some instances our informants referred to 'the Japanese technology lag' and attributed this to culturally specific causes. We heard that, on the one hand, Japanese management does not feel comfortable being first with technology. Conversely, when the Japanese make a first move in IT they are still way behind their Western counterparts.

The view from Japan

We reflected on this episode in the light of our data from Japan and gave thought to the issues facing senior management at a head office of a Japanese multinational company. One aspect of their concerns, that of corporate governance, was raised with senior managers at Sony Corporation, who said that one strand of their company's philosophy is 'the future is a shared responsibility'.This is easier said than done. The managers continued by describing the difficulties of making sure that the Sony philosophy extends to all parts of the organization, however remote these may be. Sony's Management and Engineering Information Systems (MEIS) translates philosophical goals into reality. The problem for MEIS is how to align itself to corporate philosophies as, unlike other divisions, it has no tangible product. Other support divisions e.g. accounting, human resources and ISD, are faced with similar problems.

Relationships between head office and subsidiaries

As we described in Chapter 14 our research data indicate that Japanese multinational companies face two opposing demands. On the one hand, some head offices in Japan feel a need to control certain business aspects of their overseas subsidiaries, particularly matters of finance, strategic direction and manufacturing. On the other, head offices are aware that overseas subsidiaries are closer to local markets, and that group interests are better served if subsidiaries make their own decisions locally.

The companies in the case studies vary in terms of industry sector, size of subsidiary and length of time that the subsidiary has been established. It is therefore not surprising that head offices have varying relationships with subsidiaries.

The most fundamental relationship between a head office and its overseas subsidiaries is for the latter to carry out corporate policy. A subsidiary may or may not contribute to corporate policy and decision making. In some industries (for example, the financial services industry) head office guidelines are quite rigid. Head offices closely monitor a subsidiary's performance, particularly when subsidiaries have set up in Europe relatively recently. Daily reporting to head offices is often mandatory.

At the opposite end of the spectrum, subsidiaries can be devoid of corporate governance except for reporting trading for information purposes. Some head offices in other industries (e.g. consumer goods) concede that group interests are best served when overseas subsidiaries make certain strategic decisions. Subsidiaries which have been established in Europe for some time are more likely to be allowed this degree of decision-making autonomy. However, there are notable exceptions in the banking community where a subsidiary might have been established in Europe for several decades but still be subject to head office control for certain corporate issues.

Needless to say, the situation is rarely so polarized. There has been a reduction in the amount of control exerted by Hitachi and Sony over their subsidiaries Hitachi Europe and Sony (UK) – both relatively long established in Britain. Sony Corporation is committed to the policy of 'local globalization' and managers in Sony subsidiaries are empowered to make decisions locally. Mr Akio Morita, chairman and joint founder, says 'standardization would dilute the Sony culture if subsidiaries are instructed too much from head office'.

Similar corporate goals are in place at Hitachi, where a major management theme for eighty years of corporate history has been localization of subsidiaries. Consequently, there are relatively loose relations between head office and overseas subsidiaries. However, head office still controls some business areas (for example, manufacturing output). Head office is concerned to change this relationship in the future by giving more control to sales divisions over manufacturing. This has already happened in Hitachi's operations in the United States, where the holding company controls manufacturing in its subsidiary.

In some companies, head office abdicates control of certain company functions (e.g. human resource management, local procurement) while retaining strict control of certain pan-corporate issues such as treasury and financial matters, manufacturing output and IT systems. Other companies prefer local management to direct its own destiny. This relationship can change over time, for example as the subsidiary gains greater experience in its local market area.

Concerning IT, head office control can take the form of necessary approval procedures for IT systems to be used by subsidiaries. Larger companies have extensive home-based Systems Development Departments to ensure global conformity of systems. A head office might control local IT decision making through budgetary ceilings and expenditure guidelines. In some companies, financial approval is needed from head office for local 'add-on' enhancements to systems.

As the companies researched have a varied range of relationships with their head offices, we thought it would be useful to analyse these more closely to clarify how these affect IT issues. We returned again to the case studies to clarify the situation. These data are augmented by data gathered during a research visit to Japan. We examined the head office perspective on a number of issues, including corporate policy, budget procedures, IT development and IT management.

Setting corporate policy

Corporate policy and its relationship with subsidiaries are ways in which head offices exert control and influence over those subsidiaries.

In some companies this control may extend into IT-related matters. One way which delineates relationships between head office and subsidiaries is the area of corporate policy and setting business goals. In some companies, departments that play a part in strategic decision making are located in head office, which is consequently the source of strategic direction.

For example, JTB's Sales Planning Division in Maranouchi, Tokyo, is responsible for global sales promotion strategy, while the Corporate Planning Department decides overall business direction. In collaboration with corporate executives from other relevant departments (e.g. finance, marketing) the Corporate Planning Department makes recommendations to the JTB board of directors. The Overseas Travel Division located in head office is responsible for strategic business development.

All relevant divisions in JTB's head office contribute to corporate Action Plans; each part of the plan is divided between the divisions according to their specific responsibility. For example, the Overseas Travel Department plans global business strategy; the Global Planning Department is responsible for producing long-range (3–5 years; time horizon), and short-range (1-year) plans. JTB's strategy for the years leading to the twenty-first century is the initiative GO JTB 21. GO JTB 21 has three 3-year components: 1992–1994; 1995–1997; 1998–2001.

In terms of corporate strategy, some subsidiaries may make their own decisions and may also be closely involved in advising corporate decision making, particularly where these affect their own trading areas. For example, the head office of Daiwa Securities sets overall corporate policy, including strategic business direction and new business initiatives. One such initiative is Daiwa's 'Golden '90s': a statement of Daiwa's corporate principles for the decade to the year 2000.

Daiwa's corporate culture encourages subsidiaries to make local business decisions relating to its own market environment to encourage a quick response time to new business opportunities. This is a competitive strength in the financial sector where market movements can be volatile. Reaction speed is particularly advantageous in the currently liberalizing markets of some countries in the former Eastern bloc. DEL's Business Committee consults head office as a matter of policy and practice.

JVC (UK) is another company where local senior management contributes to head office policy. The managing director, finance director and sales director of JVC (UK) visit Japan for global planning discussions and negotiations with their counterparts at head office.

In the motor industry NMGB has autonomy to make business decisions within the framework of the annually agreed business plan. As a matter of routine NMGB reports to its parent company, Nissan Europe NV (NENV), in Amsterdam. Strong communication and commercial links are maintained between the two companies. NMGB reports to Tokyo headquarters via NENV. IT strategy is decided jointly between NENV and Nissan head office in Tokyo.

Sony recognizes that it operates in a global market (domestic sales in Japan account for 20–25 per cent of total group sales). Global guidelines are flexible and head office actively encourages 'local globalization' as a part of corporate policy. Sony as a company goes ahead, not necessarily driven by head office. Sony has organized its global activities into a number of zones: Asia, the United States and Europe. Each zone has its own needs according to the business group requirements. Each zone management produces annual IT plans. If an IS system is necessary to compete and profitability is an issue, this is the business of the local subsidiary.

Until 1989 Hitachi was organized into autonomous functional divisions (Semiconductor Division, Computer Division, etc.). Each functional division made its own decisions about overseas organization, including choice of computer systems. In early 1989, following a management reorganization in Japan, it was decided to reorganize the company from a functional to a geographical basis. This is a prime factor which shapes IT decision making.

At ANA's head office in Chiyoda-ku, Tokyo, the marketing automation department (part of ANA's marketing division) has responsibility for international projects. The department holds half-yearly meetings attended by representatives from sales, marketing and management. These meetings have a twofold purpose. First, they address requests from each of these departments for responses from marketing automation. Usually each meeting generates between ten and fifteen requests (for example, to make modifications to the customer control system so that 'frequent flier' passengers can be identified for marketing opportunities). Second, the marketing automation department attempts to match the discussions with the 'concrete image' of higher management strategic objectives. Discussions with relevant departments help the marketing automation department to redesign and modify existing systems in order to gain optimum benefit from available marketing data (for example, flight details, load factors).

The marketing automation department also manages the integration of CRS systems and oversees investment in other CRS, with major and minor partners.[1] Such investment obliges the marketing department to attend board meetings and consider operational issues and voting rights. The *Abacus* investment is a global alliance which helps ANA to reduce its CRS development costs. Joint ventures with other airlines in management partnerships of CRS give an airline opportunities to reduce its operating costs.

Financial control of IT

The head offices of some companies control local IT systems expenditure as a means of exerting considerable control and influence over the IT systems in use overseas. In such instances, a subsidiary's IT department requests support from head office for IT investment and recommendations for IT development. The head office investigates recommendations for new IT systems for potential profitability before giving approval for the requests to proceed.

In general, a senior manager in the subsidiary vets and possibly approves the IT manager's investment requests. These are submitted to head office showing proposed IT investments in priority order. At head office, requests from subsidiaries are evaluated according to whether they are a feasible IT investment able to meet specific business needs. A head office is more likely to approve systems that can be used by a number of subsidiaries and tends to give a higher priority to requests from several subsidiaries. A low priority is given to a request from a single subsidiary. Head office approval procedures can take time, particularly when issues need to be clarified via messages between head office and subsidiary. The more subsidiaries affected by a proposed system, the faster a head office decision is taken.

A head office usually closely monitors returns on IT investment. The costs of this investment are balanced against the return in terms of increased profitability for the company as a whole. Anticipated financial returns on the proposed investment are a usual prerequisite in many companies.[2]

Currently, Kobe Steel does not maintain a centralized IT strategy. At departmental level where decisions are made about PCs and related software, Kobe Steel Europe (KSE) has freedom to choose its own IT systems. This can be illustrated by the corporate accounts facility where IBM mainframes are centralized. Head office has sole responsibility and KSE has no need to link directly into the system. Consequently it has the freedom to select and operate its own systems independently of the main accounting system.

As long as it conforms with general corporate guidelines, SUK makes its own IT decisions. Where decisions are thought to be contentious, or where corporate policy is unclear, ISD seeks guidance from its European Operations Office (EOO) situated in Cologne, Germany (Sony's corporate headquarters in Europe), or from Tokyo.

Where a subsidiary has local decision-making authority, these procedures become superfluous, although they may be replaced with report-back mechanisms to inform head office of current and changing situations. For example, at NMUK the ISD is not required to refer to headquarters in Japan for advice or approval and the ISD general manager reports to a local British director.

One way in which a head office is able to control and influence a subsidiary is through continuous financial monitoring. When a head office imposes budget ceilings, local IT decision making is particularly constrained. During our research we encountered a number of companies whose head offices supplement local budgets and by so doing are able, either intentionally or otherwise, to control local IT expenditure.

The head offices of several Japanese companies in the financial services sector impose a local budget ceiling. Head office approval is required for any expenditure above this ceiling, which may sometimes be fairly low. The head office of one Japanese bank in the City of London retains control of the bank's financial and accounting functions. The head office of another bank maintains control over the 'core' IT system in common use in its branches worldwide. Even the few overseas branches that have their own systems departments are not authorized to make modifications to this core system.

In a number of other companies the relationship between head office and its subsidiary in Europe is less rigid and more bi-directional. At JVC (UK), Kobe Steel Europe (KSE), Daiwa's subsidiary DIREL and Hitachi Europe Ltd head office controls or approves local budgets but allows the subsidiary to make local decisions within this framework. At JVC (UK) the computer manager reports to the finance director who is responsible for local IT budgets up to Y5 million. Larger IT investment decisions are referred to head office in Japan.

KSE has two half-yearly business plans. These are incorporated into Kobe Steel's capital and expenditure budgets for the following year. Applications made by KSE for budget funding are usually granted if they are supported by a sound explanation of expenditure intentions. Each division of Kobe Steel has its own IT plans which are amalgamated into a pan-divisional budgetary framework. This is submitted to the data-processing department as part of the annual budgeting routine. IT strategy is not rigidly controlled by head office and IT departments of each division are allowed sufficient scope to make their own IT investment decisions. Within this framework some departments establish their own LANs which access company-wide MIS systems. Head office accepted the proposal which led to the establishment of a LAN.

At Daiwa Europe the executive director of DIREL (which has responsibility for IT matters) receives a budget subsidy from head office in Tokyo. This is intended to cover purchases of hardware and marketing information services, and to maintain DIREL's operational facility. IT investment decisions are made by DIREL's executive director, although he naturally consults regularly with local senior managers and with managers in head office. Head office in Tokyo provides DIREL's Executive Director with a budget subsidy, intended to cover purchases of hardware and marketing information services and maintain DIREL's operational facility.

Most financial aspects of IT at Hitachi Europe Ltd (HEL) are controlled by head office funding. HEL's managing director visits Tokyo twice a year for discussions to gain approval for his budgetary requirements for the following six-months' budget. Senior board members from head office in Tokyo visit HEL at Maidenhead for discussions on strategy at regular (approximately quarterly) intervals. HEL's corporate MIS manager is on an assignment from head office in Japan. His main task is to monitor IT strategic planning, particularly when this involves the international networks. He reports daily to the Overseas Systems Department in Tokyo. In this way, he can alert head office to the ideas and suggestions from local staff and influence head office decisions.

Some companies apply to head office for funding for particular European projects. At the request of several senior managers in Europe, the JTB's Board of Directors in Japan agreed to fund a pan-European accounting system. Such a system would cope satisfactorily with accounting practices in any of the European countries where JTBE maintained an office, as well as standardizing accounting procedures throughout JTBE's European network.

Sony Corporation gives overall guidelines on IT expenditure. However, within agreed staffing levels the local divisional management has the responsibility to assign staff to each job function. The headcount level assigned to its ISD is determined by local management. SUK's ISD budget is decided by SUK directors as part of the overall company budget. As a separate exercise by Sony Corporation to gather information about the IT function, details of the ISD budget are reported to European Operations Office (EOO).

Budgetary controls (for example, local budget ceilings, head office budget approval) are a means of monitoring and directing local IT. Head offices can also control local IT by controlling new systems.

Identifying new IT systems

Although a subsidiary may comply with its head office in corporate matters, it may be allowed local decisions on some IT issues; for example, the type of computer hardware, or software programs that are appropriate for local trading conditions. The situation changes from one company to another and depends on the industry in which companies operate.

In the travel industry the need for speedy communications from the head office hub to subsidiary outposts and system compatibility demands that head office decides new systems. Similarly, the procurement function which Kobe Steel Europe undertakes for its head office makes it more likely that new systems will be initiated by head office. When a subsidiary performs a local marketing and sales function, it is more probable that systems to support these activities will be initiated by the subsidiary.

As we would expect, the head offices of ANA and Kobe Steel identify new IT systems for their overseas subsidiaries. Conversely, Sony subsidiaries follow corporate IT guidelines issued by Sony Corporation.

The nature of ANA's operations means that while London office chooses its own back-office systems, it must make requests to head office for new systems for the front-office travel booking operations. Similarly, Kobe Steel subsidiaries are free to choose PCs and related software. These remain independent of systems by head office (for example, corporate accounts, for which head office has sole responsibility).

At ANA's head office in Tokyo a team of programmers enhances systems. End users suggest additions to existing system at CRS development meetings which are held annually, in February. The new development is usually in place prior to the next development meeting the following February, although some proposals take a little longer.

Sony head office maintains rigid controls over the corporate communications network. It also gives guidelines for other IT issues (for example, the type of operating system subsidiaries should use). Previously tight controls over database management have recently been relaxed.

A company which is truly global in its IT vision will invariably have an established Systems Development Department in Japan. The Tokyo head office of one bank employs approximately 1000 specialist engineers and systems designers, supplemented by outside contractors who join particular projects for the duration of development. Approximately 250 people are involved in systems development for international operations. Of this number, 50 per cent have banking expertise; the remaining 50 per cent are systems development specialists.

Hitachi's head office develops IT systems and provides platforms for IS systems (including software interface) for subsidiaries within the Hitachi group. The systems development department at Omori near Tokyo has between seventy and eighty staff, of which five develop IT systems for overseas operations. Hitachi's manufacturing experience in Japan has enabled the company to establish a 'home-grown' IT platform throughout its manufacturing sites. In Europe, electronic communication networks facilitate the transmission of procurement information between Maidenhead in England and Landshut in Germany.

Naturally, it is important for electronic links between head office and a subsidiary to be mutually compatible. Most systems are initiated by head office and subsidiaries like Hitachi Europe Ltd (HEL) fall into line with head office. That said, each of Hitachi's global trading zones has a degree of internal autonomy and IT projects proposed by the MIS Department at HEL are invariably accepted. However, budget and staff quota parameters allocated by head office determine the work capacity of HEL's MIS department. The head office of Kobe Steel customarily initiates projects for international communications links (for example, a global VAN designed to link all overseas offices through an E-mail system. KSE makes proposals to head office where new IT developments affect its own working practices).

Subsidiaries of JVC use standard software systems developed by head office in Tokyo. Within the common standard system local offices are allowed to develop their own domestic applications. Where several JVC subsidiaries have similar local requirements, EDP managers request head office Systems Development Department to amend the master system. Pan-European IT projects involve EDP managers from European subsidiaries together with personnel from JVC Information Centre in Tokyo, which manages IT projects for the whole JVC group. In April 1992 head office in Japan developed a computer package to manage inventory, sales ledger and customer orders.

At Sony, a corporate project team in the IS Department in Tokyo provided the initial impetus for the STREAM project, a communications systems whose purpose is to speed information between manufacturing and sales divisions. The project was subsequently developed jointly between Tokyo and Europe.

When software is developed in head office, its migration onto a subsidiary's hardware will most likely be controlled by head office. The migration exercise will involve a specialist head office team coming to the local branch for the duration of the migration period. This may also include pre-migration training for local staff and will undoubtedly involve some team members remaining on-site to monitor the new system in use for a period of three months.

Global communications networks

Global companies, whether they are banks or financial houses, manufacturers of consumer products or travel service providers, now rely heavily on the global transmission of commercial data. Predictably, global communications are inevitably closely controlled by head office. The reasons for this are fairly obvious: consistency and control (especially of manufacturing output). For example, JVC's manufacturing facility in East Kilbride, Scotland, has its global communications links with head office in Japan, and is not part of the JVC (UK) network.

For the most part, electronic pathways are of the 'hub-and-spoke' variety with head office serving as the hub and links to subsidiaries forming the spokes. However, there are alternative configurations. The triangular pattern for Sony's international digital communications system links Tokyo, the United States and Europe. Sony's European Network Centre (ENC) in The Hague forms one corner of the triangle and is the conduit for communications from headquarters to Sony's European subsidiaries and from the European subsidiaries back to Sony headquarters.

Daiwa's Global Communications Network consists of two triangular pathways. The first triangle links the three largest financial centres of Tokyo–New York–London. A second triangle links Osaka–Chicago–Paris; important centres for futures and options trading. Costing Y100 billion to start up in 1991, these twin high-speed digital global communications networks allow global securities trading on a 24-hour basis. They are connected through an apex to most regional offices and can be accessed by almost all other offices.

Daiwa's IT decisions take into account systems in use in other parts of the company. However, the size and global spread of the company's activities preclude any single IT delivery system throughout the organization's worldwide network. Additionally, the quest for commonality of IT systems is impeded by different levels of technology available throughout the world (e.g. fibre-optic technology, high-speed information services).

The relationship between the head office of Kobe Steel and its European subsidiary is more rigidly defined. Overseas subsidiaries provide head office with data for the group's global trading operations. However, Kobe Steel Europe (KSE) is able to make suggestions concerning the IT systems that it thinks will best serve the mutual interests of itself and head office. The subsidiary saw that mutual compatibility of communication systems was an essential aspect for electronic links. Following an investigative exercise, a G4 fax network was established at key offices in Japan and overseas.

Hitachi global network (HITNET)

Hitachi's global communications are managed by the Information Network Centre (INC) in Tokyo. The INC operates 24 hours a day, 365 days a year and reports to the president. The Hitachi Global Network (HITNET), which cost US$1 million to install, is a global network linking head office with a total of 160 international and domestic sites. The network uses optical fibre cabling and includes an interactive business TV system for corporate messages.

Within HITNET each division has its own LAN which is separate from the main system. Each division has its own IT strategy and its own MIS group whose manager reports to the general manager of the division. End-user support for computer systems is usually organized locally. Divisions buy their own computer equipment.

Each division's different requirements from the network emanate from the section manager to the central group. When a subsidiary requests extra communications lines, head office either decides to allocate these or postpones providing any extra lines until the additional cost is justifiable in business growth.

Head office must link between the different LANs. The LANs in Hitachi's factories are also separate from each other. The corporate network solution is to have different requirements for different sections of the company. At Hitachi the corporate networks do not need to provide the same service to all sections of the user community.

Each division has specific uses for the network. For example, the semiconductor division has a LAN interworking for CAD; the computer division has video-conferencing facilities. The sales support system is common to all divisions. Systems to facilitate production control (e.g. delivery of raw materials, production scheduling, delivery of finished product) tend to be different systems and are developed locally according to local needs. However, some subsidiaries use common production control systems.

Head office EDP staff help subsidiaries to install new systems. For example, in the semiconductor division four EDP staff will help to install a new order entry control system. Head office provides IT services on a non-profit-making basis, at a cost 10–20 per cent cheaper than publicly available services. Communication charges for using HITNET are charged to subsidiaries and depreciated annually.

Video-conferencing

A number of companies in our study have investigated introducing video-conferencing links between head office and the local subsidiary. In some cases, for example where it is necessary to exchange visual information, such links have been established. However, in some subsidiary companies, the currently low volume of 'traffic' between the overseas subsidiary and Japan may not justify operating a video-conferencing facility between the two sites.

Furthermore, in situations where the need for visual contact is limited, most subsidiary companies feel that current equipment costs are too expensive. In a business environment where companies are continually seeking to reduce their cost base, reduced communications costs are an attractive target. Most companies feel that video-conferencing costs outweigh potential benefits, at least in the short-term. Companies may review their policies when there are noticeable reductions in current capital and operating costs of video-conferencing facilities.

Additionally, video-conferencing is logistically awkward when head office and subsidiary are located in different time zones. However, in some industries it is crucial to exchange more detailed information than can be captured in a faxed message. In the financial services industry, for example, financial market movements in one time zone can affect trading in another. In this environment it is an occupational necessity to arrive at the office early or remain late to confer with colleagues on the other side of the world.

In Japan a number of our companies operate extensive video-conferencing facilities. For example, Kobe Steel's video-conferencing studios in Tokyo relay meetings of company executives in Kobe and Tokyo. However, in Europe, exchange of visual information between KSE and its parent company is rare. The range of business services provided to head office by KSE do not urgently need face-to-face communication. For KSE the current status of procurement purchase orders can be relayed satisfactorily via faxed messages or E-mail. In the opposite direction, head office information relates mainly to the current status of projects.

However, Kobe Steel's Machine and Engineering Division has a pilot project to use Businesstalk 2000 for global communication. Head office drives the momentum for international communication links and if this pilot project is satisfactory, KSE expects to link into this system at some future date.

Managing IT

An example of the complexity of managing IT for global operation is to be found at Sony Corporation as shown in the following detailed description. At its head office, Sony has established a number of committees to manage IT strategic direction and policy at various organizational levels. The corporate IS committee oversees all these committees. Directly below the corporate IS committee are two sub-committees which deal respectively with corporate MIS and international IS.

A number of sub-committees report to the corporate MIS function. Meeting groups, which are structured less formally than committees at higher corporate levels, decide priorities for particular IT issues. The CAE (computer-aided engineering) meeting consists of representatives from Sony business groups, research centres and functional groups. Other MIS meetings deal with IT issues within Sony head office and for subsidiary companies in Japan. The management of IS issues needs to satisfy two goals: corporate and divisional.

The International IS committee manages issues relating to IT in overseas subsidiaries. Committee membership at this level consists of the head of zone and the vice president from each of the trading zones. At a lower corporate level, the international IS workshop addresses issues of concern to Sony's global enterprise. Each trading zone organizes its own annual IT meeting.

Key issues for business group management are production management systems and the MPG 'Seihan' (STREAM) system. At the zone level, issues relate to the management of the sales control system and the zone STREAM system. From the perspective of head office, it is necessary to maintain close relations between zone management and business group management.

MEIS

At the head office of Sony Corporation MEIS (Management and Engineering Information Systems) consists of several divisions which encompass a range of functions. Planning and Control Division deals with coordination and planning. Information Service Division is responsible for network services, training, end-user computing and code management. The MIS Division consults with IS Divisions within Sony Corporation. CAE is responsible for design systems. The Project of Advanced Workstyle is charged with investigating the automation of personal and individual work procedures.

Global IT architecture is developed by MEIS in collaboration with representatives from the various zones. Control is at three levels: global, zone and subsidiary company. However, there are flexible differences in each country, e.g. local support, software. Interaction between the manufacturing and sales divisions with MEIS includes reporting procedures from the divisions to MEIS.

In common with other parts of the Sony organization, MEIS works to the concept of local globalization. In terms of their work this means the development of global systems supporting overseas needs. There have been several phases of local globalization, roughly matching the phases of company growth. During the 1960s and 1970s subsidiary companies were allowed to develop their own systems except for strategic support. By the early 1980s the situation had changed and head office in Tokyo managed the entire range of systems at Sony. From 1984 to 1987 Sony head office instigated STN (a sales and marketing support system) for its domestic operations. STN was replicated in the United States (from 1982 to 1985), and was subsequently introduced into Sony manufacturing plants in Wales, Spain and France.

The early 1980s saw IT as conceptually centralized with management controlled by Sony head office. In the late 1980s to early 1990s decision making was delegated to local managers, reflecting the spirit of local globalization. By the same token, head office is now concerned that there is too much centralization and that control mechanisms are too tight. In the opinion of senior managers in Sony Corporation in Tokyo, the 1990s

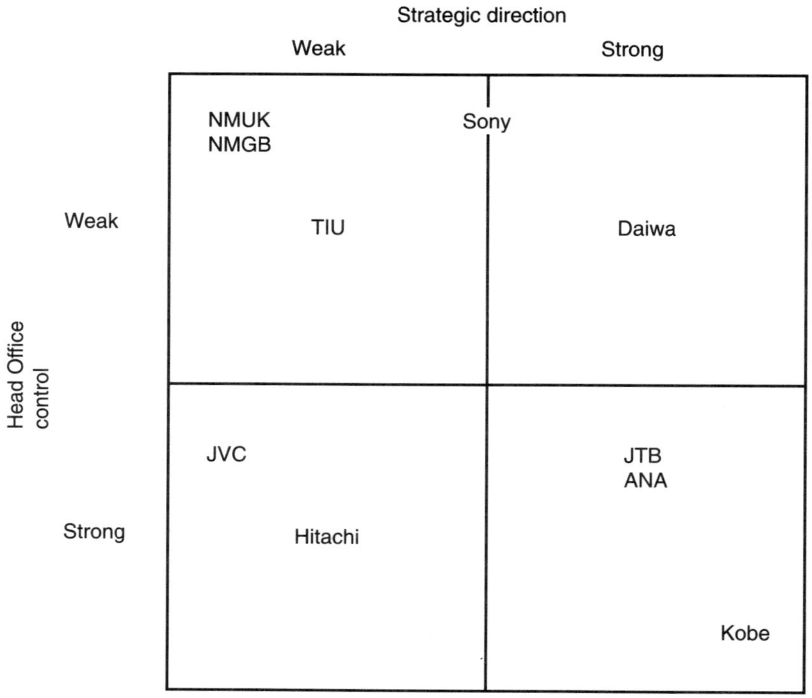

226 *The Japanese Advantage?*

```
                        Strategic direction
               Weak                       Strong
      ┌────────────────────────┬────────────────────────┐
      │  NMUK                  │                        │
      │  NMGB           Sony   │                        │
      │                        │                        │
 Weak │         TIU            │         Daiwa          │
      │                        │                        │
      ├────────────────────────┼────────────────────────┤
      │                        │                        │
      │         JVC            │         JTB            │
      │                        │         ANA            │
Strong│       Hitachi          │                        │
      │                        │                Kobe    │
      └────────────────────────┴────────────────────────┘
```
Head Office control (vertical axis)

Figure 16.1 Relations between head office and subsidiaries. ANA – All Nippon Airways; JTB – Japan Travel Bureau; NMGB – Nissan Motor GB; NMUK – Nissan Manufacturing (UK); TIU – Toshiba Information Systems

will see more control being devolved away from head office towards senior management in subsidiaries.

How the companies manage subsidiaries

We considered two aspects of head office management: strategic direction and head office control. We placed the companies on a four-sector grid with two axes as in Figure 16.1. The two axes of strategic direction and head office control are separated into weak and strong elements, which refer to the degree of influence that the head office has on its subsidiary.

By strategic direction we mean policy decision making, business strategy and similar corporate responsibilities. By head office control we mean control of financial, manufacturing, marketing, IT investment and other ways which makes the subsidiary dependent on head office decisions.

We define each of the segments in the grid as follows:

Strategic direction
Weak: Head office allows the subsidiary scope to decide its own strategic direction on a range of issues, although head office may set broad guidelines.
Strong: Head office provides strategic direction for subsidiaries. Subsidiaries play a relatively minimal role in deciding their own strategic direction. Beyond routine reporting back, subsidiaries may not have a very strong input into head office strategic planning.

Head office control
Weak: The subsidiary is not required to refer back to head office for decision making beyond routine reporting of subsidiary activities. The subsidiary is empowered to make a range of business and investment decisions, including those relating to IT.
Strong: Head office requires the subsidiary to refer back for approval on most decisions. There may be strict procedures for requesting head office approval. The subsidiary may have control over some local issues, e.g. personnel.

Below we illustrate our reasoning for the location of each of the case study companies on the grid.

The head office of *ANA* in Chiyoda-ku, Tokyo, has a number of departments which inform and guide strategic direction (for example, for negotiating and establishing new routes, calculating appropriate fare structures, marketing and systems development). ANA's marketing automation department (part of the marketing division) is responsible for international projects.

The global nature of ANA's business operations means that overseas subsidiaries make requests to head office when new systems are required. Head office identifies new IT systems for overseas subsidiaries, and subsidiaries can suggest additions to existing systems at CRS development meetings which are held annually, in February. Subsidiaries choose their own back-office systems, including business intelligence databases, and can select the type of PCs preferred by staff. We place ANA on the strong strategic direction, strong head office control quadrant.

Daiwa's head office in Tokyo sets overall corporate policy, including strategic business direction and new business initiatives. The 'Golden '90s', Daiwa's statement of its corporate principles for the decade to the year 2000, is one such initiative. However, Daiwa's corporate culture encourages each local subsidiary to make local business decisions in response to its own market environment. Local business committees consult head office as a matter of routine, and there is constant interaction between senior managers in Tokyo and London.

Head office provides Daiwa Europe with a budget subsidy, which is intended to cover local purchases of hardware and marketing information services, and to maintain the operational facility. IT investment decisions are made locally although the relevant executive director consults regularly with local senior colleagues and with managers in head office. We have placed Daiwa in the strong strategic direction, weak head office control quadrant.

Hitachi supports the concept of localization of subsidiaries. As a result, relations between head office and overseas subsidiaries are relatively loose. In early 1989 the company reorganized itself from a functional to a geographical basis. This reorganization reshaped decision making. Each trading zone which Hitachi has established throughout the world has a degree of self-contained decision-making autonomy, although head office in Tokyo expects regular report-back from each local head office.

Head office in Tokyo retains control of some business areas (for example, manufacturing output). Future plans are intended to give more control over manufacturing to sales divisions. Already, in Hitachi's operations in the United States, the holding company can control manufacturing in its subsidiary.

Head office controls funding for IT-related decisions at Hitachi Europe Ltd (HEL), and HEL's managing director is involved in twice-annual budget discussions in Tokyo. During these visits he requests approval for HEL's budgetary requirements for the following six months. For its part, at quarterly intervals, head office sends senior board members to HEL for discussions on strategy.

Head office provides the lead for IT development. The company's systems development department at Omori near Tokyo has between seventy and eighty staff, of which five develop IT systems for overseas operations. Head office develops IT systems and provides platforms for IS systems (including software interface) for subsidiaries within the Hitachi group. Hitachi's manufacturing experience in Japan has enabled the company to establish a 'home-grown' IT platform throughout its manufacturing sites. Head office allocates budgetary and staffing parameters for HEL's MIS department. We have placed Hitachi in the weak strategic direction, strong head office control quadrant.

In *JTB*'s head office in Maranouchi, Tokyo, there are a number of departments responsible for elements of global strategy. For example, Sales Planning Division manages sales promotion strategy; Corporate Planning Department decides overall business direction; Overseas Travel Division is responsible for strategic business development; Overseas Travel Department plans global business strategy. These, and other, relevant head office divisions contribute to corporate Action Plans according to each division's area of expertise. Action Plans are coordinated by the Global Planning Department. The initiative GO JTB 21, JTB's strategy for the years leading to the twenty-first century, falls into this category.

In Japan, the European Travel Centre (ETC) coordinates enquiries and bookings for European holidays via JETS. This is currently the only access to JETS within the Japanese domestic operation. The company's next phase of IT development will see the interface between TRIPS V and JETS.

When funding is required for a particular local project, say, in Europe, local head offices apply to Tokyo. This happened when senior managers in Europe requested funding from head office to support a pan-European accounting system. We have placed JTB in the strong strategic direction, strong head office control quadrant.

Local senior management at *JVC (UK)* contribute to head office policy making. Discussions and negotiations for global planning take place annually in Japan between JVC (UK) directors and their head office counterparts. The finance director is responsible for local IT budgets up to a certain amount, but refers to head office for larger IT investment decisions.

Head office develops standard software systems for use by subsidiaries, which are allowed to develop their own domestic applications within the common standard. EDP managers request the systems development department in Japan to make changes in the master system, where several JVC subsidiaries have similar local requirements. Head office decides what changes should be made after evaluating requests. In April 1992 head office developed a computer package to manage inventory, sales ledger and customer orders. This package is to be used by all JVC subsidiaries throughout Europe, including JVC (UK).

IT projects for the whole JVC group are managed by the JVC Information Centre in Tokyo. Local systems for the UK are the responsibility of JVC (UK). Subsidiaries report large IT projects to head office. When a system affects all subsidiaries these are discussed with departments in Tokyo. We have placed JVC in the weak strategic direction, strong head office control quadrant.

The head office of *Kobe Steel* controls local budget expenditure. However, with this framework subsidiaries are allowed to make local decisions. Subsidiaries prepare two half-yearly business plans, which are incorporated into head office capital and expenditure budgets for the following year. KSE applies to head office for budget funding.

Head office identifies new IT systems for overseas subsidiaries (for example, international communications projects such as a global VAN to link all overseas offices electronically). IT plans prepared by each division of Kobe Steel are amalgamated into a division-wide budgetary framework. This is submitted to the data-processing department as part of the annual budgeting routine.

Each division's IT department makes its own IT investment decisions. Some departments access company MIS systems via their own LANs. However, the corporate accounts facility is the sole responsibility of head office. Outside this system KSE can select and operate its own office systems. We have placed Kobe Steel in the strong strategic direction, strong head office control quadrant.

NMGB's corporate links are with its parent company, Nissan Europe NV (NENV), in Amsterdam, which acts as the intermediary for communications between NMGB and Nissan head office in Japan. One function of NENV is to allocate output from the Nissan manufacturing facility (NMUK) in Sunderland, UK. NENV sets NMGB's commercial objectives (for example, sales targets).

NMGB and NENV maintain strong commercial and communication links, although reporting is of a 'dotted line' rather than a formal nature. NMGB and NENV 'pool' resources and share expertise and development costs. NMGB makes its own business decisions (through an executive committee) within the framework of the annually agreed business plan.

While IT strategy is decided jointly between NENV and Nissan head office, NMGB has an IS steering committee to manage its own IT projects. This consists of senior managers from all company departments and decides overall company business objectives and priorities. The ISD and the IS steering committee work together to manage available resources to meet business needs. At NMGB, business strategies and IT strategies are closely connected.

NMGB sets its own budgets through the executive committee, although there are times when NENV is asked to provide additional funding. We have placed NMGB in the weak strategic direction, weak head office control quadrant.

When NMUK was being established a number of Japanese senior managers were involved in setting up the company. Apart from this, there has been no influence from Nissan head office on how NMUK should conduct its business. Indeed, the first NMUK Japanese managing director emphasized his policy of 'anglicizing' the company.

Occasionally, NMUK is called upon to introduce a corporate IT initiative. Such corporate projects are funded by additional budgets which the ISD manager receives from NMUK's finance and engineering departments. Apart from these instances, most of ISD's expenditure is for in-house issues. Priorities for in-house IT projects are decided between the ISD manager and his managing director. We have placed NMUK in the weak strategic direction, weak head office control quadrant.

Sony's company policy of 'local globalization' stresses that local managers of subsidiaries are empowered to make decisions. Co-founder and company chairman Akio Morita advocates that 'standardization would dilute the Sony culture if subsidiaries are instructed too much from head office'.

Sony has organized its global activities into a number of zones: Asia, the United States and Europe. Each zone has its own needs according to the business group requirements. Each zone management produces annual IT plans. If an IS system is necessary to compete and profitability is an issue, this is the business of the local subsidiary.

Head office defines corporate IT guidelines which are followed by subsidiaries, including SUK. These define the framework of Sony's corporate IS issues. Where corporate policy is unclear, SUK's ISD seeks guidance from its corporate headquarters in Europe, European Operations Office (EOO) situated in Cologne, Germany, or from Tokyo. Controls for the international communications network are very tightly defined, as were the guidelines for database management, although these have now become less stringent.

Head office also gives guidelines on IT expenditure. As long as it conforms to general corporate guidelines, SUK makes its own IT decisions. SUK directors decide the budget for the SUK ISD as part of the overall company budget.

At Sony, a corporate project team in the IS Department in Tokyo provides the initial impetus for a project, which is subsequently publicized to overseas sales companies. One example of a joint Tokyo–Europe IT development is the STREAM project. We have placed Sony on the borderline between the weak and strong strategic direction quandrants and in the weak head office control quadrant.

At *Toshiba Information Systems (UK) Ltd (TIU)* budgets are set every six months for the following trading period. The ISD budget for in-house projects is decided by the TIU finance director. TIU has no formal business strategy which includes IS/IT, but IT projects are managed by two committees: the Information Systems Planning Committee (ISPC) and the ISPWG (Information Systems Planning Working Group). The ISPC, whose members are directors, decides major strategic issues pertaining to IT and makes decisions on IT projects, particularly those that are likely to involve extensive resources. A European Steering Committee, based at Toshiba in Germany, decides pan-European systems, including developing various business systems for TIU.

ISPWG membership is drawn from lower managerial levels (for example, department heads and senior managers responsible for marketing, finance and distribution). The ISPWG is charged with overseeing in-house IT projects, under the chairmanship of the ISD manager.

Audit teams from Toshiba Corporation carry out an internal audit at TIU. Following a recent audit, TIU was awarded an A1 rating (which means that TIU is one of the best-run Toshiba subsidiaries worldwide). We have placed TIU in the weak strategic direction, weak head office control quadrant.

Summary

Relationships between a head office and global subsidiaries can be complex, and in many ways each company will evolve its own solutions to the problems of managing transnational operations. A number of factors influence the nature of head office–subsidiary relationships, including the nature of the industry, the length of time a subsidiary has been established and the function of the subsidiary (i.e. its purpose in serving perceived head office needs).

This chapter has outlined several of these factors. We have described some of the ways in which head offices set corporate policy and how policy decisions are passed onto subsidiaries for implementation. This is sometimes tempered when a subsidiary makes an input into corporate decision making.

There are a number of ways in which a head office can control IT systems, and a company of the size of Sony Corporation may progress along several different paths of managing its global operations in respect of IT. Whichever way a company decides, the result will undoubtedly be complex. Even when a subsidiary is allowed to make its own decisions, there may be financial control by head office, possibly through control of budgetary or local expenditure request procedures.

Large global companies will most likely have a development facility as part of their head office structure. However, the number of development staff devoted to work on systems purely for overseas operations may vary considerably. Some companies allow local subsidiaries to set up an in-house IT development facility. However, as we saw in Chapter 14, some companies are debating the advantages and disadvantages of outsourcing IT needs, including buying IT expertise and software packages from local specialists. When IT systems are developed at head office there may be initial problems during migration of the system onto local hardware. However, these may be overcome through sensitive and diplomatic contact between the subsidiary and its head office.

Global communications is one area of IT that is invariably controlled by head office. Companies in a wide range of industries now rely heavily on their global communications for the transmission of commercial data. Communications are inevitably controlled by head office in the interests of consistency and control (especially of manufacturing output).

We concluded this chapter with an analysis of the place of each of the companies in terms of strategic direction and head office control. In the following chapter we will consider all the evidence we have presented and make predictions about the ability of Japanese companies in managing strategic IT.

Notes

1. For example, the 13.5 per cent equity stake that ANA bought in Abacus Distribution Systems Pte Ltd in March 1992. Abacus is a consortium of principally South-east Asian airlines that operates an extensive CRS in the region. (Source: ANA press release dated 17 March 1992.)
2. Currie, W. L., 'The art of justifying new technology to top management', *OMEGA International Journal of Management Science*, **17**, No. 5, May (1989).

17
Eclipsing the sun?

We started with a scene from 1968 in which the managing director of a large British manufacturing company was being dismissive of any threat from Japanese rivals. We have little doubt that he was typical of British and indeed Western senior management of the time.

The situation is now very different. Western management has spent the last ten years or more dissecting Japanese management methods and importing the many useful concepts it found – in parallel with the unprecedented popularity of Japanese goods in the West. Some of these concepts enjoyed no more than a brief flourish but many have endured, withstanding overselling by consultants to provide real value to those organizations which have persevered. JIT, supplier partnerships and quality circles are examples.

However, the pendulum may have swung too far. In the West there is sometimes a respect for Japanese techniques which borders on awe. For example, business bookshops often appear to be dominated by publications extolling the virtues of Japanese management styles. Business conferences on 'meeting the Japanese challenge' continue to attract interest. It might even seem that in any business battle in the foreseeable future the Japanese are the certain victors. Our evidence suggests otherwise. Rather, the outcome is likely to be a close call and in this chapter we review our earlier discussion and debate the nature of this delicate balance. We believe that this hinges on the difference between evolutionary and revolutionary change, between incrementalism and radicalism, between continual improvement and a paradigm shift.

The term 'paradigm shift' is key to the debate. A paradigm is a set of beliefs and assumptions about how things work. In the business context it means a framework of expressing the way business is done in a particular industry – the unwritten rules by which people work and which determine success and failure. When these beliefs and assumptions change, then usual, practised methods for achieving success may no longer be viable. IBM provide an example. Until the 1990s IBM was an extremely successful organization, its business based on mainframe computers and excellent service. In the 1990s, as computers were decentralized, mainframes lost their popularity. Smaller computers became more commodity-like and the route to competitive success switched to software. IBM were slow to spot that the paradigm in the computer industry had changed. We are suggesting a connection here because Japanese companies have been compared to IBM: 'Suddenly many of them [Japanese companies] are beginning to look a lot like IBM – too fat, slow-footed and cautious for their own good.'[1]

In Part One we highlighted three concerns. First, we re-examined the battle so far, discussing the remarkable successes of Japanese companies to date and analysing the many, often conflicting, reasons put forward to explain them. We also outlined our arguments for believing that the next international business battleground will be Europe. Second, we put forward the view that the strategic deployment of IT will be a critical weapon in this battle, with the capability to bring victory to one side or another. Third, we described the relationship, as we see it, between national culture and management thinking. We have done so on the grounds that national cultural traits must surely influence management thinking, including management thinking on IT.

The case studies presented in Part Two considered in some detail the European operations of ten major Japanese organizations. The case study information allowed us to pull these issues together. In each of the cases we focused on the business impact of IT and the way the companies had managed the IT resource.

In Chapters 14–16 we analysed the evidence collected from the case studies and discussed the relevance of these findings. Now in this final chapter we return to the battle. We will now be looking at the strengths and weaknesses of the combatants and making predictions about the outcome.

Both the West and Japan have some clear advantages while other issues are more neutral. We look first at the factors which suggest, however strongly or weakly, that Japan will win. Then we consider factors suggesting that they will not. Finally, we weigh all these factors in the balance.

Factors for Japan

From an unenviable position as exemplars of low-quality products and workmanship Japanese organizations have learned how to change. No-one makes jokes about shoddy Japanese goods any longer,[2] and the day of the 'transistor salesman' is over.[3] Japanese companies have learned, in a surprisingly short time frame, how to make high-quality products and how to deliver high-quality service. They have also learned what the customer wants, sometimes before the customer does. In electrical goods, cars and other sectors new products have hit the market at bewildering speed – and they have usually been 'right first time' in terms of quality and customer service.

Clearly, Japanese organizations have demonstrated that they are 'learning' organizations, at least in the context described. This might prompt a Japanese manager to suggest modestly, 'Does it matter if our companies have not used IT strategically up to now? Your case studies demonstrate that we have managed IT well at a non-strategic level and when we *must* use it more strategically, we will do so, and quickly.'

As a nation the Japanese have been through such situations before and emerged successfully: recent Japanese history is a litany of adversities overcome. Why should they not do so again? Japan has a sufficiently highly educated workforce to throw numbers at any problem, and half of their workforce (women – who still tend not to work in managerial positions) is held in reserve. The Japanese are good at learning and this is a key factor for businesses of the future.[4]

There is no better evidence of their capacity for learning than in the way they have imported technology. In the immediate post-war years Japan's strength was not technology, as their industries and machinery were in ruins. Now technology is a major strength. More than any other nation, it seems that Japan knows how to apply technology for business success. A catalogue of achievements in technology-based products and methods of manufacturing testify to the years of successful Japanese experience in these areas.

In the first place, the technology was not their own. Even now it is debatable whether their technology-based products have been more than successful implementations of foreign innovations. Nevertheless, the Japanese have still exploited technology successfully. They have done so in different ways: by taking products apart and copying, by buying in foreign expertise, by buying patent rights, and by joint ventures, collaborations and take-overs. Of course, they have improved on others' technology. Why should they not do so again? Even now, Fujitsu, the largest Japanese computer company, offers scholarships to IBM people to work in their R&D laboratories on their most 'blue sky' projects. It is easy to see why Fujitsu values the arrangement.

When developing this arrangement Fujitsu may have had in mind the following anecdote. With rucksacks on their backs, a Japanese businessman and a Western businessman had become separated from the rest of the safari while out walking in lion country. Suddenly, they saw a lion, moving menacingly towards them. They carried no weapons so their situation looked awkward. To the surprise of the Westerner his Japanese colleague started to unpack his rucksack, calmly taking out a pair of running shoes and putting them on. 'What's the point of that?' the Westerner asked incredulously, 'you don't think you can outrun a lion, do you?' 'Of course not,' came the reply, 'But I don't have to outrun the lion, I only have to outrun you.'

This illustrates a shrewd ability to understand the essentials of a competitive situation. For the last few decades the Japanese have had to do so. Just after the Second World War they lagged behind the West in nearly all industrial sectors. This is no longer the case. They have caught up or overtaken the West in many important industries, and in the skills of management. In doing so, their ability to understand markets and competition has been a decisive factor.

So while the West's experience is in trying, and often failing, to defend a significant lead, the Japanese experience is in coming from behind. This experience is relevant to the strategic deployment of IT. The Japanese may well lag behind at the moment but, as we have seen, this is nothing new for them. Why should they not catch up? Whenever they play, they seem to win.

These successes of the last two decades have brought Japanese organizations and the Japanese nation immense financial resources, substantial amounts of which have been invested in overseas assets. The result has often been offended national pride, as the front pages of newspapers have reported. In the United States there was some alarm that such symbols as the Rockefeller Center and some Hollywood studios were in Japanese ownership.

More alarming is the suggestion that Japan could bring about the collapse of Western financial markets. No-one has suggested that they would do this deliberately, but one scenario is that a major earthquake in Tokyo, which, after all, does lie on a major fault, and the consequent need for rebuilding funds could result in the repatriation of sufficient funds to damage seriously Wall Street and the City of London.[5]

Less newsworthy but equally important is that fact that the Japanese can afford to hire Western experts in areas where they feel they have a weakness. They have done so in Association Football (and who doubts the Japanese have a weakness here) with the purchase of the leading English goalscorer of his day, Gary Lineker.

However, success is not always imported. Many aspects of Japanese culture militate towards success; few seem to push in the other direction.

First, failure would cause loss of face, something to avoid in Japanese society in general and Japanese business in particular. When combined with the concept that 'the group is everything: one goes down, we all go down', this is a significant force for failure avoidance. Second, the importance of the group extends beyond the immediate group in a company or the company itself to the whole of the country. The Japanese certainly believe that they are different from and probably that they are better than foreigners to whom they refer, with mild disparagement, as *gaijin*, literally 'outside people'. Third, Japan has no national resources such as oil, minerals or landmass. Some commentators[6] believe that this apparent weakness is their greatest strength: the Japanese *know* that success lies in themselves. Their skills and abilities have to be the best in the world. Fourth, the concept of 'the customer is king' is deep-rooted in Japanese management thinking. Although the West is also aware of the importance of this concept, companies are acquiring it by means of training courses. As a result, the effects may be not be as deep or all-pervading as for the Japanese, who do not have to be trained. For them it seems to come naturally, and, of course, such a natural approach may convey greater sincerity to the customer. Last, even the negative aspects of Japanese culture can promote success. Some writers describe an innate Japanese sense of inferiority. In spite of all their successes and their feelings of being different, there is an admiration, even adulation, of things Western. This is not just the designer-label symbols of success: Porsche, Gucci, Burberry, etc. but everyday items: MacDonald's, baseball, Clint Eastwood, Doc Marten's boots. A slight sense of inferiority may be a reason why the Japanese are so hard working and conscientious.

These attributes are most apparent in the remarkable Japanese educational system, which produces more science and mathematics graduates than any other national education system. Japan leads the world in the number of hours students study. This allows Japanese students to cover more ground, age for age, than their Western counterparts. Age for age, Japanese students also have higher IQs,[7] by around 15 per cent. Some authors[8] believe this to be one of the overriding reasons for Japanese business and economic success.

Japanese successes of the last few decades are principally the rewards of the previous generation's efforts. A new generation is moving into the higher echelons of management. This takes more time than in the West, given that Japanese companies tend to promote by seniority ('the Japanese love grey hair'). Undoubtedly, however, the new generation will bring new ideas and approaches. The weaknesses of the past may be eliminated...but so may the strengths. The factors which suggest a Japanese victory in the battle are:

- Major Japanese organizations are demonstrably 'learning' organizations.
- The Japanese know how to use technology.
- The Japanese are skilled at coming from behind.
- Financial strength.
- Some national pressures are success oriented.
- The Japanese educational system.
- Japan is changing.

Factors for the West

Japanese management, like Japanese society, operates in inner and outer circles.[9] The inner circle is the board of directors which receives advice through the *nemawashi* process from the various elements of the outer circle. The inner circle has its eye on key business issues such as market share, finance and business strategy.

IT is not yet generally recognized as a strand of strategy. It is seen as a support service and thus the responsibility of the outer circle. IT and business strategy are compartmentalized and we characterized this as a 'dependent' view of IT management (Chapter 15). Some organizations are trying to bridge the gap but there is little evidence that they have yet done so sufficiently to provide any appreciable competitive advantage. IT managers, not board members themselves, make presentations to the board for approval. As our research shows, board members who are sympathetic to IT or who have an IT background are highly prized exceptions. The psychological gap between business decision makers and IT decision makers appears from our evidence to be wide.

At the same time, Western companies see a different role for IT and take a different approach to its management. They see IT as strategic and are well aware of the problems caused when this role is not perceived and distinguished: 'If you try to blend an operational role with a strategic one, the operations side tends to dominate.'[10]

In our case studies we found that the operations side did dominate and it is evident that Japanese management is good at implementing continual, incremental change and improvement. On the other hand, there is little evidence from our cases that it is good at radical or revolutionary change. We detected this when we considered the different levels of transformation achieved by Japanese companies (Chapter 15) and found few examples of revolutionary transformation. The small numbers of Japanese Nobel prize winners is further evidence for this opinion.

To suggest that the Japanese are poor at radical innovation may seem surprising given the impressive rate at which new products are turned out. The emphasis, however, is on *radical*.

It may be that any lack of creativity is rooted in the strengths of the past: 'The roots of failure are found in victory.' Consensus management and the *nemawashi* system have many virtues, including attention to detail, cautious and prudent management, and good implementation, but this is not likely to promote a radical approach. Nor is it likely to encourage the individualism that is often at the root of innovation. 'The nail that stands out will be hammered down' according to a Japanese proverb.

We must stress that we are pointing to a clear difference between revolution and evolution, between automation and transformation. If they are to be implemented successfully, the two approaches require very different mindsets. In terms of IT, the difference between automation and transformation is that the latter requires fundamental management, structural and business changes to go alongside the IT. Evidence that Japanese businesses are good at making such parallel changes is scarce.[11]

This is reinforced at the global level. History shows that all empires come to an end eventually and recent history shows them coming to an end in increasingly shorter times. The Egyptian Empire lasted longer than the Roman; the Roman longer than the British; the British longer than the Soviet and so on. A simple time-series projection leads us to suppose that the Japanese economic empire will be lucky to last more the three decades – which could mean that time is running short.

We can add some cause and effect to this argument. Japan is facing a number of difficult domestic and international problems. At home the stock market has crumbled and the problems of land speculation have come home to roost. The younger generation is developing different attitudes to traditional Japanese values such as the work ethic. The role of women is becoming an issue. Ageing is a more serious problem for Japan than other nations and so on. Even the sacred cow of lifetime employment is being seriously questioned. Internationally, Japan is facing pressure to take up a role and responsibilities more in keeping with its financial strength.

In the past, such pressures, particularly the internal ones, have caused the decline and fall of empires. Japan may now decide to settle for its present position and concentrate on its domestic problems. And Japan is no stranger to introspection. For centuries Japan had an official seclusion policy under the *Tokugawa* shogunate: foreigners were virtually excluded and, in effect, Japan had no contact with the outside world.[12] This lasted until the arrival of Commodore Perry in 1853.

In recent years it has not proved so easy to exclude the rest of the world. Japan now has a number of threats in its backyard, for example the 'tigers' of South-east Asia (South Korea, Malaysia, Singapore, Taiwan, Thailand), the emergence of other rapidly growing economies such as Vietnam and Indonesia, and the ever-present threat of China, especially when strengthened by Hong Kong. Viewed from the Japanese perspective, these may well present more important economic threats than does the West. These economies threaten not only Japan's overseas markets but also its home market. Overseas investment by Japan may slow down as it looks to pressures on its domestic economy.

The Japanese government recognizes the problem of an ageing population as a major component of these domestic pressures. Japan is a gerontist society where the old are respected more than in the West. Without total support from superiors, the young are not able to get things done in the way they would like. Our case studies revealed some interesting attitudes which make it clear that, as in the West, older managers are set in their ways while younger colleagues try to promote change. Older managers are responsible for strategy while younger subordinates are more likely to have support roles – such as managing IT. A younger manager could only lead IT-induced change under the auspices of an older one.

However, even the most innovative young manager has just emerged from the Japanese education system which, for all its virtues, is not likely to stimulate creativity. At schools much of the learning is still by rote, relying on good memories and attention to logic, detail and the 'correct' answer. Criticism of received wisdom and teachers is almost unheard of. Indeed, the enormous classes of evening or weekend *jukus* (cramming schools) do not encourage questioning – only copying down from lectures.

Within organizations, management education while thorough and, in its own way, excellent is not likely to promote serious challenges to the established ways of doing things. New managers are indoctrinated into company culture by extensive training courses at which they mix solely with colleagues from their own organizations. Innate respect for their elders, a natural reluctance to criticize the group, a strong company culture and well-established working practices mean that sparks are not likely to fly. By contrast, in the West much management education is based on mixing people from different organizations and cultures. These situations provide opportunities to compare, contrast and criticize norms, beliefs and practices. However, there are signs that Japanese educational methods are changing but the signs are few and the changes will inevitably be slow.[13] So we come to the need for a paradigm shift.

A paradigm is a framework which defines accepted assumptions about the way things are and the way things are done. There comes a point when the paradigm breaks down. The assumptions no longer hold and new ways of doing things must be found. At the turn of the twentieth century in the field of physics the Newtonian paradigm began to break down. It left too much unexplained. Einstein's theory of relativity is now the basis of a new paradigm.

For a person, organization or nation, the trick is to move to the new paradigm before you are forced to. For example, Benetton, the European

240 *The Japanese Advantage?*

clothing retailer, found a new paradigm before others in the retail trade. Benetton is a 'virtual' organization with the coverage and presence of a large organization but the overheads, staff numbers and flexibility of a small one. Nearly all Benetton's activities are sub-contracted to other organizations while Benetton's management looks after strategy and coordination. On the other hand, IBM recognized the new paradigm in the computer industry (the move away from centralized mainframe computers) only when its revenue and reduced profitability, and threats from leaner competitors, forced it to do so. The market and the way business was done had changed but IBM was reluctant to change from its wonderfully successful formulae of the past until it had to. The delay seems to have been costly.

The problem facing Japan is this. The country has been wonderfully successful in the past based on a paradigm of 'the customer is king', a continual search for incremental improvement and other factors already discussed. But the paradigm must change at some time. When will this be? And what will the new paradigm be?

Even if these two questions could be answered, could Japan move sufficiently quickly to the new paradigm? Japan has a reputation for taking a long time to decide but then getting it right first time. Change takes time in Japan and time may be in short supply. Present strengths – centre up and down, *nemawashi, ringii*, etc. – may become future weaknesses. Fast decisions and incisive leadership from the top may be the key to the future. How quickly can the Japanese change? Remember, this is not incremental product change but management *process* change.

A thought-provoking book[14] devoted to the issue of paradigm shifts in business suggests that IT is the keystone of these innovations in the management arena. The problem for Japan is, as our cases demonstrate, IT is not yet on the senior management agenda. The factors which suggest that the Japanese will not be victorious in the battle are:

- IT is not on the senior management agenda in Japan.
- Japanese management is poor at *radical* innovation.
- Nothing lasts forever.
- Emerging powerful economies on the Pacific Rim.
- Some national pressures encourage failure.
- The Japanese educational system.
- The difficulty of making a paradigm shift.

Weighing the Balance

Table 17.1 summarizes the points for and against Japanese success in any strategic battle based in Europe.

The table summarizes some of the major factors influencing future international business competition. They suggest clearly that the determinants of success and failure in the past are not likely to carry such weight in the future. Major Japanese organizations face two problems.

Table 17.1 The factors for and against Japanese success

For	Against
'Learning' people and 'learning' organizations	Not good at radical innovation
Good users of technology	Strategic IT off agenda
Have experience of coming from behind	Now under attack from emerging economies
Exceptional financial strength	Nothing lasts forever
Many national pressures encourage success	Other national pressures do not
Excellent educational system for some purposes	Educational system has flaws
Japan is changing	Paradigm shift is required

The first is to recognize that there is a problem. The second is knowing how to solve it.

The problem is certainly recognized in some quarters. No less a person than Akio Morita, in his essay 'Japanese style management in jeopardy',[15] stresses the need for substantial change in Japanese management practices and organizations. If such rational arguments are not enough there is other evidence which might convince by fear rather than logic. In particular, the news from America is that widespread, revolutionary changes are taking place within its own industries.[16]

There are some signs, too, that Japanese organizations are tackling the problem. Some of the solutions may seem aggressive by Western standards. For example, one organization is using shock tactics to try to educate its managers to be more creative.[17] The purpose of this education is reported as follows:

> Their goal is to crack the rigid hierarchical structures and consensus management system that have served Japanese enterprises so well but may...prove to be their undoing.

The same article, in describing this education, demonstrates the difficulties faced. It reports that Japanese managers are often shy at proposing new ventures. Note that this remark is about new ventures, not improvements to old ones.

Throughout this book we have emphasized the strategic role of IT in transforming businesses to prepare them for the challenges of future international competition. We suggest that here again the size of the problem is daunting: 'Japanese companies...are years behind the Americans in designing these so-called distribution systems [corporate management networks].'[18]

Weighing all the arguments in the balance, including those in Table 17.1, it may seem unlikely that Japan can win. If pressed, this is where we would lay our bets. However, we would do so with some trepidation because Japan is a 'learning' nation and their organizations are 'learning' organizations. The issue is finely balanced. For us the clear sign that Japan would lose would be if, right now somewhere in Japan, a managing director is saying to his new graduate trainees, 'Western businesses present no threat to Japanese economic success'.

Notes

1. Schlender, B., *Fortune*, 22, March 1993. In the same article, 'Japan: hard times for high tech', Kazuhiko Nishi, president of ASCII Corp, says: 'Japan's electronics industry until now has been catching up, just copying what America has already made. Now there's not much left uncopied, and we are all facing the much tougher question of what to do next.'
2. In the early post-war years Akio Morita, chairman of Sony, was in the United States. While drinking cocktails with an American businessman, Morita asked why he did not do more business with Japan. Holding up a tacky plastic cocktail umbrella, the businessman replied, 'These are made in your country'.
3. In the 1960s General de Gaulle is reported to have dismissed the Japanese as 'a nation of transistor salesmen'.
4. Handy, C., *The Age of Unreason*, Business Books (1989).
5. Reading, B., *The Coming Collapse*, Orion Books (1993).
6. See, for example, Chapter 11 of Ohmae, K., *The Borderless World*, Fontana (1992).
7. IQ (intelligence quotient), is a measure of intelligence, particularly logic and reasoning, less so creativity.
8. Oppenheim, P., *The New Masters*, Business Books (1991).
9. Katzenstein, G., *Funny Business*, Grafton Books (1989) gives an amusing account of the effect of this on a Western individual working for Sony in Japan.
10. Guy Hains, IT director of Rover, quoted in 'The Rover route to computing', *Management Today*, October (1993).
11. See, for example, Thornton, E., 'Japan's struggle to re-structure', *Fortune*, 28 June 1993.
12. See, for example, von Wolferen, K., *The Enigma of Japanese Power*, Papermac (1989).
13. See, for example, Concor, D., 'Japan: Future of a Superpower', *New Scientist*, 2 October (1993).
14. Tapscott, D. and Caston, A., *Paradigm Shift*, McGraw-Hill (1993).
15. Described in the London *Evening Standard*, 21 January (1993).
16. See, for example, the article in *Fortune*, 17 May (1993).
17. Thornton, E., 'Japan's struggle to be creative', *Fortune*, 19 April (1993).
18. Schlender, *op. cit.*

Index

Airline profitability, 58, 65
All Nippon Airways Ltd (ANA):
  case profile, 57
  company background, 58–62
  impact of IT, 62–6
  IT decision making, 191
  managing IT, 67–8, 195, 217, 220, 227
Appearance, importance of, 41

Budgeting, TIU, 174–5
Business needs, identification, 189–90
Business network redesign, IT-induced, 30–2, 208
Business process redesign, IT-induced, 28–30, 208
Business scope redefinition, IT-induced, 32–3, 208
Business transformation (five-level graph), 25, 198
  business network redesign, 30–2
  business process redesign, 28–30
  business scope redefinition, 32–3
  internal integration, 26–8
  localized exploitation, 25
Buying-in IT expertise, 193–4

Centrex communication system, 76
Communication systems, KSE, 112–13
Company behaviour, 50–1
Companyism, 11
Competition:
  domestic, 8–9
  future, 10–12, 199–200
Computer reservation systems (CRS), 57, 63–4, 65, 217
Conflict aversion, 185–6
Consensus decision making (*nemawashi*), 47–8, 127, 184, 197–8
  HEL, 88
Consensus, importance of, 40
Corporate family, basis of, 42–3
Corporate hierarchy, 42, 44–5
Corporate policy, setting, 215–17
Costs, control of, 5

Daiwa Europe Ltd (DEL):
  case profile, 70
  company background, 71–3
  corporate culture, 216
  Global Communications Network, 75
  impact of IT, 73–4
  managing IT, 74–6, 219, 227
  Systems Planning Department, 74–5, 189
  use of outsourcing, 188
Daiwa Institute of Research (Europe) Ltd (DIREL), 71–2, 219
Daiwa Securities, 71
Dealership network, NMGB, 118–23
Decision making:
  consensus, *see* Consensus decision making
  functional boundaries, 49–50
  uncertainty avoidance, 51–2
Design cycle, HEL, 84–5

E-mail, 155
  TIU, 172
Electronic data interchange (EDI):
  HEL, 83–4
  JVC, 104
  SUK, 155–6
Employment, lifetime, 43–4
End-user reporting (EUR), NMGB, 125, 184
European market, competition for, 10–12

Fare pricing, 58, 60–1
Finance factors, importance of, 7
Financial control, information technology (IT), 217–20
Financial services industry, 73–4
Five-level graph, *see* business transformation (five-level graph)
Fujitsu, 235

Global communications networks, 222–4
  DEL, 70, 75
Global localization, SUK, 148

Harmony and conformity, importance of, 40
Head office, relations with subsidiaries, 213–15, 226–31
Hierarchy, corporate, 42, 44–5
Hitachi Europe Ltd (HEL):
  business needs identification, 189
  business strategy, 79–82
  case profile, 78
  company background, 78–82
  Electronic Components Division (HEL-ECD), 80, 82, 83
  head office control, 215, 219, 228
  impact of IT, 83–5, 187
  IT decision making, 184, 191, 192
  management information system (MIS), 86–7
  managing IT, 86–9, 195, 210, 221
  procurement, 85–6
  Product Marketing Information System (PMIS), 88–9
  reorganization, 217
  Support Computer Centre, 81
Hitachi Global Network (HITNET), 223
Hitachi On-Line Information System (HOLIS), 81

IBM, 233
In-house IT development, 193–4
Index matrix, 21–4, 200, 204–207
Information flows, 8
Information technology (IT):
  for administrative support, 186–7
  auditing, 176
  business benefits, 20–4
  changing role, 15–18, 34–6
  core uses, 17–18
  decision making, 191–2
  expenditure cost, 187–8
  financial control, 217–20
  identifying new systems, 67–8, 88, 106, 115, 220–2
  independent approach, 210–12
  interdependent approach, 210–12
  Japanese management attitudes, 185, 186
  learning from experience, 196–7
  managing strategic, 210–12, 224–31
  outsourcing, 188
  project organization, 195–6
  strategic potential, 198–200
  systems development, 193–5
  see also under individual companies names

Insiders/outsiders view, 39–40
Interlinked economies (ILE), 11–12
Internal integration, IT-induced, 26–8, 208
International communications, DEL, 75
Inventory, Purchase and Sales (IPS), JVC, 103–4
Investment:
  KSE, 116
  NMUK, 141–2

Japan:
  background view, 38–9, 52
  business failures, 9–10, 236
  business success factors, 5–9, 234–7, 240–2
  company culture and behaviour, 39–42, 50–2, 183
  competition with the West, 10–12, 237–40
  management practices, 184–5
  overseas investments, 10–11
  technology lag, 213–14
Japan Travel Bureau (JTB):
  case profile, 90
  company background, 91–3
  corporate philosophy, 93–4, 216
  funding IT, 219
  head office control, 228
  impact of IT, 93–4
  Travel Reservation and Information System (TRIPS), 94, 228
Japan Travel Bureau Europe (JTBE), 95
  accounting system (POP), 98
  decision-making, 184
  managing IT, 95, 186, 196–7
  outward-bound project, 97–8
  Personnel Department, 98–9
  special projects adviser, 194
  Tehai Systems (JETS), 95–7, 196–7, 228
Job rotation, 44
JVC (UK) Ltd (JVC):
  case profile, 101
  company background, 101–2
  Computer Room, 189, 192, 196
  corporate planning, 216
  impact of IT, 102–4
  IT decision making, 186, 192
  managing IT, 104–8, 195, 209, 219, 221, 229
  pan-European projects, 102–3

Index 245

Kaizen (constant improvement), 132, 184
Kan-doh (feeling or emotion), 128
Keiretsu (company groupings), 7
Kobe Steel Europe Ltd (KSE):
  case profile, 110
  company background, 110–12
  impact of IT, 112–13
  IT decision making, 186, 191
  managing IT, 113–16, 218, 219, 220, 223, 229
  video-conferencing, 224

Laptop computers, JVC, 107–8
Lifetime employment, 43–4
Localised exploitation, IT-induced, 25, 207

Management information:
  JVC, 106–7
  NMGB, 124
Marketing, airline, 66
Matrix management, NMGB, 129–30
Ministry of International Trade and Industry (MITI), 8, 9
MIT90s Research Programme, 17, 25
  business transformation,
  see Business transformation (five-level graph)

Nemawashi, see Consensus decision making
Networking, 128
  NMGB, 184
  SUK, 151–4
  TIU, 172
Nissan Europe NV (NENV), 131, 216, 229–30
Nissan Motor (GB) Ltd (NMGB):
  business needs identification, 190
  business strategies, 126, 216
  case profile, 117
  company background, 118–19
  Dealer Communication System (DCS), 117, 121–2
  Dealer Development Department, 118–19
  Dealer Management System (DMS), 117, 122–3
  dealership network, 118–19
  decision making, 127–30, 184
  end-user reporting, 125, 184
  impact of IT, 119–23

Information Systems Department (ISD), 117, 123–4, 139, 192
IT decision making, 191, 192
IT investment, 131
kaizen philosophy, 184
managing IT, 123–33, 187, 196, 209, 229–30
matrix management, 129–30, 196
supplier relationships, 132–3
Nissan Motor Manufacturing (UK) Ltd (NMUK):
  business needs identification, 190
  case profile, 135
  company background, 135–8
  corporate principles, 136, 142
  ILU board, 137
  impact of IT, 138–40
  Information Systems Department (ISD), 140–2, 144, 185
  managing IT, 140–4, 196
  production teams, 136, 137–8

Office systems, DEL, 76
Organizational turbulence, 17
Outsourcing, for IT, 188

Pan-European projects:
  JTBE, 98–9
  JVC, 102–3
Pareto effect, use of time, 48–9
Passenger information, airline, 64–5
Personal computers, 154
Planning IT:
  JVC, 105–6
  NMGB, 130–1
  NMUK, 141
  SUK, 162–3
Pool agreement, airline, 65
Process technology, 181–2
Procurement:
  HEL, 85–6
  JVC, 103
Product design, importance of, 6–7
Product Marketing Information System (PMIS), HEL, 78, 88–9
Product technology, 181–2
Productivity, 10, 11
Project management, 195–7
  JTBE, 195
  NMUK, 143–4
Promotion patterns, 46
Prorated fares, 61–2

Quality Circles, 6
Quality, importance of, 5–6

Rank and status, importance of, 42
Risk avoidance, 51–2, 185–6

Software, development in Japan, 194–5
Sony Total Network (STN), 153
Sony (UK) Ltd (SUK):
  business needs identification, 189, 190
  case profile, 146–7
  communications networks, 151–4
  company background, 147–51
  Computer Services Department, 161
  Development Services Department (DSD), 160–1, 162, 190
  European Computer Services (ECS), 157
  European Network Centre (ENC), 222
  European Operations Office (EOO), 218, 230
  European Spares Centre (ESC), 156–7
  impact of IT, 151–7, 186
  Information Systems Division (ISD), 158, 160, 162–5, 187, 220, 230
  IT decision making, 192
  local globalization, 215, 216–17, 230
  Management and Engineering Information Systems (MEIS), 214, 225–6
  managing IT, 157–65, 209, 218, 220, 221, 224–5, 230
  project teams, 162
  STREAM projects, 154, 157–8, 209, 221, 230
  System Enhancement Project (SEP), 160–1, 192
  Technical Support team, 161–2
Spare parts ordering, JVC, 104
Spare parts storage, SUK, 156
Statistical Quality Control (SQC), 6
Strategic Grid, 18–20, 200, 201–4
STREAM projects, *see under* Sony (UK) Ltd (SUK)
Structural Impediments Talks, 8
Subsidiaries, management of, 226–31
Supplier relationships, NMGB, 132–3
Systems Development Departments, in Japan, 194
Systems Planning Department, DEL, 74–5

Task sharing, 46–7
Team work, 46–7
Toshiba Information Systems (UK) Ltd (TIU):
  business needs identification, 189
  business strategy, 168–9
  case profile, 167
  company background, 167–9
  distribution system, 170–1
  Executive Information System (EIS), 171–2, 197
  impact of IT, 169–72
  Information Systems Department (ISD), 173, 231
  Information Systems Planning Committee (ISPC), 174, 231
  Information Systems Planning Working Group (ISPWG), 174
  managing IT, 173–7, 210, 231
  planning IT, 173
  warehousing, 170
Training courses, JVC, 108
Transformation benefits, IT-induced, 25–33

Uncertainty, aversion to, 51–2
Unfair practices, 8

Video-conferencing, 115, 223–4

Warehousing and distribution systems, TIU, 170–1

Yield factor, airline loads, 61

Zaibatsu (company groupings), 7